Exile & African Literature

Editor:	Eldred Durosimi Jones, Fourah Bay College, University of Sierra Leone, Private Mail Bag, Freetown, Sierra Leone
Assistant Editor:	Marjorie Jones
Associate Editors:	Simon Gikandi Department of English Language & Literature, University of Michigan 7609 Haven Hall, Ann Arbor, MI. 48109-1045, USA
	Nnadozie Inyama Department of English, University of Nigeria, Nsukka, Nigeria
	Francis Imbuga Literature Department, Kenyatta University, PO Box 43844, Nairobi, Kenya
	Emmanuel Ngara Office of the Deputy Vice-Chancellor, University of Natal, Private Bag X10, Dalbridge 4014, South Africa
	Ato Quayson Pembroke College, Cambridge CB2 1RF, UK
Reviews Editor:	James Gibbs, 8 Victoria Square, Bristol BS8 4ET, UK
	[Publishers wishing to submit books for review should send them direct to the Reviews Editor]

African Literature Today

'one of the best authoritative journals of African literature today ...' *Matatu*

'a journal consistently immersed in all the ongoing issues of African literature ...' *World Literature Today*

Editor: Eldred Durosimi Jones
* 1, 2, 3, and 4 Omnibus Edition
  5 The Novel in Africa
  6 Poetry in Africa
  7 Focus on Criticism
  8 Drama in Africa
  *9 Africa, America & the Caribbean
  *10 Retrospect & Prospect
  11 Myth & History

Editor: Eldred Durosimi Jones
Associate Editor: Eustace Palmer
Assistant Editor: Marjorie Jones
  12 New Writing, New Approaches
  *13 Recent Trends in the Novel
  *14 Insiders & Outsiders
  1-14 were published from London by Heinemann Educational Books and from New York by Africana Publishing Company

The new series is published by
James Currey Publishers and Africa World Press
*ALT 15 Women in African Literature Today
*ALT 16 Oral & Written Poetry in African Literature Today
*ALT 17 The Question of Language in African Literature Today
*ALT 18 Orature in African Literature Today
*ALT 19 Critical Theory & African Literature Today
*ALT 20 New Trends & Generations in African Literature
*ALT 21 Childhood in African Literature
*ALT 22 Exile & African Literature

*Copies of back issues marked with an asterisk may be purchased from your bookseller or direct from James Currey Ltd. Place a standing order with your supplier for future issues.

Next Issue
ALT 23 will focus on South and Southern Africa. With the end of political apartheid, South Africa once more enters the mainstream of world literature.
Deadline for submission has passed.

Future Issues
Before embarking on articles contributors are advised to submit proposals to the Editor: c/o James Currey Publishers, 73 Botley Road, Oxford, OX2 0BS. Proposals can be discussed with the Associate Editors.

All articles should be well typed, double spaced on A4 paper with a wide margin. References to books should include the author or editor, place, publisher, date and the relevant pages. Please submit disks wherever possible as well as the hard copy.

Contributors must keep a spare copy in case of loss in transit.

Exile & African Literature

A Review

Editor: Eldred Durosimi Jones
Assistant Editor: Marjorie Jones

Associate Editors: Simon Gikandi
Nnadozie Inyama
Francis Imbuga
Emmanuel Ngara
Ato Quayson

Reviews Editor: James Gibbs

JAMES CURREY
OXFORD

AFRICA WORLD PRESS
TRENTON, N.J.

James Currey
www.jamescurrey.com
is an imprint of Boydell & Brewer Ltd
PO Box 9, Woodbridge, Suffolk IP12 3DF, UK
and of Boydell & Brewer Inc.
668 Mt Hope Avenue, Rochester, NY 14620, USA
www.boydellandbrewer.com

Africa World Press, Inc.
PO Box 1892
Trenton NJ 08607

© Boydell & Brewer Ltd 2000
First published 2000
Transferred to digital printing

A catalogue record is available from the British Library

ISBN 978-0-85255-522-4 (James Currey paper)

Typeset in 9/10 pt Melior by Long House Publishing Services, Cumbria, UK

Contents

EDITORIAL

Eldred D. Jones, *Fourah Bay College*   vii

ARTICLES

Concepts of Exile in Dambudzo Marechera's Early Works   1
Annie H. Gagiano, *University of Stellenbosch, South Africa*

Mindblasts: Narrative Technique & Iconography of Sexual   13
Stereotyping as Patterns of Defilement/Cleansing in
Bessie Head's *A Question of Power* & Dambudzo Marechera's
The House of Hunger
David Kerr, *University of Botswana*

Shriek of Nerves: The Rational Voice of Dennis Brutus   23
& the Poetry of Exile in *Salutes and Censures*
Ezenwa-Ohaeto, *Alvan Ikoku College of Education, Nigeria*

Culturo-Textual Exile: The Changing 'Faces' of African Poetry   32
Lekan Oyegoke, *University of Swaziland*

Shades of Home & Exile in Ayi Kwei Armah's Novels   44
Nnadozie Inyama, *University of Nigeria, Nsukka*

Crisis of Filiation: Exile & Return in John Munonye's Trilogy   53
Amechi Nicholas Akwanya, *University of Nigeria, Nsukka*

An Exile Writing on Home: Protest & Commitment   64
in the Works of Bessie Head
Sophia O. Ogwude, *Federal University of Technology, Nigeria*

Changing States: Exile & Syncretism in Buchi Emecheta's *Kehinde*   77
Ana María Sánchez Arce, *Universitat Autonoma de Barcelona*

Exile & the Female Imagination: The Nigeria Civil War, Western   90
Ideology (Feminism), & the Poetry of Catherine Acholonu
Ode S. Ogede, *North Carolina Central University, USA*

REVIEWS

Abdourahman Ali Waberi's *L'Oeil nomade* (Adele King)	100
Maishe Maponya's *Doing Plays for a Change*; *At the Junction: Four Plays by the Junction Avenue Theatre Company*; Barney Simon's *Born in the RSA*; & Zakes Mda's *And the Girls in Their Sunday Dresses* (Geoffrey V. Davis)	103
Chirikure Chirikure's *Hakurarwi*; Charles Mungoshi's *The Milkman Doesn't Only Deliver Milk*; Chenjerai Hove's *Rainbows in the Dust*; & Zimbabwe Women Writers' *Poetry & Short Stories*; (Pauline Dodgson)	111
Bernth Lindfors's *Conversations with Chinua Achebe*; & Ezenwa-Ohaeto's *Chinua Achebe: A Biography* (Douglas Killam)	116
R. E. Obeng's *Eighteenpence*; Ama Ata Aidoo's *The Girl Who Could and Other Stories*; & Amma Darko's *The Housemaid* (James Gibbs)	122
Chukwuemeka Ike's *To My Husband from Iowa*; & Femi Olugbile's *Batolica* (Folake Shoga)	127
Rayda Jacobs' *Eyes of the Sky*; W.P.B. Botha's *A Duty of Memory* (Folake Shoga)	130
S. N. Ndunguru's *A Wreath for Father Mayer of Masasi*; A. M. Hokororo's *Salma Spirit*; Charles Mungoshi's *Walking Still: Nine Short Stories*; & Julius Ocwinyo's *Fate of the Banished* (Margaret Macpherson)	132
Sue Kossew's *Pen and Power: A Post-Colonial Reading of* *J. M. Coetzee & Andre Brink* (André Viola)	136
Hans M. Zell's *The Electronic African Bookworm: A Web Navigator* (James Gibbs)	138
Arthur Gakwandi's *Kosiya Kifefe*; Alexander Kanegoni's *Echoing Silence*; Yvonne Vera's *Butterfly Burning*; Marjorie O. Macgoye's *Make it Sing and Other Poems* (Fiona Johnson Chalamanda)	140
F. M. Genga Idowu's *My Heart on Trial*; Barbara Kimenyi's *Beauty Queen*; Ciarunji Chesaina's *Oral Literature of the Ember and Mbeere*; J. Roger Kurtz's *Urban Obsessions, Urban Fears* (Fiona Johnson Chalamanda and Angela Smith)	144
Index	148

Editorial

Eldred D. Jones

The mass displacement of peoples resulting from the internal wars which have plagued the African continent in the last twenty-five years or so have yet to produce a significant body of literature but already some exiled communities have evolved an ephemeral refugee culture in their countries of exile from which have flowed patriotic songs, stories, skits and reflections which might lead to a more abiding literature. Such a body of material, not yet subject to systematic study, has emerged, for example, from the mass exile of Sierra Leoneans forced into Guinea by the nine-year-old civil war.

Exile, however, a condition of physical or mental alienation from the habitual environment, seems to have been always a part of the human condition. One author, Chinua Achebe, explores this theme in its many variations. His representation of a pristine African society in the first part of *Things Fall Apart* shows an Okonkwo alienated in spirit from his own people by his obsessional character which indeed subsequently drove him into physical exile among his wife's clan. Once this society has come into contact with the imperial Christian civilization, a further alienating factor is introduced, resulting in Okonkwo's son deserting his father's *obi* from which he had in turn been spiritually alienated, for the compound of the Christian missionaries, a spiritual journey equivalent to thousands of physical miles. Okonkwo's eponymous grandson found himself 'no longer at ease' in the old dispensation when he returned from his educational exile. The hero of *Anthills of the Savannah* also becomes increasingly alienated from the dictatorial regime in which he served, becoming a quarry of his erstwhile employers to find a casual death as he fled into a physical exile. Chris Oriko thus typifies the dozens (hundreds) of exiles of conscience who have fled various forms of tyranny and misrule in their own countries.

The most spectacular of these oppressive systems which generated exile is South African apartheid but many other regimes have driven significant sections of the African intelligentsia but also ordinary people of conscience into disorientating but sometimes mentally productive state of exile. Thousands more remain within their societies in a state of mental alienation. Ayi Kwei Armah's 'man' in *The Beautyful Ones Are Not Yet Born*, Soyinka's interpreters, Achebe's Nwoye and Chris Oriko as well as most of Ngugi's heroes are as much exiles within their societies as if they had been thousands of miles away.

The recurrence of the theme of exile in the literary tradition of many societies since ancient times should not be surprising because it is the internal distancing of the individual from the environment that frequently produces art. When physical alienation is also introduced, the creative art may even be intensified. In spite of the image of the Babylonian exiles hanging up their harps on the trees of their country of exile, the author of Psalm 137 produced one of the most lyrical exilic lamentations in all literature while ironically doubting: 'How can we sing the Lord's song in a strange land?' But exile can also be crippling as Mandla Langa writes in *The Naked Song*, 'Exile was not so much a geographical dislocation as a state of mind, something that consumed and branded and left one marked for life. Many, like animals whose limbs were left in a snare, walked through life crippled, their minds locked on that fateful moment of rupture.' (71) Though it is the hope, perhaps forlorn, of all civilized people that the conditions which force persons into exile – tyranny, intolerance, inhumanity – will disappear, the internal alienation which produces literature will remain part of the human condition.

The next issue of *African Literature Today* (ALT 23), the last which will be edited by Eldred Jones, will be on the subject of South and Southern Africa. With the end of political apartheid, South Africa once more enters the mainstream of world literature. Articles address major developments in South African literature, the role of writers and institutions such as publishing houses and theatre groups in the struggle against apartheid. This issue has now been broadened to include contributions on related themes from other countries in the southern African region.

Concepts of Exile
in Dambudzo Marechera's Early Works

Annie H. Gagiano

The theme of exile has interested authors from ancient times. Ovid's *Tristia* being one of the classics of this line. In Shakespeare's *Richard II* (1.3 124–272) the banished political rivals Mowbray and Bolingbroke movingly discuss the condition they face, while in *Othello* the African hero, who 'fetch[es his] life and being/From men of royal siege' (1.3. 21–2), becomes (in the play's title) 'the *Moor of Venice*' (emphasis added to point the irony). In his 1930s poem 'The Capital', describing the twentieth-century urban condition, the British poet W.H. Auden recognizes as one of its features the 'Café[s]' where 'exiles' establish 'a malicious village' (Auden: 122–23) – an impression confirmed by Nuruddin Farah's brief description of exiled Somalis in his 1982 novel *Sardines* (Farah: pp. 167–9). In a posthumous collection of 1973, significantly titled *Dead Roots* (from one of his poems), the South African poet Arthur Nortje – who died by probable suicide in Oxford – records his tragic vision that 'Exile was implanted/in the first pangs of paradise' (Nortje: 140). George Lamming's 1984 essay collection (with its reference to the author's move to England from his native West Indies) deliberately startled with its title, *The Pleasures of Exile*. In the eighties, Andrew Gurr's *Writers in Exile: The Identity of Home in Modern Literature* appeared in 1981 and Seidel's *Exile and the Narrative Imagination* in 1986. Edward Said's widely influential 1990 essay 'Reflections on Exile' judges it a severe 'Contemporary political punishment', especially characteristic of the twentieth century – a condition whose 'achievements ... are permanently undermined by ... loss'. He finds that 'exile is strangely compelling to think about but terrible to experience' (Said: 357–8). Noting the ambiguities of the state, but generally more cheerful about its possibilities, is Madan Sarup in the essay 'Home and Identity' (1994).

Even a small selection like the above gives an indication of the varied and ample range of treatments of this theme in literary and (in a wide sense) philosophical writing, especially in this century. What this article will attempt to validate is that within the still somewhat neglected (Buuck: 118, 129–30; Pattison: 221) and even underrated *oeuvre* of Dambudzo Marechera (1952–87), his writing on the exile theme presents one of the most complete, wide-ranging and vividly original treatments of this condition presently available. The scholarly commentaries

1

2 Concepts of Exile

analysing his work that have hitherto appeared tend, however, to focus on the 'anti-nationalist' trend of his writings (see the essays by Gaylard, Pattison, Gurnah and Veit-Wild). David Buuck's 1997 analysis is one of the few to highlight Marechera's exile experience, noting that

> In Britain he came face to face with his own 'otherness', as he was not only an outsider within the British culture which he was drawn to, but found himself also estranged from fellow exiled Africans. (Buuck: 123)

In part of her 'Introduction' to *The Black Insider* (1990: 14–18) Flora Veit-Wild notes its author's concern with 'the struggles and conflicts of exile, of African identity in exile, and of being black in Britain' (14).

Marechera's meditations on and delineations of the state of exile occur chiefly in *The Black Insider* (1990), which might be loosely termed (See Veit-Wild's *Source Book*: 1993: 199 and her 'Introduction' to the novel) his second major work (after *The House of Hunger* – 1978), although it was only posthumously published. The long title piece (23–115) in *The Black Insider* is Marechera's lengthiest exploration of the issue, but the very brief pieces 'Oxford, Black Oxford' (118–21); 'The Sound of Snapping Wires' (122–4) and 'Night on my Harmonica' (126–7) published with it, extend his map of this territory. So, too, do several of the short stories which appeared (earlier) with the title piece 'House of Hunger' in the collection titled *The House of Hunger*, i.e. 'Black Skin What Mask' (93–9); 'The Writer's Grain' part 1 (100–15); 'Protista' (or 'The Writer's Grain' part 3: 127–33) and 'Thought-tracks in the Snow' (142–8). Some of Marechera's poems from the posthumously-published collection *Cemetery of Mind* (1992) throw light on the issue, especially those composed during the latter part of his stay in Britain. In *Dambudzo Marechera: A Source Book on his Life and Work* (1992), Flora Veit-Wild, his editor, champion and friend, produced a sympathetic and meticulous biography, parts of which are especially relevant to the exploration of the theme of this essay.

The bare biographical outline of Marechera's exile experience is that, subsequent to his expulsion from the University of Rhodesia for participation in political demonstrations against Ian Smith's UDI regime, a scholarship to Oxford University took him to England in 1974. His 'main experience' here (he later said) was 'loneliness'; his purpose, he declared, like that of others in a similar position, was

> not so much [to] gain educational certificates, but survive mentally, to hospitalize ourselves in a country where police dogs and other forms of brutalization were not a day-to-day affair. At the same time, there was this feeling that our generation had more-or-less been raped and that like any rape case we would never really recover. (Veit-Wild, *Source Book* 1992: 152)

The Warden of Marechera's Oxford college (from which he was sent down after one and a half years) commented later:

> I don't remember anyone, in all my eighteen years at New College, who caused so much trouble to the college as Charles [as Marechera was then known] did. Of course, it is a cultural shock for anyone coming from a Third World country to a place like Oxford. But I don't remember anyone reacting with the same kind of destructive violence that Charles did. (ibid.: 167).

That Marechera did 'react' to the 'cultural shock' in a much more meaningful way than the flamboyant 'destructive violence' which cost him his scholarship and his place at Oxford is proved in the deeply thoughtful way that he managed to write about it and especially in the way he was able – both poetically and philosophically – to enlarge his understanding beyond his merely personal experience (see the comment on Yevtushenko which he quotes, cited in the *Source Book*: 366). Because he knew that 'to see takes time' (ibid.: 362), Marechera returns again and again, each time from a different angle, to the ironies, paradoxes and challenges of exile, as an almost insurmountable psychic disturbance. His writing reflects (and reflects on) not only his Oxford university period, but the next five and a half years in Britain – which he would spend as a homeless drifter, squatter and temporary house guest in Oxford, Wales, Sheffield and London, a period during which his social encounters ranged over and included aristocratic British fellow-students, compatriots and fellow-exiles, and other 'tramp[s]', both English and African (Marechera, *Hunger*: 95)

Because of the complex nature of the material – the intellectual density and the brilliant originality of Marechera's writing – the approach adopted in this article (in the interest of accessing his ideas on the issue as effectively as possible) is classificatory, exemplificatory and exegetical and does not use a pre-cast theoretical frame. Born and brought up in poverty under conditions of urban squalor (*Source Book*: 1–19) Marechera manifested early on that intellectual giftedness we term 'genius' – in his case, a rapidly developing talent for articulation. His work is simultaneously metaphorically vivid, philosophically probing and precise, as well as deeply compassionate and socially aware. The notorious 'difficulty' of his work (the frequency of his allusions to world literature and his fondness for disconcerting narrative shifts and surrealist techniques) is less of a barrier to the reader who recognizes that Marechera's writing is that of an author engaged in the analysis of a topic, but one who (unlike a conventional philosopher or scientist) approaches this topic simultaneously from as many perspectives as possible in the interest of achieving a fullness of understanding. Moreover, although he never trivializes his subject, Marechera's style is not solemn, but supremely open and playful – showing a fascination with paradox, contradictions and irony – and it can switch from tragedy to comedy in an instant, or hold both visions in balance.

At least seven notions of, or ways of experiencing and imagining, exile are distinguishable in Marechera's work. These imaginings or apperceptions are *concepts*, but they are presented as *experiences* – either 'autobiographical' (i.e. the narrator's own) or 'anecdotal' (i.e. his acquaintances'). The concepts of exile which I distinguish here do not occur in such tidily distinct ways in Marechera's work, where they intertwine, intersect or relate concentrically to one another. Marechera's own indication of this point occurs early in *The Black Insider*, when the narrator tells us that the work is 'more than [a story] because a novel is like a big toe with little toes ranged down one of its sides' (24). One most important factor that counts in the communicability of the often intricate ideas

4 Concepts of Exile

addressed by the author is the successful establishment of a highly distinct narrative voice – a 'voice' which is characterized firstly by candour and secondly by intellectual confidence and erudition, as well as by a type of 'social ease' – addressing any reader with an assumption of familiarity and recognised dignity; what one might call 'fellow-feeling'. This is significantly paradoxical; in a novel whose main theme is a (multi-layered) condition of exile, the issue is discussed by a narrator whose tone is that of a person supremely 'at home'. I would suggest that by means of a number of balanced impressions (the work's title, the symbolic wall painting, expressions like 'us blacks' and the reference to English as 'foreign' (23, 24) indicate an African identity, whereas the young white woman who visits, the European reading matter of the narrator and the 'Faculty of Arts' setting (23–9) point to Western presences and influences) Marechera negotiates the space in which he can gain any reader's attention. By this technique, Marechera initially 'internationalizes' the notion of exile; not the Internationale, but the condition of exile here 'unites the human race'.

Helen (the white girl) later tells the narrator 'we [are] all changelings'; 'something indefinable was taken out of us long ago' (102). A world where 'multitudes each day succumb to the despair of hunger, disease and homelessness' (32) has lost its humanity and can offer human beings no home. In terms of this profoundly sceptical, yet humane vision, most human 'achievements' are a mockery: 'culture', 'tradition', 'history', or 'civilization', are merely 'endoparasites which actually live permanently in our minds' (33), and all human endeavour is false – mere 'attitudes' (38–42). Marechera's most inclusive sense of the exiled state (the first concept) might thus be termed ontological – it reads exile as the metaphysical condition of humanity. 'There was nothing out there or inside me which I could see was the wire between the life inside me and the actual geography of living', he writes in a central passage. 'This was the tearing cloth of exile' (61).

Interlinked with this notion is, however, the narrator's suggestion that exile is (and this is the second idea) the colonial (or political) deprivation suffered by Africans and others who have been communally, psychically 'disembowelled' by the more powerful Western cultures.

> We stand each to each like sides of rock once quarried mercilessly by blind Victorian adventurers who only sought the few gold veins in us. They have extracted the best part of our being and left us like this. (38)

Although the futuristic war which rages as the setting of *The Black Insider* is said no longer to be 'a black against white chess game' (24), the Armageddon-like hordes of paratroopers who seem set to overrun everything by the end of the novel are significantly 'face-blackened' (115). Elsewhere, too, a distinctly, bitterly African perspective – a notion of dispossession – is conveyed when the narrator refers to 'a world that had rapidly ceased to be ours and had become a whiteman's playground for investment, good living, and casual tormenting of Caliban' (105). One of the ironies in the novel's title – or its sarcasm – is brought out when the character Otolith refers to the experience of *discrepancy* registered by those 'born black in a white environment' (87) – which is the twentieth century. So the character identified as 'an African Schweik' (72) defines colonialism as 'that great principle which put anyone who was not white in the wrong' (97) – that is, 'exiled' them. All of Africa becomes 'a continent of refugees' (79). In a tone of lamentation, an *alter ego* of the narrator's notes both a desire and its frustration – the urge to '[hurl]... the white world out of us' (73). In a clear echo of Fanon's terminology, another character is described as 'coal black, disillusioned, transfigured, damned, and as it seemed prey to his nerves' (54). The narrator, too, knows that he grew up 'in the very midst of the cultural cerebral rape of my people' (51).

The sort of sneering criticism to which Marechera has been subjected – the lines he incorporates into the fabric of *The Black Insider*, '"It is clear that the writer does not have a high opinion of the black man. He is ... trying to fight liberation from western capitals while all the time wishing he was white"' (109 – cf. *Hunger*: 45) are taken directly from an actual reader's report (*Source Book*: 182–3) – a line of criticism implying that he is a traitor to the African cause, is patently unjust and inaccurate if the deep indignation informing the examples in the previous paragraph is taken into account. Yet his position is not characterized by a simple chauvinism. Marechera combines mockery and compassion when his narrator notes that 'Talk of self-realization and "identity" and their attendant pathos and banality are the poorest of summings up' (46). This can be linked with his recognition of the irrevocable effects of colonialism: 'This Indo-European group of languages ... has been carried .... to the far corners of the earth' (35), 'exiling' Africans 'within' their 'own' cultures, as the long discussion (34–7) of the invasive force of language makes clear. Its subjecting power includes naming (or labelling); 'The word "primitive" is applied' (34), notes the narrator, to the less technologized areas of the world. In his brief sketch 'Oxford, Black Oxford' (118–21) Marechera contrasts 'the dull gold inwardness, narrowness' of the British university city with 'The reek and ruin of heat and mud-huts' of his area of origin, where people live exiled from 'education, good food, even dignity' (118). About to be expelled from Oxford, he juxtaposes himself with the *actually* corrupt and intellectually lazy insider, the suave fellow-student whose condescending drawl immediately brings the expression 'The language of power' (119) to his mind (compare *Hunger*: 111). This language embodies the 'thoughts that think in straight lines [and] cannot see round corners: the missionaries and teachers saw to that' (37). Césaire, Fanon and Cabral have all emphasized this 'de-culturising' process of colonization, of which Marechera is so deeply aware.

Perhaps the most vividly depicted is the third dimension of exile addressed in Marechera's early writing: the experience of Africans in Britain. One might name this the social dimension of exile (as Marechera understands it). In one of the narratively most complex sections of the novel (56–69) the narrator offers the reader a series of intertwined memories, triggered by the sight of Otolith: 'a burnt-out case clutching Africanity in one hand and a bottle of whiskey in the other' (56), both

6   Concepts of Exile

props equally inadequate. The core memory here is of the eventually harrowing 'chance meeting in London' (56) with Nyasha (69), a fellow Zimbabwean exile who had been the narrator's best friend in that country (56). A series of other, circling memories contextualize the account of the meeting, to explain the careful and sensitive social negotiations (fruitlessly) attempted by the narrator. He recalls (for the reader) a whole series of ejections and rejections experienced by himself (the narrator, whose experiences closely resemble the author's). These range from the knowledge that a black in white working-class Britain is socially unwise if he parades his intellect (57) and includes his memories of becoming *persona non grata* to fellow Africans when expelled from university (58) and of being unnecessarily and humiliatingly stop-searched in full public gaze by a smart black policeman (58–9), as well as of an unsuccessful reunion with a (white) ex-girlfriend (59–61). Shortly after the latter episode he was ejected from his lodgings and jailed (on a complaint from a West Indian landlord) (61). Here the narrator's concentration shifts suddenly to Nyasha and their London encounter. Nyasha is unhappily married, but more seriously (it seems) also socially alienated in England. With no consideration or knowledge of the narrator's own difficulties, Nyasha complains and accuses:

> Exile in London is so demoralizing ... everyone looks phoney and suspicious and cynical and there's no black feeling among us any more. You're all scraggy at the seams.... *What's happened to us? What's happening to blacks here in London?** (62).

In its combination of deep empathy ('So it had *also* happened to him' – 62) with clear-eyed analysis, the full account of the narrator's and Nyasha's encounter is one of the most moving and significant sections of the novel. The narrator recalls their earlier mutual, passionate commitment to their country's political liberation (62) and the way their fervour had subsequently faded and become compromised. In the role of 'Emigrés in a racially colour-conscious country', their political and personal integrity becomes tainted with 'artificiality' and is simultaneously gnawed at by 'the inner unspoken discontent inside' which undermines the legitimacy of political aspirations (63). Adding another dimension to Fanon's sense of 'wretched[ness]' (65), the narrator sees the weakness and pathos of the émigré huddle (like Auden's 'malicious village' referred to earlier): a 'black laager' as inadequate defence against the 'whiteman's sneer' (65). Marechera's is no comforting vision, although it is both emphatic and compassionate, but offers a *searing* insight into the way these uncomfortable sociopolitical circumstances produce 'a strange *obsequious assertiveness*' (65). The psychological ambivalence of this state is elsewhere in the novel represented in a sarcastic, vivid image: 'the careless abandon of *assimillados* who have not forgotten their place' (106). It is notable how profoundly (morally and politically) critical Marechera is of black demoralization consequent

---

* In this and subsequent quotations from Marechera's work, I have italicized for emphasis.

upon the pressures of exile, much as he understands it (from both personal experience and social observation) – and the cover-ups (66) or the scapegoating, mutually recriminatory malice (68, 62) which result from such alienation.

As a fourth type of exile Marechera focuses (in an unusual transposition of this notion) on the *postcolonial* African state which supposedly regained or rebuilt a 'home' (106) for its citizens, but became merely a further instrument of their alienation and exploitation. Whilst castigating power corruption and failures of social responsibility among the new political elites, Marechera nevertheless does not overlook African artists' and intellectuals' complicity in the process: 'we raise the African image to fly in the face of the wind and cannot see the actually living blacks having their heads smashed open with hammers in Kampala' (84), he writes. This 'African image' (105), the narrator declares, 'did not teach us the simple preciousness of all life' (106) – instead, 'the machine of the nation-state gave the citizen a prefabricated identity ... made up of the rouge and lipstick of the struggle and the revolution' (105). In articulating these deeply-felt criticisms Marechera's position is not (any more than Fanon's, in his chapter 'The pitfalls of national consciousness' from *The Wretched of the Earth*: 119–65) that of the comfortably detached outsider-satirist, but that of a social and political 'gadfl[y]' (*Source Book*: 370) who is wholly committed to his people. (Marechera did, indeed, maintain this socially critical role – distinctly uncomfortable as it was – upon his return to Harare, as his other posthumously published works *Mindblast* of 1984 and *Scrapiron Blues* of 1994, as well as his poetry collection of 1992, all testify.)

What I classify as the fifth or autobiographical 'dimension' of Marechera's analysis of exile, the record of his personal anxieties and difficulties caused by the experience, is not his main focus (as I have attempted to illustrate heretofore). It does, however, add the quality of a particular authenticity or *testimony* to what he writes about the exiled condition – it was no mere sociological subject to him, but something he felt to the bone. The South African writer Lewis Nkosi's reference to the 'strange fate' of exile (Nkosi 1978: 93) is apposite to Marechera's sense of the 'soulless waitingroom' of exile in 'a world always without' where 'There is nowhere to go Mister' (Marechera, *Cemetery* 1992: 28, 29). The profound stress which the author's exile experience aroused is frequently alluded to, although often thinly disguised through attribution to narrator-figures, as in 'Thought-tracks in the Snow' (Marechera, *Hunger*: 142–8), with its reference to 'years of desperate loneliness' unsuccessfully alleviated by 'whiskey' and 'other self-destructuve poisons' (144). The assaults on the psyche recorded here are not only internal (like the refrain 'You're crazy, you're crazy, you're crazy' which buzzes through the narrator's head – 142), but external as well (illustrated in the taunting questions from the Nigerian student – 'Why did I not write in my own language?' and 'Was I perhaps one of those Africans who despised their own roots?' 142–3 and the racist insult from his white wife that he is a 'nigger jackass' – 145). Having escaped from the Rhodesian 'House of Hunger', he finds in England 'stone rather than bread' (*Hunger*: 144), and

8 Concepts of Exile

'truths packaged in lies' (Marechera, *Insider* 1990: 117). Relationship after relationship (especially with white women) fails and leaves him in derelict circumstances (*Insider*: 125–7).

One of the most interesting angles on exile in Marechera's many variations on this theme occurs in section 3 of 'The Writer's Grain', titled 'Protista', which features on pages 127–33 of *The House of Hunger*. I would term it the author's mythological exploration of the exile theme (the sixth type of conceptualization among those I have identified). 'Protista' is dramatically intense and dreamlike in its presentation, and its mythical references contain a number of elements from Shona folklore. In this story the protagonist has been 'exiled' to a 'raw region', stricken by a twelve-year 'drought', for unspecified 'political crimes' (127) – his state being referred to as 'this exacting punishment of exile' (129). His partner has left him to undertake a quest of her own, although she had 'long endured the barren fire of exile with [him]' (128). Layers of memory add density to the protagonist's symbolic situation. One is 'the story [his]father had told[him] … about the resilience of human roots' (128); the impossibility of getting away from one's origins (128–9). Marechera's own strange tale with its Rhodesian and Shona references metafictionally illustrates the point. So, for instance, the protagonist explains that he has named the valley to which he was exiled 'Lesapi after my birthplace where once I had learned to fish, to swim and … to relax' (129). This calls to mind Marechera's many references to 'Lesapi' in his poems (*Cemetery of Mind*: 116, 161, 200) and as noted in his biography (*Source Book*: 1, 51). Although he grew up in slums these references deliberately mythologize his origins (the general squalor of which is elsewhere clearly described) to include a paradisal, rural element – a verdant scene from which he has been exiled. Yet even in 'Protista' this ideal scene is transformed by an intrusion which calls colonialism to mind. The protagonist refers to '[Mr?] Robert's side of the river, *where it was fenced and there was a notice about trespassers*' (129) – an exclusionary device which is another suggestion of being exiled and deprived, *dislocated*. Especially poignant and resonant is the following passage:

> I had named the valley to give it the myths and faces of moments in my own life. But as the years went by, the waterless valley – paralysed by the cramping effects of an overwhelming oppression – emitted its own symbolic mists which overpowered my own imagination [with the shapes of] … this eerie region. (131)

False 'roots' (132) later entrap the protagonist, but although his beloved returns, now dead, to release him, his escape seems at best ambiguous, and finally he is (it seems) overcome and defeated (133). The story is rich in symbolic detail and far too subtly complex to be adequately analysed in so brief a space, but that it offers a mythologically clothed reflection on the cultural dislocation caused by exile, seems clear.

Finally, it may be noted that Marechera probes the psychological effects of exile. The author is certainly 'following' Fanon in his reading of exile as a cause of trauma (exacerbated by racism in the new environment), as the clear Fanonian reference in the title of the story 'Black Skin

What Mask' (*Hunger*: 93–9) makes evident. In this sketch, the narrator's own black skin is (in the opening paragraph) described as endowed with a life of its own:

> My skin sticks out a mile in all the crowds around here. Every time I go out I feel it tensing up, hardening, torturing itself. It only relaxes when I am in shadow, when I am alone, when I wake up early in the morning, when I am doing mechanical actions, and, strangely enough, when I am angry. But it is coy and self-conscious when I ... begin to write. (93)

Evidently it is an intensely, even virulently alien environment that can turn the body's most natural home, the protective envelope of one's skin, into a source of danger and discomfort. Yet the power of the new environment gazing upon the individual 'others' him from him*self*: The exile's environment allows it to impress its distorting perception on his consciousness. In a story that focuses its analysis chiefly on the narrator's reluctant 'friend', one so alienated that he can be seen 'trying to scrub the blackness out of his skin' (93), the opening paragraph quoted above is doubly important – it makes clear that, although the narrator appears mostly scornful and mocking about the absurd extremes to which his fellow African's racial neurosis drives him, he (the narrator) does understand and even share these anxieties induced by exile. The narrator may be sardonic, but he is not contemptuous; being himself too ambiguously 'close' to the (finally suicidal) protagonist – although the narrator's defiance towards the system (99) sets him off from his pathetic 'friend'.

A similar psychologically focused analysis, this time comically surreal in its presentation, occurs in Part I of 'The Writer's Grain'(*Hunger*: 100–13). It is made clear only fairly late in the story that this narrator, who appears at first to be the typical (i.e. white, British) Oxford don, is in fact African, and that, consequently, the splitting of his self (100–101, *passim*) is caused by his exiled, culturally alienated condition.

> I was cracking up. I did try to tell [my wife] something of what was oppressing my mind: more than half of all English words directly or indirectly slur blackness – and I was teaching the bloody language and the bloody literature and also actually writing my novels in it ... there was always at the back of my mind a smouldering discontent ... (111)

Partly satire, partly social analysis, and partly a wild, hilariously weird comedy, this story is strewn with barbs to prick the unwary reader. The narrator-protagonist is both the black victim and the figure of racial-sexual vengeance, the latter role being especially evident in the deliberately shocking scene where he frenziedly kills 'a cat ... called Melinda the Bloody White' (112) who is *also* (maybe) his mistress. The cat is battered to death with tomes representing English literature, and the fierceness of the protagonist's onslaught is explained or justified by his resentment at the (in his eyes) exaggerated concern Europeans like the British show towards animals, in contrast with their victimization of 'black people everywhere' (111). The mauling of the cat is also a projection of the narrator's psychic 'disintegration' (105) and his 'humiliati[on]' (101). All this is the long-term consequence of 'parents starv[ing] themselves' to 'give [their child] education', in the process 'sell[ing] you mind and soul to the bloody whites' (112) – a familiar theme of these writings. The difficulty of charting or profiling Marechera's complex, intertwined concepts of exile proves neither confusion nor immaturity on the part of this still unjustly neglected writer. It shows (instead) the arduousness of his learning how 'exile' might be understood, and the uncompromising, vividly immediate – as well as deeply considered, *pondered* – nature of his expression of these ideas and experiences. In a style by turns sombre, amusing and perplexing, Marechera's writing records the working of a mind both incisive and subtle, as well as a profound, socially responsible sensibility, in his engagement with the theme of exile.

WORKS CITED

Auden, Wystan Hugh, *Collected Shorter Poems 1927–1957*, London: Faber & Faber, 1966.
Buuck, David, 'African Doppelgänger: Hybridity and Identity in the Work of Dambudzo Marechera', *Research in African Literatures* 28.2, Summer 1997: 118–31.
Cabral, Amilcar, *Return to the Source: Selected Speeches of Amilcar Cabral*, New York: Monthly Review Press, 1973.
Césaire, Aimé, *Discourse on Colonialism*, New York: Monthly Review Press, 1972.
Fanon, Frantz, *Black Skin, White Masks*, St Albans, Herts: Paladin, 1970.
— *The Wretched of the Earth*, Harmondsworth: Penguin, 1967.
Farah, Nuruddin, *Sardines*, London: Heinemann, 1982.
Gaylard, Gerald, 'Dambudzo Marechera and Nationalist Criticism', *English in Africa* 20.2, October 1993: 89-105.
Gurnah, Abdulrazak, '"The Mid-Point of the Scream": The Writing of Dambudzo Marechera', in Abdulrazak Gurnah (ed.), *Essays on African Writing 2: Contemporary Literature*, Ibadan: Heinemann, 1995: 100–18.
Gurr, Andrew, *Writers in Exile: The Identity of Home in Modern Literature*, Sussex: Harvester, 1981.
Lamming, George, *The Pleasures of Exile*, London/New York: Alison & Busby, 1984.
Marechera, Dambudzo, *Cemetery of Mind / Poems*, Harare: Baobab Books, 1992.
— *Mindblast or the Definitive Buddy*, Harare: The College Press, 1984.
— *Scrapiron Blues*, Harare: Baobab Books, 1994.
— *The Black Insider*, Harare: Baobab Books, 1990.
— *The House of Hunger*, London: Heinemann, 1978.
Nkosi, Lewis, *Home and Exile and Other Selections*, London: Longman, 1978.
Nortje, Arthur, *Dead Roots*, London: Heinemann, 1973.
Pattison, David, 'Call No Man Happy: Inside The Black Insider, Marechera's Journey to Become a Writer?', *Journal of Southern African Studies* 20.2, 1994: 221–39.
Said, Edward, 'Reflections on Exile', in R. Ferguson *et al.* (eds), *Out There: Marginalization and Contemporary Cultures*, New York: New Museum of Contemporary Art, 1990: 357–68.

Sarup, Madan, 'Home and Identity' in G. Robertson *et al.* (eds), *Travellers' Tales: Narratives of Home and Displacement*, London: Routledge, 1994: 93–103.

Shakespeare, William, *The Tragedy of Othello The Moor Of Venice*, in S. Wells and G. Taylor (eds), *William Shakespeare: Complete Works*, Oxford: Clarendon Press, 1988: 819–53.

— *The Tragedy of King Richard the Second* in S. Wells and G. Taylor (eds), *William Shakespeare: Complete Works*, Oxford: Clarendon Press, 1988: 367–95.

Seidel, Michael, *Exile and the Narrative Imagination*, New Haven, CT.: Yale University Press, 1986.

Veit-Wild, Flora, 'Carnival and Hybridity in Texts by Dambudzo Marechera and Lesego Rampolokeng', *Journal of Southern African Studies* 23.4, December 1997: 553–64.

— (ed.), *Dambudzo Marechera: A Source Book on his Life and Work*, Harare: University of Zimbabwe Publications, 1993.

— 'Introduction' to *The Black Insider* by Dambudzo Marechera, Harare: Baobab Books, 1990: 5–22.

Mindblasts: Narrative Technique & Iconography of Sexual Stereotyping in Bessie Head's *A Question of Power* & Dambudzo Marechera's *The House of Hunger*

David Kerr

The superficial similarities between *A Question of Power* and *The House of Hunger* are obvious. They are both southern African narratives written in exile during the early 1970s, both running against the realistic or politico-hortatory grain of most contemporary southern African literature, and both drawing very closely on the authors' biographies, particularly their experience of mental affliction. This paper suggests, however, that the two texts problematize the issue of madness differently, and these variations find expression in contrasting narrative strategies.

I would like to argue that *A Question of Power*, although rarely dealing directly with the political struggle against apartheid, grapples intimately, from an exile's standpoint, with the psychic wounds caused by South African racist policies and attitudes. I further argue that this psychic conflict assumes a structure similar to that of a spirit possession ritual, following a basic three-part pattern of 'normality' – possession – enhanced 'normality'.

Elizabeth, the protagonist of *A Question of Power*, is much concerned with the evil of witchcraft, and when she is afflicted by mental problems, she feels she is possessed by evil spirits. The possession takes the form of a psycho-drama in which Elizabeth is defiled by violent phantoms who perform obscene actions of multiple sex, homosexuality, incest and bestiality. The phantoms also reproduce some of the most vicious sexual stereotypes generated by white racists in South Africa.

Dan is the most demonic of these phantoms. His indefatigable lust seems almost the embodiment of the white stereotype of African men as bearers of uncontrolled libidos. The reproduction of the myth requires a racist obsession which, according to Bhabha, 'vacillates between what is always "in place", already known, and something that must be anxiously repeated ... as if ... the bestial sexual license of the African that needs no proof, can never be really ... proved' (Bhabha 1996: 66). The coloured protagonist, Elizabeth, although the victim of black sexual harassment, is not a racist. Her psychic haunting by the demonic Dan, is offset by another phantom, Sello, whose apparent purity is iconically represented by his early appearances in a monk's robe. At times, however, Sello too lapses into the bestiality of Dan, so that the two characters became 'merged as horrors in her mind' (Head 1974: 148). These moments provide some of Elizabeth's worst nightmares, much like the common trope in a horror film, where a moment of security or escape from nightmare proves illusory, and the horror resumes with added intensity. It is as if Head uses these moments of ambiguity to psychically debate and eventually subvert the stereotypes of black/white sexuality, which she feels inhabit her.

The character of Medusa adds another variant to the script of this psychodrama. In much feminist literature of this period, Medusa, the Greek deity whose gaze turned men to stone, was a hero. Head's Medusa is a far more ambiguous figure. Sometimes she is an embodiment of dangerous female sexuality, associated with Elizabeth's need for masturbation; sometimes she is an accomplice in the sexual exploits of Sello and Dan, denouncing Elizabeth for her lack of African erotic appeal, and sometimes she is a malignant yet necessary force, who, while throwing the thunderbolts which cause Elizabeth's debilitating headaches, also keeps her in touch with mystical spirituality.

A Question of Power's Afro-Gothic apparatus of sexual nightmare requires objects for Sello/Dan's lust. The most flamboyant of these are the 72 (mostly black) prostitutes, with names like Miss Wriggly Bottom and The Womb, each with her own skills and proclivities. Their most important function in the nightmare is to taunt Elizabeth for her sexual 'weakness', on account of her mixed blood. At one particularly painful climax of horror the prostitutes shout at her, 'Dog, filth, the Africans will eat you to death' (46).

This example shows how the sexual persecution which Elizabeth experiences is linked to her peripheral status as a political refugee from South Africa, on the margins of Morabeng's highly structured society, particularly as a 'coloured' who does not understand Setswana or the complexity of village society. Elizabeth internalizes the sexual/racial exclusion mechanisms of white apartheid and reproduces them in a distorted form as markers of her insecurity in her new home. But where apartheid stereotypes of black lasciviousness are manifestations of a despised Other, fabricated to keep Africans weak, in *A Question of Power* the relations are almost reversed. Within the socio-cultural reference system of Morabeng, the sexual stereotypes associated with Dan, Sello, Medusa and the prostitutes act as reified indices of African power, from which Elizabeth feels excluded.

Elizabeth, like Head in her real life, is institutionalized in a mental hospital. The apparent 'cure', however, which Elizabeth enjoys as a result of the psychiatric medication is actually less important than the autotherapy Elizabeth applies through her love of literature. She throws the packet of prescription tablets out of the window (203), and finds more effective relief from reading D.H. Lawrence's poetry and Premchand's Indian novel, *The Gift of a Cow*, and from meditating on Buddhism and Islam.

I suggest that this aesthetic relief links *A Question of Power* to the therapeutic mechanisms of spirit possession rituals. Bourdillon (1990) has commented on the difference between Western and African concepts of multiple personality and madness:

In western society this [multiple personality] is regarded as a form of insanity, in other societies it might be regarded as a form of possession by evil spirits when the changes cannot be controlled by ritual (330–31).

Bourdillon notes that in an African context, rituals such as *Masabe* among the Shona act as a form of para-theatrical therapy so that the multiple personality can, through exposure, be ultimately controlled. In southern African culture madness is not necessarily an absolute evil. The Chinyanja proverb 'Wamisala adiona nkhondo' (the mad person saw the war) implies that mental stress may be associated with prophetic or spiritual power.

Head was very aware that *A Question of Power* tapped African sources of spirituality, even if she herself (despite reading Mbiti's book on African religion) did not understand it properly. She realizes that her novel might not be 'the classic struggle with God and the Devil I thought it was. It might simply be some African horror – something I don't understand ... People don't understand anything about how baloi work' (Eilersen: 150). Head seems to be acknowledging that the sexual mobsters, which haunt Elizabeth in *A Question of Power*, constitute some form of possession by evil spirits or witches (*baloi*) and that the process of writing the novel is a method of exorcizing them.

This might account for the structure of the novel assuming, at least in some aspects, the form of a spirit possession ritual. The opening pages of *A Question of Power* present a fairly naturalistic account of Elizabeth's early life in South Africa and her exile to Botswana; they also etch some of the main characters in the village of Morabeng. From about page 30, however, the naturalistic narrative begins to break down, and the word 'seems' becomes repeated frequently, as Head describes the horrors of her possession by Sello, Dan and Medusa. Despite some occasional resurfacings into the natural world, Head sustains this domain of spiritual nightmare until the end of the novel, when Elizabeth realizes that she has emerged into a state of 'lofty serenity' (202). This allows Elizabeth to re-emerge, cleansed, into the world of normality (metonymized by Kenosi and the women's agricultural project).

There are parallels between this narrative structure and the form of a spirit possession ritual, such as *Mapira* (Berliner 1978) or *Vimbuza* (Kamlongera et al. 1992). These ceremonies take the form of a nightlong descent into bestiality, a liminal atavism marked by the symbolic wearing of wild animal skins and the drinking of animal blood. This is a private, even intimate immersion into defilement, experienced by the afflicted, followed by a joyous return to society, in which the afflicted, assisted by a medium, cleanses herself by dancing the evil spirits away. Just as the spirit possession ritual uses the aestheticism of music and dance to allow the afflicted a controlled experience of irrational spirituality, Head's narrative confrontation with the psychic evil of racism, expressed in scatological and pornographic images, allows Elizabeth to purge those horrors from her soul and return strengthened to society.

Thus the racist stereotypes which Head inflicts upon Elizabeth should not be seen as a manifestation of pure racism. Head herself was aware of the necessary evil of her recourse to racial/sexual stereotypes in her own madness and in that which she creates for Elizabeth. In a letter to Randolph Vigne she declares the need to confront the demons of apartheid and the Ku Klux Klan. 'You have to look at wild, savage evil, relentless, merciless cruelty, then you understand them' (Head 1991: 160). By the end of *A Question of Power*, Elizabeth has gone through her dark night of the soul, and, just as the patient in a spirit possession ritual uses dance to reconnect herself to the world of daytime normality, Elizabeth uses literature as the cathartic agent, exorcizing the evil phantoms which had haunted her.

Although the strength is mainly psychological, it also has an ideological dimension. Several critics have complained that Head's concern with the inner psychology of her characters makes her neglect issues concerning the injustice of apartheid. Lewis Nkosi, for example, complains that in *A Question of Power* 'the autobiographical element holds sway over the novelist' to the detriment of sociopolitical analysis (Nkosi 1981: 99). I believe it is possible, however, to decode a strong ideological message in the novel. Head associates the crushing power of her spiritual tormentors with the principle of power 'in its overwhelming lust for dominance and prestige' (1974: 135). This makes Elizabeth rail against all power-hungry politicians, whether white or black, against the rich and influential who exploit the poor, and even against a patriarchal, Judaeo-Christian-Islamic God, 'some unseen being in the sky' (205) who allows his creatures to suffer. In the final analysis, *A Question of Power* asserts a utopian vision of human relations based on love and mutual trust rather than control, power, cruelty and exploitation.

Utopian is certainly not a word one would even think of associating with *The House of Hunger*. Marechera's novella seems to expunge almost all forms of the spirituality which preoccupies Bessie Head. Yet many of Head's obsessions — madness, sexuality, power, race and subjectivity — are also central to *The House of Hunger*.

Marechera's narrative is no less autobiographical than Head's. However, he eschews a fictionalized, third person protagonist, opting instead for a first person narrator. The protagonist, who has no name, seems to be very close to Marechera himself, and I shall use the term 'Ego' to refer to him in this paper. Where Head deals with mental breakdown which had happened just a few months before the writing process began, Marechera creates a Bildungsroman, where the crucial mental breakdown occurs several years earlier when Ego/Marechera was doing A levels at school. *The House of Hunger* does not focus only on the mental breakdown, but links it to Ego's total life history, and to a concrete, socio-political context in Zimbabwe.

It is clear, however, that the description of Ego's neurosis at school has strong autobiographical elements. Marechera's teacher at St. Augustine's, Father Pearce, has testified to the novelist's mental problems at the time:

> I found him charming and ingratiating one day and a real demon the next! He showed a number of signs of clinical mental sickness, including hearing voices threatening him (Veit-Wild 1992: 68).

In *The House of Hunger* Marechera describes the laughter of these voices as being obscene and 'of the crudest type' (30). The luminous description of mental stress in this part of the novella is rather similar to Head's metaphors of volcanic eruptions. 'Little thrusts of swift lights, diamond sparks, spinning maddeningly, leaped through my mind until I could not bear the headache of it' (30). For the most part, however, Marechera does not anatomize the sensation of mental breakdown, he creates a moral and aesthetic universe, which itself provides a correlative for Ego's spiritual disintegration.

The different emphasis between the two texts can be seen in the contrast between their moral tones. In *A Question of Power*, Good and Evil are dynamic forces like medieval morality characters (though Bunyan may have been a more proximate influence). In *The House of Hunger* morality only exists ironically, as Ego contrasts an idealized, heroic ethic rooted in history with the debauched and trivial reality which he encounters in his modern day-to-day life.

The irony centres on the motif of 'black heroes' which runs throughout the novella. The first major appearance of the 'black heroes' is as a design on Julia's T shirt, as she and Ego drink in a bar: 'her massive breasts ... were stamped by the gigantic legend of Zimbabwe' (20). The picture of black warriors on the bulging garment, however humorously presented, refers to a valorized, precolonial, African heroism, 'a golden age of black Arcadia' (24), in contrast to which the squalor and banality of Ego's life seem empty. When, for example, the prostitute, Nestor, physically ejects Ego and his friend, Philip, from her house, the narrator cannot resist commenting ironically, 'we could not get out fast enough. Ah heroes, black heroes ...' (56).

The implicit contrast between an ideal of male, black heroism and the anti-heroic quality of all the novella's male characters (not excluding Ego) permeates *The House of Hunger*. The black men in the book are either opportunistic cowards (like the police informer, Harry), confused bullies (like Peter and Stephen), promiscuous drunkards like Ego's father, or ineffectual intellectuals (like Philip and Ego). Even the ZANLA guerrilla, Edmund, killed by the Selous Scouts, fails to live up to the image of black heroism, owing to the memories Ego has of Edmund being mercilessly bullied at school. This catalogue of rogues and misfits stimulates Ego to call out in despair, 'where are the bloody heroes?' (43).

Nor does Marechera offer any relief by hinting at a more optimistic future, as other contemporary novelists did, such as Alex la Guma in *Time of the Butcherbird* and *In the Fog of the Seasons' End*. During a discussion about exiles and the future of Zimbabwe, Philip complains about opportunists who are 'just as bad as white shit', saying that 'there's a lot of bastards hanging around in London waiting to come back here and become ministers' (Marechera 1978: 59). This discussion between Philip and Ego bears a striking resemblance to a conversation about African politics in *A Question of Power* when Elizabeth tells Tom, an American agricultural volunteer:

> The politicians first jump on the bandwagon of past suffering ... and sweep the crowd away by weeping and wailing about the past. Then why do they steal and cheat people once they're into Government? (Head 1974: 133)

The difference is that in *A Question of Power* Head celebrates the 'African masses' or 'ordinary people' as a positive alternative to the 'politicians' and 'presidents for life'. Marechera envisages no such relief; disillusionment sullies the Second Chimurenga even before it takes place.

The narrator has little more respect for the female characters in *The House of Hunger*. They can be categorized either as victims (Immaculate, Patricia) or prostitutes (Nestor, Julia) or both (Ego's mother). Both male and female characters seem to be engaged in a compulsive and debilitating war against each other. Here Marechera shares some of Head's preoccupation with sexuality as an arena for power conflicts. *The House of Hunger* uses sexuality, especially of an inter-racial kind, as a symbol for colonialism in Rhodesia. This is partly manifested in the pressure on African women to use hair-straightening or skin-lightening cosmetics. But overt sexuality also links African women to a wider paradigm of colonial exploitation. The most vivid example of this is the description Marechera gives of a youthful Ego who spies upon a black prostitute servicing white clients.

> (W)e could see on the gravel road splotches and stains of semen that were dripping down her as she walked. Years later I was to write a story using her as a symbol of Rhodesia. (49)

The almost pathologically graphic imagery expresses Ego's disgust at the colonial penetration of Africa in both the sexual and political senses.

Marechera's employment of sexual nausea as a trope of psychological instability is only superficially similar to Head's. Where Head associates African sexuality with power, Marechera associates it with powerlessness. This is achieved not by describing the sexual/metaphysical antics of fantasy characters but by creating a series of motifemic image-chains, which link the domains of colonialism, sexuality, violence, artistic solipsism and personal alienation.

The most prominent of these motifs is encapsulated in the often-repeated word, 'stains'. At the literal level 'stains' refers to bodily fluids, semen, excrement and blood. Ego's obsession with these fluids and with the frailty/morbidity of the human body in general is an index of his psychic maladjustment. At the moral and aesthetic levels, however, it has a far more powerful significance. The references to semen, as we have seen in the above quotation, relate to colonial exploitation of Africa, but also, in a different context, to the escapism of black Rhodesian youths, 'screwing pussy as though out to prove that white men do not in reality exist' (75). At yet another level they refer to a domain of sexual licence which epitomizes the deracination of an emergent Zimbabwean society under the pressures of modernization and urbanization.

The defiling imagery of excrement and bodily corruption expresses Ego's ontological insecurity in a world without stable metaphysical or moral values. This is typified by the conceit of musical latrine flies:

> A cloud of flies from the nearby public toilet was humming Handel's Hallelujah Chorus. It was an almost perfect photograph of the human condition. (10–11)

The photograph freezes Ego's characteristic, neurotic stance – the inability to find any metaphysical meaning to life. Where, in *A Question of Power*, Head interrogates the premises of Western theology, Marechera in *The House of Hunger* recoils in existential alarm at the whole concept of God. Humanity and God seem to have no mutual contact, 'it is as if [the world] was God's wound, and we were all maggots slithering in it' (70).

The motif of 'stains' as blood is perhaps even more common than semen and excrement. This has a very personal, autobiographical context. Marechera slightly changes the circumstances of his own father's death (killed in a traffic accident) to have Ego's father killed by a more symbolically resonant vehicle, a train:

> The old man died beneath the wheels of the twentieth century. There was nothing left but stains, bloodstains and fragments of flesh... And the same thing is happening to my generation. (45)

Marechera's train carries the thrust of Western technology, destroying indigenous African rural culture, and leaving in its wake both literal death, and more widely a psychic destruction, the anomie which engulfs Ego and, even though they sometimes do not realize it, his whole generation.

The only chance of escape from internal exile is one which bears some resemblance to Head's solution to the problems of alienation – the agency of artistic reflection. Ego sums up his rather Sartrean argument for an existential view of art:

> Nothing lasts long enough to make any sense.... Only rarely do we see the imminence of wholes. And that is the beginning of art. (60)

As Gurnah comments, 'the life of the mind is valorised as the narrator's only means of keeping at bay the ugly and mocking phantom other – the 'real' world' (Gurnah: 1994:116). It is the possibility of art as a solution to the meaningless contingency of life that allows Marechera to create *The House of Hunger* at all, and he is acutely aware that the very act of writing the novella is almost an act of defiance, plucking meaning from chaos:

> Stains! Love or even hate or desire for revenge are just so many stains on a sheet, on a wall, on a page even. This page! (55)

Constantly, through such self-reflexive auto-denigration, Marechera strives to undermine any potential dignity which the art of creating *The House of Hunger* might engender.

The refusal to provide the reader with any false artistic equilibrium is largely generated through the narrative technique, the strategies of which can be usefully illuminated by a comparison with *A Question of Power*. Head's novel uses a relatively simple diagesis. The story is told in chronological order, with almost no flashbacks, and, once the reader accepts Elizabeth's fantasies as real (as they are to her), with a coherent concept of character. Sello, Dan and Medusa, despite an alarming tendency to alter their appearance and personalities, are still lucidly presented as independent characters. The narrative clarity is supported by a style which, even when it mixes metaphors, or soars from the concrete to metaphysical abstraction, always maintains a very firm syntactic grip.

In *The House of Hunger*, by contrast, Marechera uses a stream-of-consciousness style in which mixed metaphors, colloquialisms, strained similes, neologisms, complex hypotactic layering, sentence fragments, interrupted parentheses, multiple ellipses, and a provocative juxtaposition of wildly divergent registers, tumble anarchically. The characters seem to have no independent life, but to emerge or sink at the behest of the narrator's fevered consciousness.

Most confusing of all, Marechera uses a hypodiagetic narrative technique, designed to disorient the reader, particularly with respect to the time frame. The 'present' in the novel consists mostly of a conversation between Ego and Julia in a bar. This, however, provides only a skimpy frame from which Ego engages in a series of flashbacks to various stages of his earlier life, some remote, some recent, and presented without any chronological consistency. Flashbacks within flashbacks occur so frequently that the reader often feels pulled into a temporal and emotional whirlpool. Where Head coaxes the reader to give vicarious testimony to Elizabeth's neurosis, Marechera forces the reader into participating in Ego's breakdown.

The contrast between the two narrative strategies is most obvious in their endings. As we have seen, Head provides a sense of firm, if unanticipated, closure – Elizabeth's return to 'normality' in the almost oceanic epiphany of the novel's last two sentences. Marechera offers no such moment of equilibrium. The reader is expecting a return to the frame of the Julia/Ego bar scene, but it never comes. Instead, the novella ends *in medias res*, within a narrative about 'the old man'. This is an ambiguous figure. Is he Ego's dead father (and the narrative thus yet another flashback)? Or is he a totally new character, a sympathetic old man who, like some implausible *deus ex machina*, rescues notes which the Govern ment spy, Harry, is keeping about Ego?

Whatever tie-in the final narrative sequence has with the plot, it projects a studied inconsequentiality, designed to deflate any sense of aesthetic immanence, which a narrative normally achieves simply through providing a denouement. The old man's rambling series of folk-story fragments seem to pull the narrative into the realm of the aesthetic, as if aiming for closure. But by a piece of hypodiagetic sleight of hand, Marechera locks the reader within a narrative prison, achieved through the geometric trope of a circle.

Modern theories of narratology lay strong emphasis on geometry as the dominant metaphor underlying conventional narrative structure, especially through the circular plot. As Gibson explains, 'the universal irreversible, geometric scheme has become the fundamental model for our traditional conception of structure' (20). In the conclusion of *The House of Hunger*, Marechera seems consciously to play with and discard such concepts of narrative geometry. The old man has just told a folk story about a man whose wife gives birth to a blood-spattered egg (itself suggesting a geometric shape, as well as the more obvious symbol of artistic fertility), when he announces:

> A writer drew a circle in the sand and stepping into it said, 'This is my novel', but the circle, leaping, cut him clear through. (81)

In this little fable, Marechera, through the distancing agency of multiple narratives (Ego telling the old man's story of what the anonymous writer said), proffers the traditional geometric closure of narrative – the circle – only to deny its efficacy. The geometric figure, like some circular saw, slices the writer in half. This suggests the dangers of artistic creativity, but also subverts the whole narrative, as if defying the reader to find repose in the novel's ending. Once Marechera has conjured his world of contingent chaos and defilement, he does not allow readers the easy escape, which a concluding full-stop normally provides.

It is now time for me to provide my own sense of closure to this article. It would be easy to use a contrast between the Head and Marechera texts to play one off against the other. I could endorse Head's social commitment to humanity, as opposed to Marechera's solipsistic nihilism. Alternatively, I could validate Marechera's unflinching honesty, in contrast to Head's utopian sentimentality. Neither of these conclusions would be adequate. At a personal level, I find both texts compulsive testimonies to the psychic dilemmas raised by exile and other disruptive manifestations of the late twentieth-century, southern African political economy. The books' contrasting appeals are often dependent upon the fluctuations of my own idealistic or cynical moods.

Both *A Question of Power* and *The House of Hunger* offer valuable insights into the nature of post-colonial anomie. At a time when most authors were harnessing literary energies to the organized struggle against apartheid, Head and Marechera created prophetic literature which probed the psychological roots of racism and exploitation, in ways which continue to reverberate profoundly even after the formal apparatus of racism and colonialism has been dismantled. Their accounts of linguistic and cultural alienation, with both authors very self-conscious of their isolation from the bulk of their neighbours, resonate for a growing readership in a southern Africa where economic migration creates even more cultural displacement than the political exile of the sixties and seventies. Head and Marechera, in their different ways, chart the minefields of a socio-psychic realm, which Baudrillard says is 'held together ... more by arbitrary than by obvious, more by complex but transitory historical contingency than by inevitable anthropological constraints' (Baudrillard 1991: 35). The two authors provide a rough map to this terrain, which ever more of us may have to follow in a changeable, chaotic and often threatening post-colonial world.

WORKS CITED

Baudrillard, J., 'Is It Really Important to Think?', *Philosophy and Social Criticism* 9.1, 1991.
Bhabha, Homi,*The Location of Culture*, London: Routledge, 1996.
Berliner, Paul, *The Soul of Mbira: Music and Traditions of the Shona People of*

Zimbabwe, Los Angeles: UCLA Press, 1978.

Bourdillon, M, *Religion and Society: A Text for Africa*, Harare: Mambo Press, 1990.

Eilersen, Gillian Stead, *Bessie Head: 'Thunder Behind Her Ears'*, Cape Town: David Philip; London: James Currey, 1995.

Gurnah, Abdulrazak, 'The Mid-Point of the Scream: the Writing of Dambudzo Marechera' in Abdulrazak Gurnah, (ed.) *Essays on African Writing and Contemporary Literature*, Ibadan: Heinemann, 1994.

Head, Bessie, *A Question of Power*, London: Heinemann, 1974.

— *A Gesture of Belonging: Letters from Bessie Head, 1965–1979*, edited by Randolph Vigne, London: South African Writers; Portsmouth NH: Heinemann, 1991.

Kamlongera, C., Nambote, M., Soko, B. and Timpunza-Mvula, E, *Kubvina: An Introduction to Malawian Dance and Theatre*, Zomba: University of Malawi, 1992.

Marechera, Dambudzo, *The House of Hunger*, London: Heinemann, 1978.

Nkosi, Lewis, *Tasks and Masks*, Harlow: Longman, 1982.

Veit-Wild, Flora (ed.), *Dambudzo Marechera: A Source Book on his Life and Work*, Harare: University of Zimbabwe; London, Melbourne, Munich, New York: Hans Zell, 1993.

Shriek of Nerves:
The Rational Voice of Dennis Brutus
& the Poetry of Exile in *Salutes and Censures*

Ezenwa-Ohaeto

Dennis Brutus in one of his early poems captures with telling accuracy the deeper reality of South Africa when he writes:

> The sounds begin again;
> the siren in the night
> the thunder at the door
> the shriek of nerves in pain
>
> Then the keening crescendo
> of faces split by pain the
> wordless endless wail
> Only the unfree know (*A Simple Lust*:19)

These images of pain reflected in the poem are poignant, but even at that stage of his development as a writer Brutus could display a mastery of the art of containing his emotion. Thus his poetry possesses a subsumed rage that is metaphorically portrayed through the haunting phrase: 'the shriek of nerves in pain'. This metaphor encapsulatea the characteristic of the rational voice in the poetry of Brutus which arouses the reader's intellectual abhorrence as well as making significant the issue of exile. In the poetry collection *Salutes and Censures*[1] this rational voice subjects South Africa to the powerful lenses of a sensitive mind through a juxtaposition of respect and honour (salute) on the one hand and unfavourable criticism (censure) on the other. This attitude is not contradictory, for in its core lies the metaphoric depiction of the South African enigma which portrays an avowal of love for legal structures in that society at that time, in spite of the fact that it is founded on illegal structures. I shall examine the manner in which the rage of Dennis Brutus is encapsulated in a 'shriek of nerves' that emerges through a rational voice as well as the background of exile that generates that rage.

Obviously this paradoxical attitude to reality which enables Brutus to contain his rage and produce a rational poetic voice despite extreme

---

The author is grateful to the Alexander von Humboldt Foundation, Bonn, Germany and the Universities of Mainz and Bayreuth for research facilities.

provocation, has generated criticism. Bahadur Tejani in an article which has now been overtaken by the creative energy and the exile tradition in the poetry of Brutus argues that 'temperamentally Brutus is unsuitable to take on the sophisticated might of the South African government. This unsuitability leads to simplistic conclusions of hope without struggle.' (Tejani 1973: 142). That comment, derived from an examination of the prison poems of Brutus, failed to highlight his hidden strength or his ability to retain literary calmness despite the high degree of provocation; for poetry ultimately is an art form. However, Tejani was immediately taken to task and another critic demonstrated that his preconceived ideas and opinions about South Africa and about Dennis Brutus have gravely distorted his criticism.

This critic agrees that critical questions could be asked about the poetry of Brutus but that the trouble is that Tejani 'asks the wrong questions: questions which are formulated on the basis of strong preconceptions and opinions about Brutus' (Salt 1975: 141). What this literary argument highlighted is the extent to which creative efforts could be perceived as either art or propaganda. However, another critic's observations give not just the right perception of Brutus but also summarize a significant aspect of creativity: 'in the final analysis the burden of Brutus' poetry is to expose the evils of apartheid to the world, to show that he does not support such evil and that something has to be done about the situation. The politician and the revolutionary need to take off from there and effect the desired changes' (Akosu 1986: 50).

Nevertheless, Brutus has been in exile and his works have subsequently taken on new dimensions as *Salutes and Censures* reveals. In this collection the rational voice encapsulates an attitude of censure within the salute, while a pose of salute is subsumed within the cloak of censure. This paradoxical portrayal of reality emerges through a tabulation of incidents and people that deserve the poet's attention. In 'Salute to our Allies' the poet acknowledges the numerous activities of all those who abhor apartheid and who also use the forum of international sports to challenge the nonchalance signified by 'the privileged play/while the oppressed are chained/in the prisons of South Africa'. In this poem Brutus salutes the courage of all those who have brought the South African problem 'to the conscience of the world'. That observation emanates from the knowledge that exile enabled Brutus to acquire. The poet's conclusive statement is significant of his gratitude for he says:

And our message to them:
Joyfully we greet you
gratefully we salute you
in spirit we unite with you
Together we will win. (5)

The appreciation of revolutionary action in this poem does not signify parochialism. These people that the poet perceives as uniting with him in spirit include all the freedom fighters in the world. In 'In London the News Comes', the poet acknowledges the courage of the Sandinistas who overthrew the Somoza regime in Nicaragua. Although he is aware that history often forgets the contributions of the nameless ordinary fighters, his rational voice insists:

> but first
> salute the fallen
> those who purchased this victory
> with their blood and their lives. (6)

At the same time the poet-persona also recognizes the essential role of the surviving fighters. It is clearly the ordinary people whose invaluable contributions to the struggles for freedom are neither recorded nor rewarded that merit the salute of Dennis Brutus.

By contrast to the salute in 'In London the News Comes', another poem 'In London it is Dark' indicates that the Western world deserves censure through the metaphorical reference to 'Westminster, that place of shame/spawner of slavery's systems'. The censure here encapsulates issues of international politics and the consequences of policies that do not take into consideration the aspirations of other peoples of the world toward freedom.

Individuals who have distinguished themselves in the onerous task of liberating South Africa and other parts of the world are highlighted as symbolic figures. In 'A Tribute For Steve Biko', the poet uses the figure of Steve Biko, a freedom fighter killed by the South African secret police, to comment on the agony of oppression. This attitude which makes Dennis Brutus imaginatively relate himself sympathetically to all those subjected to oppression is apparently what has been identified as his 'concern for other suffering people' (Egudu 1976: 133) which makes him play the role of a spokesman. It is the instinctive sympathy generated by personal experience in spite of the fact that he is in exile which makes Brutus 'a representative of the oppressed and the victims of injustice in South Africa and elsewhere' (Ojaide 1986: 68) and it also makes his portrayal of Steve Biko as a poetic figure symbolic. The poem praises the courage, dedication and humanity of Biko in contrast to the inhumanity of his destroyers. The poet writes significantly:

> here he planned, dreamed
> waged his struggle
> and hardened his will
> to confront the butchers
> to challenge their terror
> – even if they robbed him of his life. (8)

The reference to the killers as 'butchers' connotes the impression of people who destroy without compunction. Thus, Brutus, in saluting the courage of Steve Biko, censures the inhumanity of his killers. This paradox where the poet subsumes condemnation within his praise of certain people in South Africa emerges with telling accuracy in three poems 'In the Dark Lanes of Soweto', 'Sorrow for the Children of Soweto' and 'There was a Girl'.

The three poems depict the sorrow associated with brutal sadistic destruction of life and property but the poet extends his focus to praise the resilience of the people. 'In the Dark Lanes of Soweto' portrays the squalor of the people whose 'lust for freedom stubbornly survives/like a smouldering defiant flame –/and the spirit of Steve Biko moves easily' (10). The imagery of freedom as a smouldering defiant flame illustrates the strenuous efforts of the people to prevent it from being extinguished. This defiance is magnified in 'Sorrow for the Children of Soweto', when the poet states that the death of children 'will not be forgotten' and that 'their lives will purchase our freedom'. It is also significant that in the poetry of Brutus the impersonal tone is often abandoned for the use of the first person plural which indicates the poet's intellectual involvement in the poetic exercise. The rational voice which emanates from such an involvement is thus made poignant and significant because, while the poet portrays his involvement, his clinical dissection of injustice makes the portrayal convincing. It is not that Brutus strives to be merely objective but he is aware that reason must prevail if any abnormal situation is to be fully appreciated by outsiders. His minimal use of affective words in 'There was a Girl', for instance, makes the issue of discrimination and the oppression of the human spirit insightful. The poem tells us:

> There was a girl
> eight years old they say
> her hair in spiky braids
> her innocent fist raised in imitation
>
> Afterwards, there was a mass of red
> some torn pieces of meat
> and bright rags fluttering
> a girl, once, in a print dress they say. (11)

The tragic portrait of the girl shows without affective words the pain it arouses but the rational voice of the poet explains that she was a bubbling pleasant imitative child who becomes a victim of events she does not understand. The description of her bleeding body as 'torn pieces of meat' and her dress as 'bright rags fluttering' reveals the wanton destruction and devaluation of a human life. Although Brutus was in exile it is clear that his rational voice in this and other poems indicates that it is wrong to assume that these poems written in exile 'only serve to inform us about the places Brutus has visited and people he has encountered without conveying any enduring emotional power' (Nkosi 1981: 167). The suppressed emotion in the description of the girl's death and the dismemberment of her body succinctly reveals more than a lengthy unbridled emotional essay could have conveyed.

Tha rational voice of the poet uses events and people as signposts to present a poetic territory in which the poet juxtaposes the rationality in other countries where he has sojourned with the irrationality of his home land at that time. This balancing act can only be effectively achieved when a poet has pruned his passions. The poem 'In Memoriam: Solomon

Mahlangu' like the poem on Steve Biko makes memorable the implication of Mahlangu's death. This elegy also confirms that 'through memory' Brutus 'retains the companionship of those left behind and thereby vicariously shares their privations. But memory is not a means of keeping faith alone. It is also simultaneously a way of finding the stable point for all his spiritual and physical restlessness' (Ogundele 1998: 92). However, the memory of Mahlangu is reflective of the stable point the poet seeks through the restlessness generated by apartheid and also the creative mode through which his anguish as a sensitive mind is assuaged. The figure of Mahlangu who 'singing he went to war/ and singing/ he went to his death' (13), becomes an icon of resistance. Brutus arouses significant consciousness through this death when he writes:

> One simply poses
> One's life
> against another's
> One's death
> against another's death. (14)

The juxtaposition of Mahlangu's life with the life of the poetic persona shows that no life should be regarded as substandard, and it is through this ability to arouse imaginative sympathy that Brutus makes a telling commentary on human nature.

Furthermore, the incongruity of the contemporary South African situation emerges in this poem. Brutus insists that while Mahlangu's life is a 'joyous life, a free life', the life of his oppressor is 'the monstrous life of a monstrous thing/who lives on the death of others/on our death'. The change from the impersonal of the third person plural to the first person plural once more exhibits that the poet contains his rage with amazing skill. Brutus perceives himself as involved but he does not allow his involvement to mask his perception of reality. The rational voice in the poetry of Brutus thus enables him to overcome the accusation of being a mere reporter of reality, who also presents a one-dimensional picture of life. It is not in doubt that the death of Mahlangu is felt intensely by the poet, for elsewhere in the poem he writes that 'the nail was pulled from my brain/and the drip of tears inside my skull/began' (17). But these tears are metaphorical for they are internal rather than external, thereby indicating the high degree of emotion involved but which the poet contains in order to make persuasive, objectively, the termination of Mahlangu's life.

The salutes to Damas, Aimé Césaire and Léopold Senghor are further examples of the tendency in Brutus to reflect a humanistic focus in his poetry. These three men played historical roles that are intertwined with the socio-political experience of the African. However, the poet examines their roles through an analysis of their cultural roots, thereby illustrating the need for freedom and justice. It is this same concern with historical events and social figures that is contained in 'A Friendly Question to the Native People of the American Continent'. Brutus here not only asserts his own humanity and the humanity of those he represents through his poetry, but also the humanity of other oppressed peoples in the world that he regards as 'unconquerably resilient allies' (22).

It is the poetic voice of Brutus, not his experience that is rational. Although he prunes the emotive words in order to arouse an intellectual response from the reader, he still adheres to the mass of experience emanating from his immediate and distanced reality. It is thus acceptable that the poetry of Brutus 'accepts and asserts ... the principles of intellectual integrity and in doing so avoids, or ignores, the clogging dangers of South African parochialism' (Nkondo 1981: 35). There is also the implication that even if the immediate reality of the poems becomes indistinct the works could serve as metaphors because the rational voice subjects experience, through an alchemy of imagination, to an alloy of basic human concerns. This lack of parochialism which creates human concerns features in several poems like 'For the Kent State Martyrs', 'In Memory of Agostinho Neto' and 'Terrible Knowledge'. In these poems Brutus ranges across the world from the death of those who died for justice in Kent State in May 1970 whom he swears to remember and 'keep their memory alive', through Neto: 'patriot and statesman' of the Angolan struggle and the revolutionary fighters of Chile, especially Hortense Allende, Joan Jara and Isabel Letelier who are perceived as 'clusters of fruit/swollen and rich' to the death of Karen Silkwood who died on the road from Cimarron on 13 November 1974. Karen Silkwood's death in the poem 'Terrible Knowledge' portrays the sensitivity of the poetic voice in the poems which arouses our abhorrence through its statistical tabulation of the human capacity for wanton destruction. The poet concludes thus:

Terrible knowledge
of our capacity to destroy
of our potential for destruction,
of our destructive greed:
terrible knowledge
Karen's knowledge
Our knowledge
terrible knowledge (29)

It is significant that the poem progresses from the impersonal (terrible knowledge) through the particular (Karen's knowledge) to the universal (our knowledge). It reveals the fact that Brutus conceives the flaw in human nature as a pervasive irrational urge to destroy. This is certainly a lesson that the exile experience reiterated for Dennis Brutus.

An observation which has been made concerning the prison poetry of Dennis Brutus which is tenable here is that the poet's 'objectivity lends an air of truth and sincerity to his account' (Ogunyemi 1982: 69). Quite early in his career and in an interview Brutus gives an indication of this poetic objective rationality when he confesses that 'although it is fine to fight for humanity, one must always see "humanity" in terms of real persons' (Lindfors 1976: 55). It is this perception of humanity in terms of real persons that clearly makes Brutus acknowledge the human element in the oppressor while he condemns the element of inhumanity in that same oppressor.

The exile poetry of Brutus may not appear aggressive or combative but the imagery of prison or the hardship of prison life is recurrent. Despite the view that 'his political and literary style, in its almost superhuman austerity and control, and his tight non-violent self-discipline remind one of Gandhi' (Wylie 1980: 39), this imagery of prison life with its sordid squalid existence reveals the enormity of the violence done to human lives. In these prison poems what Roscoe calls the indicative dominates and he explains that 'the indicative reports what really did, and does happen in prison, the certainties of life there' (Roscoe 1977: 163). In 'You May Not See the Nazis'. the poet equates the brutalities of the Nazis with the cruelty of South African prison life. Brutus stresses that:

> the death-rate is really quite high;
> and if you listen carefully
> You will hear the faint cries from the prison
> of people who have not been charged with any crime
> Really, we are not doing too badly (35)

These 'faint cries' signify the obvious thickness of the prison wall and also reflect the degree of insensitivity in the minds of those who put the people in prison on framed charges.

The prisoners 'squat on the floor', they 'sit like mouldy vegetables' and they 'crouch in corners' like 'emptied sacks' as they 'nurse in their broken frames/the frail flame of humanity/while monsters growl to snuff it out' (38). The monsters are human beings whose beastly acts arouse sympathy for their victims. This attitude of sympathy which may be hidden by the rational voice also emerges in the poem 'Tonight' where the poet-persona confesses that 'every night/I send my thoughts/to the men and women/who suffer/in the prisons of South Africa/because they fought for a just society/and a better world' (37). This constant mental journey back to the wombs of South African prisons is indicative that exile has not obfuscated the poetic perspective of Brutus. In 'Robben Island' with which he ends the collection, he perceives himself as a ghost among the prisoners but he is convinced that 'the will to freedom steadily grows/the force, the power, the strength steadily grows' (38). Thus Brutus through his use of a rational voice logically examines the South African reality in spite of the fact that he is in exile, and arrives at the conclusion that the land will be freed of the unjustness of its social structures through the 'will to freedom'. It is not surprising that this hope for freedom was subsequently fulfilled.

The rational voice of Dennis Brutus enabled him to cast an insight on his society while he was in exile and also to make an effective use of the twin-issue of 'Salute' and 'Censure' to portray the negative and positive tendencies in man. Although these exile poems may occasionally lack the taut style of his earlier works they still reveal that he has not lost the 'ability to write both very tightly packed metaphysical poetry and loose, unadorned, colloquial poetry' (Goodwin: 21). The consequence would have been disastrous without his rational voice which meshes experience and moulds it into a recognizable disciplined form. It is, therefore, unacceptable that Chipasula feels that 'artistically, Brutus does not fare any better in exile as his later work indicates' (Chipasula 1993: 49). It is obviously the fact that the poet is rational which leads to that erroneous conclusion. Clearly the result in this poetry is that the subsumed logic could be unravelled and clearly developed into a pattern that reveals the 'shriek of nerves', which is a metaphor for agitated emotional reaction that is enclosed within a calm exterior.

The human angle in his exile poetry therefore makes the rational voice of Brutus distinct and necessary to be heard and appreciated as he salutes and censures those who inspired his creative journey in the world.

NOTE

1. *Salutes and Censures* is not the only poetry collection published in exile by Dennis Brutus. However, it is significant that it is his only exile poetry collection first published in Africa. The collection was also published by Africa World Press, Trenton, New Jersey in 1988. But the references are to the Nigerian edition.

WORKS CITED

Akosu, Tyohdzuah,'Poetry in the Repressive State: The Example of Dennis Brutus', *Review of English and Literary Studies* 3.1, June 1986: 37–52.

Brutus, Dennis, *A Simple Lust*, London; Heinemann, 1983.

— *Salutes and Censures*. Enugu: Fourth Dimension Publishers, 1984.

Chipasula, Frank M., 'A Terrible Trajectory: The Impact of Apartheid, Prison and Exile on Dennis Brutus' Poetry', in Abdulrazak Gurnah (ed.), *Essays on African Writing: A Re-evaluation*, London: Heinemann, 1993: 38–55.

Egudu, R.N. 'Pictures of Pain: The Poetry of Dennis Brutus' in Christopher Heywood (ed.), *Aspects of South African Literature*, London: Heinemann, 1976: 131–44.

Ezenwa-Ohaeto, 'Art in Pain. A Study of the Dangers and Prospects of Protest Poetry through Two Representative South African Poets', *The Literary Half-Yearly* 25, 1, 1984: 17–38.

Goodwin, Ken, *Understanding African Poetry: A Study of Ten Poets*, London: Heinemann, 1982.

Lindfors. Bernth. Somehow Tenderness Survives: Dennis Brutus Talks About His Life and Poetry', *The Benin Review:* 1, June 1974: 44–55.

Nkondo, Gessler Moses, 'Dennis Brutus: The Domestication of a Tradition'. *World Literature Today* 55, 1, Winter 1981: 32–40.

Nkosi, Lewis, *Tasks and Masks: Themes and Styles of African Literature*, Harlow: Longman, 1981.

Ogundele, Wole, 'The Exile's Progress: Dennis Brutus' Poetry in the First Phase of His Exile', *Commonwealth: Essays and Studies* 10, 2, Spring 1988: 88–97.

Ogunyemi, Chikwenye Okonjo, 'The Song of the Caged Bird: Contemporary African Prison Poetry', *Ariel* 13, 4, October 1982: 65–84.

Ojaide, Tanure, 'The Troubadour: The Poet's Persona in the Poetry of Dennis Brutus', *Ariel* 17, 1, January 1986: 55–69.

Roscoe, Adrian, *Uhuru's Fire: African Literature East to South*, Cambridge: Cambridge University Press, 1977.
Salt, M. J., 'On the Business of Literary Criticism, with Special Reference to Bahadur Tejani's Article: "Can the Prisoner Make a Poet?"', *African Literature Today 7, Focus on Criticism*, 1975: 128–41.
Tejani, Bahadur, 'Can the Prisoner Make a Poet? A Critical Discussion of *Letters to Martha* by Dennis Brutus'. *African Literature Today 6, Poetry in Africa*,1973: 130–44.
Wylie, Hal, 'Creative Exile: Dennis Brutus and René Depestre', *NSAL* 3, October 1980: 35–44.

> Culturo-Textual Exile:
> The Changing 'Faces' of African Poetry

Lekan Oyegoke

Perhaps an article with a title like this should start with a critique of itself. This would be in consonance with the self-reflexivity and contradictory pluralism of postmodernism. A bare almost naive definition of postmodernism gives out that it is a description of certain proclivities of literary studies after the Second World War, a succession to modernism that had itself been a challenge to tradition, an assault on convention and the numerous aesthetic assumptions that were founded on a totalizing view of the literary text or literature, the arts and culture. Postmodernism, it would appear from this, owes its existence to the fact that modernism got caught up in the Russian Formalist processes of automatization and defamiliarization. The reaction in the arts and literature that led up to the radical iconoclasm of modernism is believed to have in its turn fallen into a habitual mode that has set off another 'pattern' of reaction which manifests itself in sundry ways as postmodernism. And even now there is some talk in critical circles in respect of literary studies having entered a mode that has begun to usher in post-postmodernism.

Though enveloped in a cloud of uncertainty one point seems clear: as a concept or a theory, postmodernism, like modernism, is pretty elusive, almost bizarre in its manifestations. This is probably as it should be, and true to character; it has several offerings. Linda Hutcheon proffers a good beginning point when she says:

> I offer instead, then, a specific, if polemical, start from which to operate: as a cultural activity that can be discerned in most art forms and many currents of thought today, what I want to call postmodernism is fundamentally contradictory, and inescapably political. (4)

This proposition is instructive. It is a fairly nebulous concept with a diversity of tangled convoluted strands; its practice is akin to a wild dance in a quicksand of shifting and 'shifty' borders. Notice how in the web of confusing pluralism Hutcheon is emboldened to propose a 'specific' start. The contradictory beginning should, as a proposal, be unsurprising: it accords well with the kaleidoscopic nature of our subject.

As if that were not problematical enough, 'postmodernism' as a principle is here being brought to bear on the poetry as well as the person of Okot p'Bitek. The study of the person and the poetry as recorded by

G.A. Heron (1976) indicates that Okot the person, the poet, is nothing if not controversial. As a rebel Okot's radicalism at the political level only compares slightly with the radicalism of social critics and poets the likes of the late Christopher Okigbo who laid down his pen in a season when the barrel of a gun seemed to thunder more loudly than the shaft of a pen, only to pick it up no more as he got caught up permanently in the 'lavender mists' that had been beckoning to him for half his life – Okigbo died in defence of justice, liberty, and the right to self-determination. Nobel laureate Wole Soyinka has spent a good part of his adult life pitted against the despotic forces of state terror and oppression. And Dennis Brutus was at one time shot in the back by the forces of apartheid terrorism.

This article aspires to show the multiple character of the African poetic text, a product of peculiar dynamics that converts the poet into an exile in certain literary traditions. The sands of the shifting poetic terrain comprise the cultural, textual and intertextual.

II Okot's poetry inhabits a class of its own, a feature of which seems to be the necessity to package, in the presentation, both the poet and the poetry under a common label. Separated, the poetry tends to be flat and spiritless, the imagery rather trite and devoid of poetic depth. On paper, the poetry seems so vapid and aesthetically anaemic as to render the description of it as poetry something of a misnomer. The printed lines that have survived the person, the poet himself, and which now reach us as poetry are rather more like truncated sentences, sundered works of prose arranged in imitation of lines of poetry, for example:

> I am not senseless,
> I am not cowardly,
> Not dastardly
> I am not a thug,
> I am not insane,
> This is not
> Cold-blooded murder,
> I did not do it
> For the money ...
>
> He was a traitor
> A dictator
> A murderer
> A racist
> A tribalist
> A clannist
> A brotherist ...
>
> He was corrupt
> A reactionary
> A revisionist
> A fat black capitalist
> An extortioner
> An exploiter ...

34 Culturo-Textual Exile

> A fat mosquito
> Hums a sweet song
> And soothes
> The snoring sleeper ... (p'Bitek 1971: 67–8)

These lines from Okot's *Two Songs* are typical. But then, what is poetry? From the times of Plato and Aristotle, of Sidney and Dryden, Coleridge and Wordsworth, I. A. Richards and T.S. Eliot, up to now, the search has been futile for a foolproof definition of poetry. In an anarchic postmodernist cultural dispensation the search for 'true poetry' seems in silliness comparable to the alchemical search for gold in bronze. There is probably no such thing as true poetry. What is certain, however, is that the literary arts together with their study afford some opportunity for an excursion into the grotesque and the incongruous, a setting in which the absurd and the hideous aspire to the sublime.

Okot's 'poetry' appears to be a departure from certain kinds of traditions. In their bare, almost simplistic transparency the Okot lines represent a reaction of a variety not altogether unlike the Wordsworthian romantic reaction to the neoclassicism of the likes of Alexander Pope. Wordsworth, we may recall, set an agenda of individualism, subjectivity, lyricism and commonality of poetic diction in his famous preface to *Lyrical Ballads*. Nevertheless, the simplicity of Wordsworthian poetry is deceptive: the Wordsworthian lines have a pithiness, a depth that fragments their pretensions to referentiality and lucidity, for example:

> A slumber did my spirit seal;
> I had no human fears:
>   She seemed a thing that could not feel
>   The touch of earthly years.
> No motion has she now, no force;
> She neither hears nor sees;
>   Rolled round in earth's diurnal course,
>   With rocks, and stones, and trees. (*The Norton Anthology of Poetry*, 722)

The object of this article is not to compare the poetry of Okot and Wordsworth as such, but to attempt an outline of a literary development and so to place the unique character of Okot's poems or songs in perspective. The Okot lines seem, as noted earlier, bone-dry and commonplace for a number of reasons, some of which oral literature scholar, Isidore Okpewho, discusses in chapter ten of his acclaimed *African Oral Literature* (1992).

Okot might have been not a literary but an oral poet operating within a cultural ethos shaped by the oral traditions. In this equation the standards of orality are pitted against those of literacy, the African against the Western European, the communalistic against the individualistic. It is noteworthy though that the debate on orality versus literacy has, after the dialogue between, especially, Walter J. Ong and Ruth Finnegan, fallen into abeyance. Orality in culture seems now to have attained a respectable status, having been newly rehabilitated after years of denigration at the hands of Western anthropologists and ethnologists who found it convenient to equate orality with primitivism.

That Okot has worked in the oral traditions is nothing unique: the oral traditions are not the preserve of the African literary experience. What is remarkable is that in adopting the oral traditions Okot retrieves the indigenous African language as well. And this has happened, as we have noted, at a time when the nouveau educated African gloried in his new Western-style enlightenment and hugged his coveted cultural status symbol: English or French or Portuguese, depending. The quality of Okot's grasp of the cultural politics of Africa is comparable to Ngugi wa Thiong'o's and is indeed commendable. In *Horn of my Love* Okot makes the following observation:

> Missionaries, anthropologists, musicologists and folklorists have shown some professional interest in the oral literature of African peoples. They have plucked songs, stories, proverbs, riddles etc. from their social backgrounds and, after killing them by analysis, have buried them in inaccessible and learned journals and in expensive technical books. I believe that literature, like all the other creative arts, is there, first and foremost, to be enjoyed. Here is the poetry of the Acoli people: their lullabies and love songs, their satirical verses, their religious songs and chants, their war songs and funeral dirges. Going through them we may get a glimpse of what these people think and believe life is all about; their moral values, their sense of humour, their fears and joys are presented here in these songs. (p'Bitek 1974: ix)

It follows that Okot's poetry should properly be in Acoli, not English, and it should be performed, not read. As Finnegan and Okpewho make clear in their studies, oral poetry, or for that matter literature, is best in the language of its original composition, and is better in the oral performance than in the written medium. The conversion of the literature from the indigenous or natural language to another through translation, and from the oral to the written medium impairs its value, quality and significance.

Song of Ocol, *Song of Lawino*, *Song of Prisoner*, *Song of Malaya*, for example, strike one as insipid in print and in translation. In the performance in Acoli they are not vapid lines, but vibrant songs. The performance stirs the feelings and moves the heart like any good song should do. The issue of meaningfulness is rendered secondary; but for the Acoli audience there is no problem whatever with the nuance of the language, the imagery or poetic strategies of sarcasm, satire, irony and humour. And all this is as it should be, for the natural audience for Okot's poetry is the one that is defined by the language: Acoli.

This point raises a whole set of problems, the most basic yet most controversial being the question: What is African poetry? Clearly, it is no easier to define or rather describe 'African poetry' than it is to define 'poetry' in general. Yet, perhaps the starting point is to ask – assuming literature to be a cultural product of an intellectual and creative kind expressed in language – what is African literature?.

Already discredited is the tendency to adopt a racialist premise for a definition of African literature which described the literature in terms of Africa and the black diaspora, and another which adopted a continental premise that made no allowance for cultural diversity and individual literary identity. As Africa was viewed as a monocultural landmass for decades, colonialism and cultural imperialism in Africa helped to formulate a cultural fixture that expressed itself in English or French or Portuguese, in the main, and attached the label 'African literature' to itself. The tag 'African literature' is unlike similar terms used elsewhere to describe specific literatures, because it is silent on the existence of literary works in the indigenous African languages. The confusion that surrounds the true character of African literature renders it unclear as to who its proper audience is. Writings in English, French and Portuguese in Africa occupy the centre of cultural life in Africa, having driven cultural activity in the African languages to the margin.

Cultural expression in the colonial language should give way to literature in the indigenous African language such as Acoli, siSwati Shona, Yoruba, Zulu. So reconstituted, the natural language for Acoli poetry becomes Acoli rather than English, and the natural audience for Acoli poetry becomes the audience literate in or just familiar with Acoli rather than the minority intellectual class versed in the erstwhile language of colonialism.

III According to Heron, Okot is said to have repudiated all contacts with Western literary influences in spite of having received formal education in the Western tradition and in Western institutions of higher learning. Okot's claim was that his creative skills and materials derived exclusively from the African oral literary traditions. However, a close inspection of his poetry reveals a curious incidence of intertextuality:

> A Saharan thirst
> Engulfs me,
> My tongue hangs out
> And I pray to Lazarus
>   Brother Lazarus,
>   Please,
>   Just a drop...! (1971: 23-4)

This intertext in *Two Songs* points away from the African oral traditions, strictly speaking, and is hitched in the direction of the biblical New Testament. The setting is hell versus heaven, and the scenario is one involving a dead rich man and a dead penurious Lazarus, playing reversed roles in the life-after-life. *Two Songs* is rife with biblical Christian intertexts:

> Let the black Bishops
> And priests
> Preach against us,
> Let them sow their seeds
> In snow white fields
> As they pray
> To Saint Peter

Not to allow us
Through Heaven's Gate ...
Let the Lord
Grant their prayers
And condemn us all
To flaming eternity ... (1971: 183–84)

The intertext 'heaven's gate' in the above lines is fluid and apparently originates from the Holy Bible. But it has been popularized by Okigbo on the African literary scene. Okigbo acknowledged the influence on himself and his writings of poets such as Ezra Pound, Gerard Manley Hopkins, and T.S. Eliot. Okigbo's poetic imagery is fused with visions of immortality and a ritual passage through 'heaven's gate'.

'The Passage'

BEFORE YOU, mother Idoto,
    naked I stand;
before your watery presence,
a prodigal

leaning on an oilbean,
lost in your legend.

Under your power wait I
    on barefoot,
watchman for the watchword
    at Heavensgate;

out of the depths of my cry:
    give ear and harken ... (Okigbo 1971: 3)

Both Okigbo and Okot might have been fascinated by Shakespeare's Sonnet 29: 'When in disgrace with fortune and men's eyes'. Shakespeare's lyric speaker takes a philosophical look, or so it appears, at the fallen condition, involving total isolation from fellow humans. It is a desperate situation in which the persona is bereft of hope. The lyric speaker's Adamic state is, however, transformed by love or the thought of love – love conquers all and God is love – and is brought up

From sullen earth, sings hymns at heaven's gate;
For thy sweet love rememb'red such wealth brings
That then I scorn to change my state with kings. (*Norton*: 236)

Okigbo's excursion to heaven's gate is both spiritual and cultural, as several scholars have noted. After years of cultural immersion in Western philosophies and literatures, Okigbo is re-baptised at the 'watery presence' of the goddess Idoto, and there is a return to roots, there is spiritual and psychological healing. The process of transformation is a noble one, its solemnity eminently otherworldly. Okot's attitude to heaven's gate, on the other hand, is rather iconoclastic. Having taken the position that he had never been subjected to cultural cleavage, never been separated from cultural roots, his treatment of Christianity is one of scorn, of utter contempt.

Okot's irreverence seems similar to that of the lyric speaker in Soyinka's famous dramatic monologue: 'Abiku'. Abiku is self-assured, unruly and arrogant. He cares little about his parents' suffering or feelings, and scoffs at attempts to alter the course of destiny by his parents and the charmer paid to reshape his itinerary. The sadistic and callous tone of Abiku is, however, appropriate to the personality and presentation of the spirit-child in the Yoruba metaphysic. The many faces of Abiku continue to be explored in interesting new ways not only in folklore but also in written literature: for example, Ben Okri's Azaro in his magic realist prose works.

The poet in Africa can also be multi-faceted. The poet of the oral traditions is, as has been suggested, first and foremost a performer in a more urgent sense than the writer. The sense of urgency about the content and form of what may be described as traditional African performance is a feature of its orality, a function of the symbiotic link between the performer and his audience, as oral literature scholars have pointed out. Even greater urgency might be imposed on the performance if it is linked with ritual.

The audience is implicated in the term 'oral poetry' in a sense that it is not in written poetry — even if it is assumed that poetry is expected to be heard, usually, not read. The 'oral moment' is, as Okpewho points out, important to a meaningful definition of oral literature. The traditional performer is an artist because he has a live audience, while the writer requires neither the immediacy nor the specificity of a real audience for self-definition. It is ironical that African literary study all but completely ignored the issue of audience in African literature until its recent problematization in postcolonial discourse.

The professional praise singer among the Yoruba is an artist or poet whose duties are defined by the functional relationship between him and his audience. He or she praises individuals or families for moral and material favours. The modern counterpart to the traditional praise singer is often not a writer but a musician using indigenous and foreign musical equipment to perfect his trade and take advantage of new opportunities. If they were not musicians the likes of I. K. Dairo, Ebenezer Obey, and Sunny Ade would have been praise poets.

Ong (1982) is right in observing that literacy effects important changes in 'mental and social structures'. The craze among the Yoruba to include poetry reading on the agenda at wedding receptions and funeral ceremonies is a relevant illustration. The ewi or iwi poet who recites poetry is the praise poet who cannot be a singer. His audience today is the elite class. The poet collects the relevant biographical details of the celebrants and members of their families and works them into poetry which he then performs. In the oral context, as has been noted, the poet and performer were one.

Literacy subverts the traditional equation between poet and performer. The appearance of writing means the poet need not also be a performer. A poet may elect only to compose and contract out the performance. If the poet is unhappy with the arrangement with gifted performers he could dispense with their services and just communicate by writing. He could decide to turn to some printer or publisher for mass circulation among the reading public. The audience becomes rather more anonymous with the advent of writing and print: the surviving character index is language. The above model is almost Platonic, Plato having argued a linearity of connection between Muse, Poet, Rhapsodist, Actor and Audience. This inspirational link is at its best at the level of orality; literacy prises it apart. The ewi or iwi poet's new audience is anonymous because of the new distance between him and them; and because there is a distance and anonymity the poet discovers greater freedom that effects thematic and structural changes, in the texture of his poetry. Ong's observation is pertinent:

> A deeper understanding of pristine or primary orality enables us better to understand the new world of writing, what it truly is, and what functionally literate human beings really are: beings whose thought processes do not grow out of simply natural powers but out of these powers as structured, directly or indirectly by the technology of writing. (1982: 78)

As the close connection between poet and audience is sundered with the appearance of writing, the iwi poet who writes is no longer defined by the exigency of the 'oral moment' and in consequence ceases to be a 'traditional artist'. The new poet by virtue of literacy has moved into the category of literature designated as 'indigenous', and indigenous because the poet retains the indigenous African language in his literary compositions. It should be conceded though that the transition from an oral to a literate poetic culture is not always neat: there can be overlapping, for example, the indigenous poet shares the literate audience with the national or African poet who is literate in a European language, that is, those members of the literate audience who are bilingual.

The class of literature known as 'national' or 'international' or 'African' is the one supported by the former European language of colonialism such as English. The audience for this differs from the one for indigenous literature on points not of literacy but of language choice. When the modern African poet decides to perform in addition to being an African or 'national' or 'international' poet, the decision and its execution do not make him a 'traditional artist' because his text would have been 'technologized', in Ong's word, before being oralized.

Okot p'Bitek and Atukwei Okai are two modern poets who sometimes performed their own poetry. Chanting their own poems does not make them more traditional or more African. But if, as Okot often did, the poet gave up the English language and performed in Acoli, he became an Acoli poet, and only a performer before non-Acoli audiences. However, although Okot is dead, it is only the performer who is dead: the poet lives on in print and is still available to literate audiences. But when the traditional artist dies the continuity of his art is maintained by the community who own the material and ensure its upkeep in surviving performers who may have been trained by the departing performer who himself inherited the substance of his art from the great bards before him.

It is perhaps the case that a writer is just another 'text' as postmodernists argue. And as a text, the writer does not, perhaps cannot, operate in isolation, but must relate to other texts in a 'bizarre' interplay of discourse. Michel Foucault proposes an 'archive of the positive Unconscious' as the source of much of the discourse that constitutes a text. For Roland Barthes intertextuality is evidence of the inability of a poet to live clear of the infinite text to escape other texts or intertexts to which the poet as a text is daily exposed: newspapers, radio, television, etc, and in the case of Okot, like other educated poets, one might also add, books, both African and otherwise.

So, it might be asked, what sort of a text might Okot be? – to borrow Robert de Beaugrande's (1988) engaging way of framing this kind of question – is this text an oral text, or what?

The earlier argument might have given the impression that the question about Okot's textuality was an easy one to answer. But that is not the case. Okot's textuality is complicated by the fact that he sometimes translated the oral text from Acoli to English and at other times he composed his own distinctive materials while borrowing extensively from the oral traditions. From the oral traditions he gets his lyricism, his sense of rhythm and the musical ideophonic nuance of the Acoli language which also provides the imagery, the figurative play of language and capacity for pluralism in agreement with the ways of poetry.

One of the by-products of the interplay of orality and literacy is, as we have seen, the necessity to separate written literature from oral literature in much the same way that the modern writer must not be confused with the traditional artist or performer. The modern African text cannot be evaluated using values, criteria or expectations deriving from the oral traditions, nor is it proper or acceptable to assess the oral text using exclusively the principles, rules or laws of the written form.

Take the case of the Senegambian griot. His performance is profound and elaborate though not always tied to ritual. The griot has supplied ethnographers and literary scholars with sundry items of African folklore, from straight historical accounts to lengthy epics, yet cannot summon copyright laws to protect his interests even where some of the materials include aspects of his own imaginative composition. He is unable to make specific claims because it is believed that the material extracted from him is communal property that can be used by anyone who is interested. If the griot is literate and can record his own materials the arrangement is less problematic. But usually the griot is not, and perhaps would not have been a griot were he able to write.

Perhaps from the point of view of the griot such as the Nyanga bard, Mr Candi Rureke, the source of Daniel Biebuyck's *The Mwindo Epic* (1969) and 'three of the Gambia's leading bards: Bamba Suso, Banna Kanute and Dembo Kanute' who were the original sources for Gordon Innes' *Sunjata: Three Mandinka Versions*, the scholars and writers who importune him for a performance are only unusual members of the audience. The main substance of the griot's performance, the material he uses, is still lodged in his mind, preserved by his memory, and can be returned to and used as the need arises, subvertible only by death.

Okot died long after postmodernism had pronounced the author dead and torn down the structuralist edifice of transcendental copy. So, reducing the traditional text such as *Horn of My Love* (1974) from the oral to the written medium does not make the text any less communalistic – although traces of individuality may still be found in the transcripts as in the actual performance of the same material, as folklore scholars have noted. However, the same argument cannot be made for the more individualized works of Okot p'Bitek.

There is no way a reader of poetry can avoid paying in time for the satisfaction of having poetry. William Empson's truism about ambiguity being a vital ingredient of poetic composition is reinforced by new theories of the multilateral ways of literary language and the essential instability of a text. Assuming the plurality of a text to be a given, still some poems would demand more from a reader than will others. Now when a poem seems so singularly transparent, what may the reason be? Does it deserve to be called poetry? Is the simplicity a failure of craft?

At the risk of turning irredeemably banal, it seems appropriate to restate the obvious: The process of puzzling out a meaning, assuming there is such a thing, varies from poem to poem as from reader to reader, given that more of modern poetry is read than heard. Oral poetry is often cited as an example of poetry that is marked by simplicity of both diction and imagery. Some scholars of African poetry have gone so far as to suggest that modern African poetry be marked perforce by this kind of oralized simplicity. The truth, however, is that not all oral poetry qualifies as simple: for example, the Ifa mantic poetry of the Yoruba.

It should seem pretty obvious by now that Okot's simplicity is the simplicity of the oral traditions and thus scarcely qualifies as a failure of craft. The transcribed oral text, as we have noted, is a disembodied text in many ways: first, it derives from the community; second, the text is physically separated from the performer; thirdly, linguistically the text is deprived of its natural cultural context of Acoli. A similar argument is relevant to those of Okot's poems that are the products of his own individual imagination: for these Okot is heavily indebted to his Acoli oral traditions and they suffer a stillbirth appearing in English. Ogo A. Ofuani quotes Okot as having made the following observation himself about his literary exertions trying to translate from Acoli to English in a different context:

> I have been trying to do it ever since, but it doesn't come through ... Well, I don't know the reason, but I put it into English and it becomes watery, you know? (1996: 185)

However, not using English does not free the Okot text from the consequences of the freeplay of texts in the 'archive of the positive Unconscious' and the result is conspicuous evidence of intertextuality. Okot is thus a many-faced poet and text, bearing the imprints of the traditional bard, the indigenous African poet and the modern African writer of African poetry in at least two languages. The Okot text suffers permanent loss of integrity or perhaps purity on exile linguistically (Acoli to English and back) and textually (oral medium to written text, and back and forth).

There seems to be something compulsive, something inevitable about the play of intertextuality. In an unguarded moment an intertext from classical literature, or at least Graeco-Roman mythology, slips into play in the African world outlined by Okot's sarcasm in *Song of Ocol*:

> No street
> Will be named
> After Mansa Sulayman
> Of ancient Mali,
> He is as irrelevant
> As the Greek goddess Artemis
> A miserly king
> He passed nothing on
> To us (1971: 85–6)

These examples are not meant to show that Okot lied in his claim to have eschewed the influence of Western literature on his creative endeavours, but to illustrate a postmodernist suggestion that the world of literature, the arts and culture is an open-ended and dynamic one involving an interplay of texts regardless of the times and climes, and that the traditional attempt to suggest the contrary, that the world of the literary text or product is fixed and hermetically sealed, is false, and that this conventional view is constantly being subverted in the text itself.

Intertextuality contradicts the traditional notion of a text and this point of contradiction is what in a text Jacques Derrida has described as aporia. Abiola Irele's description of this dynamic in a related context as 'Euro-African intertextuality' seems apt:

> Even more determinant has been the influence in English-speaking Africa of that singular cluster of texts, represented by the King James Bible, John Bunyan's *Pilgrim's Progress*, and the plays of William Shakespeare. (1996: 1)

As Irele correctly observes, Western literature has had a massive impact on the consciousness and creative imagination of the African. The Okot example shows that its manifestation as intertextual play is inevitable and unobstructible by a conscious denial of its presence.

Finally, it should be conceded that a return to the indigenous African language for both creative composition and performance is an aesthetic goal that is measurable in terms of degree and not in an absolutistic sense. A return to the Acoli in the poetry of Okot will not alter the status of the intertextuality, as noted above, but will be a step in the right direction: that of greater Africanity. Acoli will be, as has been argued, of enhanced aesthetic value to both the material and the prosody of the performance, and it will reduce the gap between poet or performer and the performance as between text and audience. It is a kind of dynamics that seems to affirm that the modern African poet can aspire to no other status than that of an exile of traditions.

WORKS CITED

Biebuyck, Daniel P. and Mateene, Kahombo C., *The Mwindo Epic*. Berkeley and Los Angeles: University of California Press, 1969.

De Beaugrande, Robert, *Critical Discourse A Survey of Literary Theorists*, New Jersey: Ablex Publishing Company, 1988.

Ferguson, Margaret and Salter, Mary Jo (eds), *The Norton Anthology of Poetry* (Fourth Edition), New York: Norton and Company, 1996.

Finnegan, Ruth, *Oral Poetry*, Bloomington: Indiana University Press, 1992.

Heron, G. A., *The Poetry of Okot p'Bitek*, London: Heinemann, 1976.

Hutcheon, Linda, *A Poetics of Postmodernism*, New York: Routledge, 1988.

Innes, Gordon, *Sunjata: Three Mandika Versions*, London: School of Oriental and African Studies, University of London, 1974.

Irele, Abiola, 'Shakespeare and Company', *Research in African Literatures* 27, 1, Spring 1996.

Ofuani, Ogo A., 'Old Wine in New Skins? An Exploratory Review of Okot p'Bitek's *White Teeth: A Novel*', *Research in African Literatures* 27.2, Summer 1996.

Okigbo, Christopher, *Labyrinths*, London: Heinemann, 1962, 1971.

Okpewho, Isidore, *African Oral Literature*, Bloomington: Indiana University Press, 1992.

Ong, Walter J., *Orality and Literacy: The 'Technologizing' of the Word*, London: Methuen, 1982.

Okot p'Bitek, *Song of Lawino*, Nairobi: East African Publishing House, 1966.

— *Song of Ocol*, Nairobi: East African Publishing House, 1971.

— *Two Songs*, Nairobi: East African Publishing House, 1971.

— *Horn of my Love*, London: Heinemann, 1974.

Shades of Home & Exile in Ayi Kwei Armah's Novels

Nnadozie Inyama

The experience of exile is a phenomenon that quite a few African writers are familiar with. Virtually all African writers of note have found themselves, at one time or other, living outside their homeland against their wish. Usually, this situation is precipitated by the writer's stance against an unjust political system, which then responds by making life unbearable. There is hardly any region of Sub-Saharan Africa which has not contributed to this pool of writers-in-exile: Ngugi, Farah, Brutus, Mphahlele, Nkosi, Armah, Beti and others. Chinua Achebe, for a variety of reasons, has been living in America for several years, and the Nobel Laureate Wole Soyinka had to escape into exile in 1995.

Although a large, distinctive body of 'exile literature' is yet to emerge from this development, it is plausible te speculate that with time such a body of work might emerge. In the meantime, it is still possible to see exile in various shades as a substantial sub-theme in the works of some African writers. One writer whose novels embody this feature is the Ghanaian Ayi Kwei Armah, especially in his earliest novels *The Beautyful Ones Are Not Yet Born*,[1] *Fragments*, and *Why Are We So Blest?* In this article, I intend to adopt a schema proposed by the late distinguished scholar and critic of culture, Professor Raymond Williams, to examine some of the characters in these novels as 'exiles'. I wish to argue, using Williams's definitions or terms, that Armah finds the protagonists in these novels inadequate as instruments of positive, social and political transformation, essentially because they are alienated exiles – whether or not they are physically living in Ghanaian society.

In *The Long Revolution* Professor Williams writes that 'conformity or non-conformity' has become too simple and limited a model for describing subtle gradations of response from individuals to the societies in which they find themselves (1961: 84). 'We need', he writes, 'descriptions such as member, subject, and servant, or rebel, exile and vagrant, if we are to get past the impasse of simple conformity and non-conformity' (92). He summarizes these categories thus:

> To the member, society is his own community; ... To the servant, society is an establishment, in which he finds his place. To the subject, society is an imposed system in which his place is determined. To the rebel, a particular society is a tyranny; the alternative for which he fights is a new and better society. To the

exile, society is beyond him but may change. To the vagrant, society is a name for other people who are in his way or who can be used. (92)

In this article I am mainly interested in the exile, and the sub-category of 'self-exile' which Williams also describes. 'The exile', he writes,

> is as absolute as the rebel in rejecting the way of life of his society, but instead of fighting it he goes away. Often he is like the subject in that unless he conforms he will be destroyed, or will be unable to maintain his life. But he is unlike the subject in that he has managed to escape, or has been allowed to get away. In some cases ... he will get away to membership of another society in which he finds his personal reality, his vital system of values and attitudes confirmed. More usually, perhaps, he will remain an exile, unable to go back to the society that he has rejected or that has rejected him, yet equally unable to form important relationships with the society to which he has gone. (89–90)

The most distinguishing characteristic of this person, then, – the conventional exile – is physical removal, by himself or by others, from the society with which he has come into conflict. We may state immediately that this distinction would apply to almost all African writers in exile, since their continued stay in their countries of birth could lead to their being 'destroyed' or 'unable to maintain' their lives.[2]

However, the conventional exile thus described is different from the 'self-exile' who Williams also calls the 'internal émigré' (quoting the Bolsheviks). In his elaboration,

> The self-exile could, if he chose, live at ease in his society, but to do so would be to deny his personal reality. Sometimes he goes away, on principle, but as often he stays, yet still, on principle, feels separate ... This kind of self-exile lives and moves about in the society into which he was born, but rejects its purposes and despises its values, in terms of alternative principles to which his whole personal reality is committed. Unlike the rebel he does not fight for these principles, but watches and waits. He knows himself to be different, and the pressure of his activity is to preserve this difference, to maintain the individuality which is the term of his separateness. There is great tension in this condition, for theoretically, at least, the self-exile wants society to change, so that he can start belonging to it, and this involves him, at least notionally, in relationships. (90)

Armah's main protagonists in *The Beautyful Ones* (the man, Teacher), and *Fragments* (Baako), seem, in varying degrees, to fit into this social type – the self-exile; physically he is in society, but emotionally, socially, intellectually and psychologically he is fundamentally alienated from this society. The man, or his friend Teacher, as well as Baako 'could, if he chose, live at ease' in the Ghanaian society of the novels. But, for each of them, this would be to deny his 'personal reality' and to compromise his principles through the corrupt pursuit of the material goals of the immediate society. Each man feels separate from this societal passion, and this society is closely represented for the man (and for Baako) by his disappointed family. For Teacher, also, society is represented by the nagging memory of the family whose hopes he had disappointed and from whom he has withdrawn. For each of these characters, to conform and live according to society's (and family's) present temper would be a kind of death: 'They will destroy me, Teacher', the man wails, talking about the morally destructive actions which his wife and mother-in-law want him to take for family comfort (54). The agony of this conflicting situation is no less searing for Teacher. He says to the man:

> yes, but I am not free. I have not stopped wanting to meet the loved ones and to touch them and be touched by them. But you know that ... all they want is that you throw away the thing in your mind that makes you think that you are still alive, and their embrace would be a welcome unto death. ... And so I run. I know I am nothing and will never be anything without them, and when most I wish to stop being nothing then the desire to run back to those I have fled comes back with unbearable strength. Until I see again these loving arms outstretched, bringing me their gift of death. Then I stop and turn around and come back here, living my half-life of loneliness. (1976: 55–6)

The 'great tension' in the lives of these two characters emanates from the conflict between their 'theoretical' wish for a changed or different society 'so that they can start belonging to it', and the insistence of their families and those around them that they function in society as it is presently constituted and tempered. This they refuse to do, and as a consequence find themselves on the edge of things: uninvolved spectators in the daily happenings around them, watching, agonizing, but not initiating any action to bring about change. What indeed they have with their society is a 'notional relationship', and for all the involvement they have with the ways of this society they might as well be physical or conventional exiles.

One consequence of this man–society distance is the negative transformations it creates in family relationships. The man seems to exist on the emotional periphery of his household; his wife has no sympathy with his moral scruples, and his mother-in-law cannot tolerate him. The essential nature of husband–wife relationship is crystallized in this passage:

> There was nothing the man could say to his wife, and the woman herself did not look as if she thought there could be anything said to her about what she knew was true. But inside the man the confusion and the impotence had swollen into something asking for a way out of confinement and in his restlessness he rose and went out very quietly through the door, and his wife sat there not even staring after him, not even asking where he was going or when he would come back in the night, or even whether he wanted to return at all to this home. (47)

As for his children, 'It seems their eyes are also learning this flat look [from their mother] that is a defence against hope, as if their mother's message needs their confirmation' (41). Having refused to 'die' for his family's nourishment, the man becomes an emotional exile from them, like Teacher. In the man's case, he is further suppressed in his mother-in-law's emotional/kin hierarchy by an outsider – the politician Koomson whom she now calls 'Brother' because he seems to offer the prospect of a materially full life. It is a fact that is not lost on the man, because he tells his friend Teacher about it. The emotional distance that has developed between the man and his family, and between Teacher and the family somewhere, which he has fled from, parallels the distance between both men and the society whose ways and values they spurn so intensely.

Both men share a longing for a different order, a nostalgia for what might have been, the same way the conventional exile longs for the land of his birth which he has been expelled from, and which he is too distant from and powerless to change or transform. For Teacher the awareness of this impatience and the disillusionment have precipitated despair:

> I don't feel any hope in me any more. I can see things, but I don't feel much. When you can see the end of things even in their beginnings, there is no more hope, unless you want to pretend ... No. I also am one of the dead people, the walking dead. A ghost died long ago. So long ago that not even the old libations of living blood will make me live again. (61)

When we first encounter him, Teacher is lying naked on his bed, as if waiting for his burial shroud, dead to the immediate world around him. Again, he says to the man:

> I know my life is empty ... Now all I do is read books of other places and other times, listen to music of South Africa and the Congo and the Afro-Americans. (93–4)

In Teacher's catalogue of 'activities' nothing relates to the immediate Ghanaian world, unless it is bitter memories of a past that failed. 'And often I remember Maanan and the bitterness and the emptiness of life rise up in me. That's all' (94). The emotional, intellectual and cultural distance between him and the surrounding environment is almost as significant as the physical distance between Ghana and the countries whose cultural products he relates to.

Neither Teacher nor the man fights actively for the establishment in their society of the principles they feel so strongly about. Each man 'watches and waits', a fundamentally flawed position since inactivity and mere existentialist agony can not precipitate change. They refuse to be 'rebels', but remain steadfastly uninvolved self-exiles. Again, Professor Williams is helpful in explaining this impasse:

> But since, unlike the rebel [the self-exile's] dissent has remained fixed at an individual stage, it is difficult for him to form adequate relationships, even with other dissenters. He may support the principle of dissenting causes, but he cannot join them; he is too wary of being caught and compromised. What he has principally to defend is his own living pattern, his own mind, and almost any relationship is a potential threat to this. He has become or remained his 'authentic self', but this authenticity cannot be shared or communicated to others, or if the effort at communication is made, the commitment involved in it will be characteristically minimal. Whatever he may come to say or do, he continues, essentially, to walk alone in his society, defending a principle in himself. (Williams 1961: 90–92)

As if in support of this thesis, we hear Teacher say the following:

> If we can't consume ourselves for something we believe in, freedom makes no difference at all. You see, I am free to do what I want, but there is nothing happening now that I want to join. (Armah, 1976: 61)

Throughout their long evening together neither the man nor Teacher advances any idea on how to actively change society, or how to collaborate to influence change. Each man continues essentially to walk alone in his society, defending a principle in himself. In *The Beautyful Ones* the word 'alone' and its cognates occur frequently in relation to the characters in the work, but particularly the man and Teacher. In spite of crowds of people around them, of even family, both men are alone. The loneliness is not the loneliness of the physically far removed, but the more intense loneliness of the one who is at home but yet is in exile. This is one shade of exile in Armah's fiction.

To a large extent, the same shade of exile is applicable to Baako, the protagonist in *Fragments*. Again, the source of his 'aloneness' is his refusal to compromise his 'authentic self', to accept both the privileges and corruptions which his 'been-to' status seems to have mapped out for him for the material benefit, as they see it, of members of his family. The moral question looms large in the conflict between Baako and his relations, and it percolates into this: whether he will do as 'everybody else' is doing – like Brempong, for instance – for the benefit of his family members. The other related conflict arises from how they see the meaning or value of his trip abroad and what it should result in, and Baako's interpretation of the essence of his overseas experience.

As Robert Fraser says in *The Novels of Ayi Kwei Armah*:

> The point of friction between Baako and his people is far from single or simple. It is determined by a whole bunch of attitudes on both sides which shape the areas of conflict. For example, a crude analysis of the attitudes of Baako's family towards him would tend to suggest that they are merely on the make. But a more searching look at the behaviour of Efua, his mother, and Araba, his sister, soon reveals that their pre-occupations are neither cynical nor demeaning ... Their love for Baako and longing for his return are undoubted; their absolute assumption that he will bring a car in his wake is one way of paying him homage. (Fraser 1980: 33)

But there is a wilfulness in the protagonist, a rigidity of perception which will not allow him to compromise even slightly on how he imagines that society should be. Yet again, like the characters in *The Beautyful Ones* Baako is basically powerless to influence or precipitate change, and those around him cannot sympathize with his attitude or vision. From being a physical exile in a foreign land, the trauma of which had partly caused his earlier illness and precipitated his return, he now gradually metamorphoses into the type of self-exile we have in *The Beautyful Ones*. His return appears itself to be a suicidal wish fulfilment, since he was aware before leaving for home that he was not in tune with the family's – and society's – expectations of him. He stands in stark contrast to Brempong, his co-passenger on the plane, who plays with relish the role his family and kinsmen want him to play, and is fully rewarded by them emotionally and psychologically. Although he has been away from home for extended periods of time (far longer than Baako, in fact), Brempong has no anxiety about his return, no sense of exile, and cannot contemplate a feeling of loneliness while among his people. Brempong is 'together' with his people, Baako is apart from his.

When he meets Juana, the psychiatrist who later becomes his girl friend, Baako

> talked, very precisely, of the things worrying him, like a doctor probing into a diseased body, ... all his talk was of a loneliness from which he was finding it impossible to break, of the society he had come back to and the many ways in which it made him feel his aloneness. She asked him about his family, thinking of some possible shelter, but when he spoke of it, his family became only a closer, intense, more intimate reflection of the society itself, a concave mirror, as he called it, and before long she was left in no doubt at all that in many ways he saw more small possibilities of hope in the larger society than in the family around him. (*Fragments* 1974: 143–4)

The society Armah probes in *Fragments* is the same as the one in *The Beautyful Ones*, and the narrative focus is once again on the individual's response to the passions of his society. Like the characters in the earlier novels, Baako is acutely conscious of the ills of his society, or what he sees as its misplaced priorities and misdirected passions and pursuits. Unfortunately, society feels differently from him and acts differently. As Juana tells him, he is 'going against a general current' (145), a sentiment reiterated by Ocran who tells him, 'If you want to do any real work here, you have to decide quite soon that you'll work alone' (112).

Unfortunately, Baako prefers to 'defend a principle in himself', thus alienating himself from his family and all around him. The family's response is to reinforce his self-exile status for him by first of all withdrawing emotional support and finally physically removing him to exile in a mental asylum. His cycle of exile is thus completed.

Fragments gives the reader the first remote hints of the exile theme as Armah subsequently explores it in *Why Are We So Blest?*. Reading this latter novel, one gets a suspicion that in terms of mental composition – though not actual publication – *Why Are We So Blest?* pre-dates *Fragments*; also, that Baako is Modin's *alter ego* who has survived the traumatic experience of exile and sought succour in a family circle that fails him.

Whatever the case, however, Armah seems to me to amplify in *Blest* the implicit point made in *Fragments*: the journey to the West, far from being a boon to the African, is in fact a destructive and traumatic experience of exile, a view that runs counter to conventional wisdom and one that precipitates Baako's problems in *Fragments*.

Armah persistently reinforces this view of the journey-as-exile through the experiences of Modin, and also through the complementary reminiscences of Solo. The perception by colonized peoples of 'the mother country' in Europe, or its trans-Atlantic extension, America, as places of enlightenment and pleasure is constantly sabotaged through the presentation of Modin's experiences – humiliating patronage, physical brutalization, moral depravity and spiritual decay. Western (white) society is presented as filled with varied dangers for the African black man who embraces it; the bait of 'knowledge' is only a disguise for luring the victim to his demise. Says Modin in his diary:

> The hunger that brought me here is not a hunger for knowledge. It cannot be. What knowledge is here when all this learning is a ritual of willful blindness?

> My hunger has been for things of the flesh, That is the wild fever that pulled me here and showed my spirit its grave. (*Blest* 1974: 129)

The African 'bright boy' who has been chosen for the journey abroad on a scholarship is badly deceived if he imagines that good fortune has come his way. All that his brilliance has brought him is exposure to the eyes of the enemy who lures him away to remould him for his own purposes, he will be subjected to

> An upbringing aimed at isolating the selected soul, then pushing it back into childhood. A plethora of images exciting desire. The massive prohibitions damning the many to deprivation. Isolation with its false solution: opportunities to surround the lonely self with things, to ease the immediate sharpness of aloneness, things that in the end cut you off further – things to lead your life energies not back to a larger life: things oriented away from life. The invitation to the lonely one: a call to suicide... (*Blest* 1974: 168–9).

Once isolated in exile the victim is then put to whatever use his 'benefactors' desire; his aloneness is deliberately plotted for this purpose:

> This loneliness is oppression's symptom of success. The blessed wave us in front of the damned – we, the desperate are made symbols of hope. Filled with the stupid puffed up pride of the impotent, we acquiesce. Looking for friendship, we search for the oppressor's ranks. The European woman, the American woman – mere shiny things to waste lonely, useless time with. (ibid)

These subtle points form the fictional core of *Blest*, but they are too subtle for the untravelled African to understand or appreciate – hence his consistent belief in the boon-laden value of the journey to America or Europe; hence, too, the inability of Baako's people to understand his stance, his failure to play the 'been-to' role for them.

Both Baako and Modin, who recognize their journey as exile, and see through to the manipulative – and to them destructive – essence of white benefaction, make belated efforts to fight their predicament – Baako by refusing to bring 'cargo' with him on his return, as this would be the most tangible evidence of his immersion in the ways of the people he has fled from, and Modin by attempting to join an African revolutionary, anti-colonial movement. But these actions are ultimately futile and merely symbolic. In Baako's case his family's acute hunger for the things he has rejected foreclose even a partial appreciation of his position. No one even tries to find out what the illness that led to his precipitate return was; it seems that no one believes that sickness actually exists out there: 'Move back, you villagers,' Brempong's sister shouts at those milling around the returning hero. 'Don't come and kill him with your TB. He has just returned, and if you don't know, let me tell you. The air where he has been is pure, not like ours ...' (*Fragments* 1974: 82). For Modin, on the other hand, the seed of his failure was sown in his involvement with Aimée: 'His mind searched for, thought it had found a way past that ordained destruction, the destiny held out to us. What he could not see was the subtler death within the general. He had found his own dissolution and he called it love' (*Blest* 1974: 170).

Ultimately, Armah seems to see these characters as useless to the struggle to liberate Africa, both physically and mentally. The redemption of Africa and African values, the regeneration of society, can neither come from self-righteous, uninvolved self-exiles within the society itself, nor from those who have been tainted by the trauma of foreign exile; not from the man or Teacher in *The Beautyful Ones*, nor from Modin or Baako. Modin's ridiculous revolutionary aspirations are negated by the irony which he seems to be unaware of in spite of his much-vaunted intelligence: that he is in love with a woman who is socially and culturally rooted in the group he wants to fight. His exile and immersion in Aimée's predatory sexuality seem to have blinkered him; at best he has been turned into a partial perceiver of the reality around him by this exile; he is unable to see his essential flaw which is immediately perceived by other workers for the revolution. It is to Solo, the other returned, emasculated exile and assembler of Modin's diary that the reader owes the deeper insights into Modin's exile-tainted mind.

In Baako's case, the experience of exile has also limited his perception of things. There is a hysterical underpinning to his actions that prevents him from fashioning out deliberate strategies for overcoming the obstacles to the realization of his vision of society. The trauma of exile has led to a simplistic reduction of his community's ills to one source – a hunger for Western material artefacts. Rigidly bound in this conviction, he is unable to make even the smallest tactical concessions.

In my view, Armah rejects all these people, exiles in various forms who do not fully know the problems of their people. For change to occur, the impetus must be home-grown and accomplished by those who are totally immersed in the ways of their people. This, I think, is where the thematic bridge between his first three novels examined here and his *Two Thousand Seasons* and *The Healers* exists. In the latter novels the task of resistance, regeneration and healing has begun, spearheaded by the genuinely beautiful ones, the people Professor Williams would describe as 'member': involved, committed, 'confident of the values, attitudes and institutions of the society', (1961: 85), those who will contribute in the argument for society's progress and change from the standpoint of full participation, not self-consuming isolation. I have resisted the insistent but hazardous temptation to draw unfounded biographical parallels between Armah and his characters especially in *Fragments* and *Why Are We So Blest?*. Perhaps such biographical correspondences exist, especially as Armah himself has experienced exile; but it is not my intention to confuse the author with the characters and situations he has invented. Perhaps also, Armah is the most substantial of African writers in terms of the 'literature of exile' I mentioned earlier.

NOTES

1. Page references are given immediately after each quotation. For further bibliographical details of works cited, see below. Dates and places of publication refer to editions used in this article.
2. A tragic example is that of Ken Saro-Wiwa, the Nigerian (Ogoni) writer and activist who was hanged, along with eight other Ogonis, in November 1995 for alleged involvement in the murders of four Ogoni chiefs. The trials and executions provoked world-wide furore and condemnation. Most of the opinions expressed on the issue were that the trials were unfair and unjustly conducted. There have been some dissenting views and refutations, however. Among the most striking is that of one Desmond Orage, a US-based son of Chief S. N. Orage, one of the murdered men, and also a nephew-in-law of Ken Saro-Wiwa, since Saro-Wiwa's wife, according to Mr. Orage, is his mother's 'full sister'. (See *NY Times* 6/12/95, A 16-A 17).

WORKS CITED

Armah, Ayi Kwei, *The Beautyful Ones Are Not Yet Born*, London: Heinemann, 1976.
— *Fragments*, Nairobi: E.A.P.H., 1974.
— *Why Are We So Blest?* Nairobi, E.A.P.H., 1974.
— *The Healers*, London: Heinemann AWS, 1979.
— *Two Thousand Seasons*, London: Heinemann AWS, 1979.
Fraser, Robert. *The Novels of Ayi Kwei Armah*, London: Heinemann, 1980.
Williams, Raymond, *The Long Revolution*, London: Chatto & Windus, 1961.

> Crisis of Filiation:
> Exile & Return
> in John Munonye's Trilogy

Amechi Nicholas Akwanya

In Munonye's writing, from *The Only Son* (1966) and *Obi* (1969) to *Bridge to a Wedding* (1978), exile and rootlessness are the most recurrent motifs. These do not occur as themes to be explored, rather they constitute the individual's situation and, therefore, influence his attitudes and outlook. Among the works of the middle period, only in *A Wreath for the Maidens* (1973), where the action is connected to a national political crisis, does the exile status of the main characters appear rather inconsequential in giving orientation to the action and determining attitudes and outlook. In *Oil Man of Obange* (1971) and *A Dancer of Fortune* (1974), exile is the state of being without a community, and the individual is obliged to try and build himself one from nothing, so to speak. What Munonye brings to the traditional novel in Africa is a mode of questioning which is prepared to go beyond the so-called African experience into the social practice and philosophy of history of traditional society in examining the nature of suffering and alienation.

Partial solutions

The best known of Munonye's works is probably *The Only Son*. Here the contradictions internal to the logic of a traditional system of authority are followed through to the point where the system itself seems to crumble to pieces. It is in John Munonye's writing that we see more sharply perhaps than in the work of any other writer of the Igbo literary movement a representation of traditional society as a system of authority articulated into natural units based on filiation and kinship bonds. In *Things Fall Apart*, for instance, we know nothing of Okonkwo's extended family; and though we know a little of Ezeulu's in *Arrow of God*, the relationship seems to play no role at all in social organization. In the latter work, the male characters are seen as individual members of the ruling class of elders, as is also the case in *Things Fall Apart*, or they are seen as citizens of one or another of the villages that make up the community; and though these may have their own localized cultic practices, there is no suggestion of their having a political structure. The exercise of power seems to be only at two levels, that of the individual household presided over by an adult male, and that of the town community. What we see, however, in Munonye is that each household is an economic unit, with its own land, thus having control over the means of production, which is vested in the adult male householder. But the extended family is a higher authority still where control of the land is concerned; hence it is a tier of the social structure, with cultural and political power attached.

As we see in *The Only Son* and *Obi*, family lands are subdivided among the male children after their father's death, when they are old enough to set up their own households. But as Okafo, the elder of two brothers, dies early, leaving behind an infant son and his mother, the family land reverts to the younger brother Amanze, who holds it till his young nephew should be able to take it over (*The Only Son*, 8). The system working at its best is seen in *Obi*. Here traditional society is truly caring; and the reason for this is the absence of a domineering male, the villain (the actual villain of the work, Jerome, the pillar of the church in Umudioba, is not involved in the main action). In the earlier text, Amanze is not only domineering, but also under the influence of his wives, who push him to exercise all the rights the tradition allows over his dead brother's house, but not the responsibilities. Apparently lacking in this society are adequate checks to prevent a man like Amanze from taking advantage of the system to the point of destroying it. The crisis of *Arrow of God* is also in some measure to be explained by some such lack. Here the antagonistic forces led by Ogbuefi Nwaka and Ezidemili on the one hand, and Ezeulu on the other, appear to be equally matched; and nothing can stop them pursuing their struggle for influence to the point of destroying the institutions which sustain and hold their society together.

In consequence of Amanze's misuse of ancestral authority in *The Only Son*, the widow and her child are forced into exile to Nade, the mother's hometown, where we find a different father figure, Oji. Unlike Amanze, the latter accepts the privileges as well as the responsibilities that go with patriarchal authority. A tension is therefore set up between Umudioba, Amanze's home, and home of Unreason, and Nade, where Oji is the high priest of Reason. The contrasting notions, Reason and Unreason, with which we are familiar in Brecht's theatre, for example, in the Prologue of *The Caucasian Chalk Circle,* may be treated as the 'symbolized universals' in *The Only Son*. As ruling oppositions in the narrative, the movement and development of the story will necessarily be articulating one against the other, to form what Kristeva (1982) calls a thematic loop; and the sequence will come to a close only by the resolution of the opposition. The pattern of this articulation of reason against unreason is repeated and varied in the two later texts; and in *Bridge to a Wedding*, the process is brought to a close in the final triumph of the positive over the negative value. Here the cause of unreason is served by Samson and his brothers who, self-centred and grasping, initiate a process of land consolidation, beginning with communally-owned family lands, using force and intimidation against their victims to further this end. The opposite interest, reason, is promoted by Ebeneto and Orazu, tireless bridge-builders, and by Obieke and Edogu, long-suffering, self-sacrificing, and community-affirming.

In *Obi*, however, the form of the binary opposition loses its sharpness as we switch to a kind of conflict in which the logic of one cultural practice, that of traditional religion, is articulated against another, the Christian one. To Chiaku and Joe's relatives in Umudioba his lack of offspring is a public issue, and they have tradition on their side in demanding that Joe should marry another wife to ensure that the situation is corrected. But the man has imbibed the Christian ethos so successfully that it is now a factor in his interpretation of experience and response to events around him. Thus he sees his childlessness as a problem private to him and his wife to deal with as they see fit; and he resents his relatives interfering. For him the path of reason is to stay monogamous, while seeking medical help over his wife's condition, and in a way that would not offend against their religious beliefs. Someone like the headmaster of the Catholic school in Umudioba, in a similar predicament as Joe, has, while maintaining the appearance of being a convinced Christian, tried every remedy he knows, including the use of charms, without success. His wife's response is to give herself away to someone else to raise his offspring.

For Joe, however, appearances are not one thing, and the reality another. He seems even to have become disconnected from his people's thought patterns to the extent that when he decides to put up a big house, he is convinced that he and Anna his wife deserve this comfort. But as a family's permanent seat, in the people's thinking, this house is an *obi*, a building that is purely symbolic, for it can be *put for* the family itself, since the word is also used for a family that is properly rooted in the community. Such a building is a figure of the family as a self-perpetuating entity. The kind of house that Joe is proposing appeals to the members of the extended family who see it as prestigious. But this is not enough to quell their unease; and Chiaku flatly rejects the idea 'That a man should undertake to build such a house for rats and lizards, and snakes' (*Obi* 142).

The structure of this text, its centring on and narration of aspects of a great struggle whose outcome is nothing less than a social transformation, opens for it the possibility of reception as a historical novel. In such a crisis, the character is often a figure representing one historical movement locked in a blind and passionate struggle with another historical movement (Lukacs 1962/81). With this the narrative may prove a way of conducting the struggle as a partisan. In Munonye's trilogy, the effect of total commitment on the part of the protagonist is the loss of a narrative centre: the story fails to connect around the 'him'. He is partisan. Just as the *obi* fails to appear in the narrative, so does the story fail to reveal a human centre: *Obi* is not Joe's story, but about an ill-fated attempt to reconnect his roots.

As long as the two opposing sides are acting out the logic of their beliefs the conflict runs on parallel lines; there can be no meeting point. What Joe sees as a useful and good investment, his people see as foolish and meaningless; a problem he sees as purely personal, and in any case calling for patience, they see as public, and requiring urgent action. Appropriately, it is by way of a 'coup' (Kristeva) that the text achieves closure. Obieke's wife taunts Joe with impotency, Joe strikes her with his fist, setting off a chain of events that leads to her death. Exile is resumed, and the resolution of the opposition of reason and unreason under the present format is deferred. But in *Bridge to a Wedding* it is no longer an issue, as it has been defused behind the scene by Kafo becoming the father of a vivacious family of six. It is the conflict over the control of family lands first opened up in *The Only Son* that is resumed in *Bridge*. But the recurrence of sequences based on the same opposed universals is only one aspect of the repetitions that we find in the three works.

Repetition and form; the forms of repetition

The Only Son, *Obi*, and *Bridge to a Wedding* form one connected story, despite the fact that each one constitutes a unified and self-contained structure. Among the connecting features are the incidents, which form a temporal sequence, such that the three works may be related among themselves in terms of a beginning, a middle, and an end. As well as this, there is continuity at the level of the subjectivities, the principal characters whose histories intersect, diverge, and then reconverge, and the domain of the action, the home the exiles abandon, and to which they return at the end. Munonye here follows strictly the neo-Classical unities of person, place, and time. However, I shall be paying greater attention to the formal aspects of these interconnections, for we do see, for example, where character is concerned, that not only are we dealing with the same individuals, having identical names, characterizing features, and basic preoccupations, but also with individuals who are functionally equivalent, even though they have different names, and appear in different sequences or portions of the story.

Nnanna and Obieke are the two characters that continue throughout the three texts, the first mobile, moving from Umudioba to Nade and Ossa, back to Umudioba, off again to Sankia, before returning finally to Umudioba – renamed Mudi in *Bridge*. His name also changes from Nnanna in *The Only Son* to Joe in *Obi*, and Kafo, a slight contraction of his surname Okafo, in *Bridge*. But Obieke is the stable centre whose place is fixed in Umudioba and in tradition. Joe encounters different adventures and changes over time; but Obieke is the same as ever. As protagonist, however, Joe is the character around whom all the others are grouped; and all these subjectivities are characters as well as functions. Hence Chiaku/Anna reflect the functioning of the caring female, who is mother or wife, the first dominating in *The Only Son* and a substantial portion of *Obi*, until eclipsed by the second in this work. Complementing this feminine principle is the figure of the protective father, who nevertheless will not hesitate to launch the son into the place of danger to prove himself – Oji, Father Smith, and in *Bridge*, Ebeneto. Opposed to the character is an adversary, who is conceptualized as evil – a type of ogre; and between them a compromise is unthinkable. The opposition is truly binary: the being of the one simply excludes the being of the other. In *The Only Son*, Amanze is the ogre; in *Obi*, it is Akueze, and in *Bridge*, it is

Angus Manns. In the last text, however, his terrors have largely crystallized in the form of the past, and we have, apart from the caring female and the protective father, the faithful friend, Orazu, a middle-aged version of Ibe of *The Only Son*, and a still youthful Obieke in *Obi*. When Joe is out of the scene, as in the Mudi section of *Bridge*, Obieke takes his place as the central consciousness, and with him, as faithful friend, Edogu, who is several times misidentified as Orazu (117).

Just as the characters may be seen as representations of participants already encountered, the story itself develops as a series elaborating and varying the same basic micro-narrative sequence, which functions as a kind of 'textual generator'. But this differs from Riffaterre's account of textual generators (1979), in that Munonye's minimal structure is produced in the text as manifest content, and therefore functions not as the 'deep structure' from which the whole derives, but as an *exemplum* that each of the following installments looks back to. Typically, an exemplum is organized as the exposition of a procedure (Beaujour 1980: 336) that will be reconstituted under different formats throughout the narrative or in subsequent works.

This minimal narrative we see early in *The Only Son* where, in reaction to cruelty from his uncle Amanze and his wives, he lodges an arrow in the calf of one of the wives. As a result he has to flee for safety with his mother. The home is forsaken, and the character is an exile, though he finds the strange place congenial. This in itself is a temptation to stop him seeking to reclaim the lost home. Hence the work is organized as an epic journey to regain the ancestral home, and the focus is not so much on the hero or on whether or not he succeeds in the implied quest, but on the various moves that lead to his achieving the goal. This goal, however, is not achieved in *The Only Son*. What we see rather is that the demands that his adopted home puts on him have begun to assume the aspect of a constraining enclosure against a free spirit, whereas the church mission newly started in Nade is promising to open to a neophyte nothing less than a vast new world. Nnanna's acceptance of this call results for the mother in a breach of the emotional link which has so far held her back from remarrying. She accepts a marriage proposal, and Nnanna responds by removing to the mission station, the first leg of the journey that will take him to Ossa to serve as a mission boy. Thus the book ends on a repetition of the first outward movement into a strange environment.

The traditional ancestral ideology, as we see it in Munonye's trilogy, has as its props the family home situated in the ancestral property, the living exchanges within the extended family, and the exchanges between the past and present members metaphorized in endless reincarnations. Hence the importance of male offspring through whom the dead fathers of the line reappear and participate again in history. The male child is not merely a privileged member of the family, but an embodiment of the line. Often in Munonye the figure of the ogre is a member of the extended family, and his role is seen in his dispossession of some other member of his means of livelihood. We see the pattern fully at work in *Oil Man of Obange*, and it is such an intention that Chiaku accuses Amanze of

58 Crisis of Filiation

harbouring against her son (*The Only Son*, 8–9). Traditional society as we know it in Munonye's fiction has no answer to a man pressing in this way the advantages the tradition allows him. But as we see in *Bridge to a Wedding*, where Samson and his brothers seize the property of their kinsman Obieke, disregard of these unwritten laws undermines and tends to destroy the ancestral system itself. This is the danger that the head men of the extended family of Udemezue are trying to ward off when they refuse to divide by a formal act the portion of the family property belonging to the house of Okoli between Joe and Obieke, the surviving head men (*Obi*, 128–31).

The expropriation of the family land by Amanze which is the remote cause of the hero's flight is rewritten in the Nade portion of *The Only Son*, with Oji as the humane interpreter of tradition, who understands that family land is given for the sustenance of the family members, and not necessarily as a stepping stone to power and affluence. That the land does not belong to the individual as such is clearly brought out by the head men of the Udemezues in *Obi*, where we are led to the discovery that part of the reason the family land will not be divided between Joe and Obieke is that the former has no offspring as yet:

> They drew their seats together, in a small circle, their knees almost touching. Then they spoke in whispers. It was not long before they came to a decision. Joe had nobody yet who would inherit his own share of the land. If he were a bad man – but may Ojukwu of Umudioba forbid! – he might give away the land to people outside the family. No, the land should remain intact as Okoli's property. When the time came for dividing they would know; there would be no difficulty about that. (129)

As we have seen, the reason for the high regard for male offspring is that they are the embodiment of the line itself. Joe's title to the land is confirmed if he has male issue. The importance of reincarnation in the trilogy is as the line's self-reaffirmation. Reincarnation is the function that perpetuates life beyond death, and enriches life by inserting within every new form a version from the past: Joe is said to be the reincarnation of his grandfather Okoli, just as Obiakizu, his young cousin, Obieke's son, is the reincarnation of Okafo, Joe's own father. In *Obi*, we find that Obieke's father Amanze has been waiting to reincarnate in Joe's seed to complete the generation loop, turn the family inside out, and start a new generation of crossings and recrossings. There seems to be a limited number of individuals in the family of man, all of whom are in the past or present.

It is obvious that the economy of reincarnation we see in these texts is quite different from what we see, for instance, in Onuora Nzekwu's *Wand of Noble Wood*, where we can make out three distinct spheres, the world of the ancestors, the world of men of flesh and blood, and the world of the unborn, the last being a form of the future, waiting to be made present. Must we conclude therefore that in Munonye we are looking at a traditional society quite different in kind from Nzekwu's, or that at least one of them is wrong, and try to demonstrate this by reference to the 'outside facts'? These are the paths to which we are led by the earlier critics, such as Larson (1971: 121), and are largely of anthropological interest. A different approach, which I am attempting here, is to treat the material as deployed for a purpose. This is an approach that does not assume that even philosophical and moral issues that occur in a work of fiction are necessarily thematic, but that they may be open to, and should first of all be examined in a purely functional analysis, questioning them on the conditions and logic of their incorporation into the narrative. This is particularly appropriate in a work like Munonye's trilogy, where the very characters themselves may be more functional than substantive.

Thus we must relate the economy of reincarnation in the trilogy to the founding oppositions, whereby the preservation of community, the path of reason, is premised on its self-identity, its continuity with the past. That this unity is threatened by the exile of one of the members is implied in *Bridge to a Wedding*, where Joe's absence has opened the way for Samson to encroach on the property of the Okolis. Before our very eyes the house of Okoli is shrinking up and dying, and the consequences are grave: the Udemezues are deep in crisis and, as a result, there is a great cleavage in the Umudioba town community itself, which defies every attempt to heal it. Before this, in *Obi*, the healing of the rift within the family which had been engineered by Obieke has ended in failure, as exile is renewed. Here, however, another kind of absence is the issue, namely, Joe's failure to bring forth offspring. All the members of the extended family are deeply concerned over this, and the ancestors too, we learn. All the while that Joe is childless, Amanze had 'refused to be reincarnated; he was waiting to return as Joe's child' (94). Now he reincarnates outside the house of the Okolis, though still within the extended family.

But reincarnation could also be seen as a model of interpretation. As a figure of the narrative process itself, it brings to mind a text bending back upon itself in endless self-repetition; as such the regaining of the lost home could be deferred indefinitely. Repetition works in Munonye not so much as a reassurance that we are on old and familiar ground, but as a device for endlessly putting off the repossession of it.

Exile as a rite of passage

The trilogy is highly cohesive as a story; the one striking variance in detail is as regards the circumstances that have led to the flight of the protagonist from Umudioba. The actual event as we see it taking place in *The Only Son*, and as accurately remembered in *Obi*, involves Nnanna shooting an arrow into the leg of Obidia, Amanze's wife. In *Bridge to a Wedding*, however, it is Amanze himself who is pierced with the arrow (217). Is this a simple error on the part of the narrator, or is he reporting Joe's consciousness forty years on, after the event has become rearranged in his memory? Joe has sufficient depth in the trilogy for his memory of events to be subject to rearrangings and reinterpretation. For instance, his memory of his second flight from Umudioba has become in *Bridge* associated with guilt (28). But this had not been the case when the incident itself happened. At this time, what is uppermost in the character's mind is that it is demanded by tradition that he should go away. And it seems that this cultural requirement is purely commonsensical:

> It was custom that demanded it, but it was also a matter of common sense. For how could he stay in the land to look at the cousin whose wife he had beaten to death? Obieke who had been very kind to him and extremely helpful! And with what eyes would he continue to see the children whom he had now rendered motherless? 'You it was who killed our mother – nobody else did.' That was what they would be saying to him in their hearts. It was perhaps more matter of common sense than custom. (*Obi*, 209)

The mind here seeks to justify the ways of custom, perhaps as a construction based on experience. At the same time, however, it reflects a sensibility for the pain it must occasion the persons directly affected by this death. We do not yet have a consciousness of guilt, only the ingredients that would later yield it as a precipitate for a perceptive and lonely soul.

The condition of Joe's existence is retreat and isolation. We find him in *Bridge to a Wedding* having adjusted mentally to this mode of existence:

> He had long resolved to remain aloof, unknown if possible, in Sankia; he was a man in hiding; his pursuer was none other than fate itself, or the devil, since, being Christian, he must not believe in fate. (28)

It is inevitable in an exile sequence that the individual is passive; for exile is an experience, something that happens *to* one. It is not a form of human action, of which Barthes (1977: 107) distinguishes three 'major articulations', namely, desire, communication, and struggle. In Munonye's trilogy, exile is precisely what frustrates these forms of *praxis* from taking their course. And this is where it differs from his *A Dancer of Fortune* and *Oil Man of Obange*. In the latter, for instance, exile is a moral condition, and results from the closure of a struggle over family lands which has led to the near extinction of one large branch of an extended family. For the remnant, it simultaneously opens an equally deadly struggle for survival.

In the trilogy, any interpersonal conflict which promises to be full of tension and decision is usually evaded. For example, when Nnanna leaves the village to become a mission boy, the second outward journey that changes his life profoundly, he is moving off from a site where a struggle has failed to take place. He and Chiaku going their separate ways turns out to be as if arranged for convenience: the mother has accepted a proposal to remarry, and he flatly refuses to consider staying alone in the house he previously shared with her. Similarly, the heavy blow to Akueze's head, and the success of Enine hospital in treating Anna's infertility, prevent the struggle with the relatives over the succession to the *obi*, a representative struggle on behalf of the values of Christianity against those of the cultural tradition, from taking place. But the original of these evasions is the pre-empting of what was to have been a vastly unequal struggle with Amanze by the arrow shot into the latter's wife's leg. As rearranged in *Bridge*, this incident is given an oedipal potential, with Amanze as victim. But this potentially productive line is not followed through.

What helps to retain a reader's interest, despite the evasions, is the distortions whereby each outward journey seems an entirely new experience. Hence the first outward journey is a flight for safety, the second into the embrace of the Christian and modern culture, and the third is ostensibly from a potentially vengeful kinsman. But the general direction of movement is from the constraints of an inward-looking traditional society outwards towards contact and affiliation to the expanding Western culture, until one can return again, having imbibed in good measure Christianity, education, and urbanism, a powerful and confident exemplar for the village to look up to.

Joe is as much pursued by fate as driven by it. For the protagonist, exile works at several levels. In so far as the past has become a source of embarrassment, certain crucial acts of the character having metamorphosed into symbolic acts with a fearful aspect, exile is a form of expiation. But it is also a form of training in self-mastery. First his early impulsiveness and physical strength transform in the young man domiciled in Ossa into aggressiveness. Under the tutelege of the missionaries, this would become repressed. The Joe we meet in the early pages of *Obi* is a smooth gentleman on the surface, but the sign of the unreconstructed brute underneath remains discernible in the vein that stands out on his forehead whenever he experiences serious provocation. This is the force that would erupt with a fatal outcome when Akueze flings the epithet 'castrated bull' at him (189). He spends the ensuing period of exile trying to get the better of the brute. We see him succeed when he feels grossly insulted by his cousin Angus in the presence of Ebenetor and Orazu:

> Kafo stepped forward; bit his lip; stared dangerously, eyes inflamed ... His body began to shake again, as did his voice when he said: 'I've had more than enough from him.' He fought very hard indeed, within himself, countering an urge to advance and strike. There, in Angus right before him, was the devil, in the form of man, dangling before him an opportunity for violence. He must resist the temptation – must hold his lip between the jaws and fold his palms in a neutralizing effect. Violence was the thing which had sent him out into a nameless world. (86)

He seems to have achieved at last the equanimity needed for coping with Umudioba. It is this non-aggressive attitude to life that the narrator projects as valid, and it is a quality that Obieke has as a natural gift. But his son Obiakizu is rather of a similar temperament as the earlier Joe; already he has served a term in prison because of it, and may need the influence of his father and Joe on either hand to help him arrive at the happy state of renunciation.

Exile, finally, is for Joe the space for the shaping of his destiny as the true son, rising from the condition of an outcast. Apart from the decision in *The Only Son* to become a Christian and to go into the service of the missionaries, the major events that affect the course of his life are either set up by him inadvertently, or they simply happen to him, having been set in motion by other people. This is a weakness notable in *Obi* and *Bridge*, and the result of the character thus becoming 'de-realized' is that

62 Crisis of Filiation

he is almost *absent* from his own story. Part of the reason for the high praise that *The Only Son* received at its first publication (Carter 1969) was really that the story was seen as convincing, and the character fully realized. This is certainly not the case in the later works.

As a child, Joe had been entrusted to Amanze by custom and circumstances, but Amanze had rejected this charge. His next home in Nade proves hardly adequate or permanent. For all this, his friends would prefer him to remain in the familiar environment, and take his chance with life. But as for venturing into the wider world, particularly in the tow of the missionaries, this to them is as good as getting lost. His first return is premature. Even though he has made good for himself, his lack of offspring, as far as his people are concerned, quite nullifies all the achievements. In the renewed exile, he succeeds in this too, and moreover returns at a time when the *obi* is most in danger of closure, for the resident survivors Obieke and his son Obiakizu, under pressure from members of another branch of the extended family, are at the end of their tether. Now they are utterly impoverished, and without a livelihood. His return is a new lease of life for a tottering house.

Conclusion

Of all the older Nigerian writers, Munonye seems to have attracted the least criticism. The reason for this has little to do with the values that are foregrounded or the so-called anthropological material in his writings. On these points he is hardly inferior to the most highly regarded in the tradition. The difficulty is with the uses these materials are put to, which touch upon the formal aspects of fiction. For instance, a non-aggressive attitude towards life is not in itself a factor of weakness in a novel, any more than an aggressive one ensures strength and success. We find these contrary qualities in Achebe's *Things Fall Apart* and *No Longer at Ease*. The success of these works is more a matter of technique than a function of the argumentative structure. It is technique that allows us to see that an aggressive attitude is Okonkwo's attitude rather than Achebe's, and the non-aggressive, Obi's rather than the author's. In Munonye's trilogy, particularly in *Obi* and *Bridge to a Wedding*, one rarely senses the characters as individual subjectivities existing in their own right, nor do they seem to enter into a living interaction with the sequence of incidents in which they are connected. We do not have the sense of a self-sufficient world, rather it is the sense that the characters and incidents are being *used* to argue a point.

WORKS CITED

Achebe, C., *Things Fall Apart*, London: Heinemann, 1958.
— *Arrow of God*, London: Heinemann, 1964.
Barthes, R., *Image – Music – Text*, transl. S. Heath, London, Fontana, 1987.
Beaujour, M., 'Exemplary Pornography: Barries, Loyola, and the Novel', in S.R. Suleiman and I. Crossman (eds), *The Reader in the Text*, Princeton NJ: Princeton University Press, 1980: 325–49.
Brecht, B., *The Caucasian Chalk Circle*, ed. E. Bentley, Harmondsworth: Penguin, 1949/66.
Carter, D., 'John Munonye: *The Only Son*', *ALT* 3, London: Heinemann, 1969, 52–4.
Kristeva, J., *Desire in Language: A Semiotic Approach to Literature*, ed. L.S. Roudiez, Oxford: Oxford University Press, 1980.
Larson, C., *The Emergence of African Fiction*, London: Macmillan, 1971.
Lukacs, G., *The Historical Novel*, Harmondsworth: Penguin, 1962/81.
Munonye, J., *The Only Son*, London: Heinemann, 1966.
— *Obi*, London: Heinemann, 1969.
— *Oil Man of Obange*, London: Heinemann, 1971.
— *A Wreath for the Maidens*, London: Heinemann, 1973.
— *A Dance of Fortune*, London: Heinemann, 1974.
— *Bridge to a Wedding*, London: Heinemann, 1978.
Okonkwo, J. I., 'The Missing Link in African Fiction', *ALT* 10, London: James Currey, 1979: 87–105.

An Exile Writing on Home: Protest & Commitment in the Works of Bessie Head

Sophia O. Ogwude

I The stultifying socio-political atmosphere of oppressive regimes and governments results in protest and exile for the visionary writers of many nations. In the African context exile literature is virtually synonymous with Black South African writing. The list of exiles from the subregion is long but a few names will suffice: Peter Abrahams, Ezekiel Mphahlele, Bloke Modisane, Mazisi Kunene and Dennis Brutus. All have had at various times in their lives to make for safer harbours to nurture and harvest their literary and artistic gifts.

Black South African creative writing started in 1870, but it was not until 1925 that protest first emerged in this corpus of writing which has by now come to have a distinction of its own. In that year, Mghayi wrote decrying the evils of the white man's presence in Southern Africa in a mock-heroic poem in honour of the Prince of Wales who was then visiting. The emergence of *Drum* magazine in 1951 further encouraged vigorous literary activity among blacks, and the protest tradition of these early years later took on the politics of challenge as well from 1960 as a result of the Sharpeville massacre which marked the close of passive resistance and the beginning of a more resolute black concern with immediate sociopolitical issues. Unfortunately, the literary scene had in much of this period been exclusively dominated by men and negrophilists as some would classify Peter Abrahams and Alex La Guma.

The concern of this article is to examine the South African tale of inhumanity as told by a female member of the oppressed class. And Bessie Head offers a unique case study. She was born in Pietermaritzburg, South Africa on 6 July 1937 through a relationship which was regarded as taboo: a white mother from a wealthy family and a black man, a domestic servant in charge of their stables. It is hard to imagine more tragic birth circumstances in that racist society. Before Bessie Head went formally into exile in 1964, she had learnt to be alone in South Africa and had been made to accept alienation as the condition for that internal calm necessary for successful self-application to meaningful and rewarding play and/or work. In other words, she had experienced the worst of racism and oppression. Therefore, it is only reasonable to expect that if she writes, this must remain for her a mine of ideas.

II Bessie Head is an exile who writes eloquently on all that she has been exiled from: South Africa and nationality, marriage, and other intimate and meaningful inter-human relationships. Significantly, all her work is concerned with protesting the evils in inter-human relationships. At this point, a fundamental question to ask is whether or not Bessie Head has any relevance in the black nationalistic struggle of her time. This question is important for two major reasons. First, earlier critics of her works have to varying degrees argued that she has not made the nationalistic struggle in South Africa her concern. Expectedly then, that school of thought cannot consider her art as protest in any sense. In fact Lewis Nkosi believes that she has little or no political commitment and that 'for most of the time Bessie Head seems politically ignorant'.[1] The premise of this article is that the author is indeed a protest writer. Therefore answering the question on her relevance will help bridge the gap. Secondly, the question of relevance is a fundamental one for every writer. A writer with no relevance cannot expect his works to be taken seriously.

There is a division between what has hitherto been said of Head's work and the thesis expanded in this study. Our position is that she is politically committed. In fact she could not have been otherwise. She may not have been a gadfly in the sense in which Socrates called himself one because she does not 'fasten upon the state' but she nonetheless 'arouses', 'persuades' and 'reproaches'.[2] Romanus Egudu summarizes our position and Head's too when he writes that:

> Although literature may not and should not usurp the office of a pulpit-sermon or political propaganda, it is difficult to see how this art, whose primary objective is communication and whose primary means of accomplishing it is language (which itself has a duty to communicate), can fail to evoke some response or reactions from the reader; for every communication system operates on the basis of a stimulus recognition – response relationship. The artist is a member of society, and the content and style of his work are affected by social reality ... one's response to a literary work may not be a simple course of physical action (and it does not have to be); it may be only a mental or emotional reaction, which can ultimately lead to action – physical or intellectual.[3]

It will therefore be argued in this article that the author is a socially relevant writer; that she is politically aware, which means that she is a socially responsible writer committed as she should be. It has been shown that her style, the basis on which she is negatively appraised on political issues, has not been given due attention and that her literary techniques in themselves are pointers to her social and political commitment. It is argued that even while in exile, Head's ultimate concern is South Africa and the lot of the black South African. The writer herself believes that this is what she has done and this is how she puts it:

All my work had Botswana settings but the range and reach of my preoccupation became very wide, ... I began to answer some of the questions aroused by my South African experience.... My work has covered the whole spectrum of Southern African preoccupations – refugeeism, patterns of evil, and the ancient South African historical dialogue.[4]

Head has been accused of political naivety and ineptitude because she has not been seen to be conforming with the set-down formula of political writing. Yet, ironically, a study of her aesthetics more readily reveals the epistemological. Stylistic differences among a select group of writers may appeal to different sensibilities without necessarily jeopardizing their common commitment to a particular cause. The point of departure is that she refuses the already established conventions, preferring instead the role of a 'pioneer blazing a new trail into the future'.[5] This prepares us to expect an unconventional exposition of the apartheid system and its numerous manifestations, for, as Virginia Woolf remarks:

> If a writer were a free man and not a slave, if he could write what he chose, not what he must, if he could base his own work upon his own feeling and not upon convention there would be no plot, no comedy, tragedy, no love interest or catastrophe in the accepted style.[6]

Because she neither uses conventional techniques nor seeks to enlist stock responses from her readers, mere peripheral study of Head's works results in much misunderstanding. Her goals are much broader than those of the ordinary protest writer and as such they demand different and diverse techniques. She sums up the task before her and explains the seeming ambiguities in her works in terms of these tasks rhetorically:

> How do we and our future generations resolve our destiny? How do we write about a world since lost? A world that never seemed meant for humans in the first place, a world that reflected only misery and hate? It was my attempt to answer some of these questions that created many strange divergences in my work.[7]

The author is as interested in her protest mission as she is about the future generations of black South Africans. Therefore, she goes beyond protest. She helps to devise other ways of maintaining and sustaining life regardless of apartheid. And she realizes that, ultimately, her success with such concerns will be dependent on a truthful and honest exposition of the many facets of the hydra-headed problem of racism and human oppression. As a result, she makes it her concern to show the South African black where he has erred in the past. Many years of white subjugation and oppressive lies have so dented the black image that any meaningful rehabilitation of it needs to begin with the unearthing of the true black image. The debris of the crumbling walls of racial pride which has been subjected to years of cultural, racial and economic battering must be collected together and put up again.

III The approach was to investigate the genres which the writer has used in her works, since favoured media reveal a lot about a writer's goals and objectives. The novelist has employed four discernible genres: the autobiography (imaginative and fictional), utopia, history and the short story form.

Her first three novels, *When Rain Clouds Gather* (1969), *Maru* (1972) and *A Question of Power* (1974) are autobiographical. The distinction between *A Question of Power* on the one hand and *When Clouds Gather* and *Maru* on the other, is that between the imaginative and the fictional autobiography. Perhaps the most fascinating aspect of the autobiography is the power and the ability to open up to the reader an integral part of the historical personality; however, this is not to say that the autobiography is more important because of the historical details of an individual. Rather, the personal pressures suffered by the autobiographer, the consequent metamorphosis and emergence of his final personality, together with the literary technique of the autobiography as a distinct genre of prose, that is, the process by which 'experience is transformed into literature',[8] bear greater claims to importance. This is so because, together, they help to elicit both our sympathy and involvement in each particular dilemma of human life which is the major subject of the genre. James Olney puts this clearly:

> Autobiography is the literature that most immediately and deeply engages our interest and holds it and that in the end seems to mean the most to us because it brings an increased awareness, through an understanding of another life in another time and place, of the nature of our own selves and our share in the human condition.[9]

The imaginative autobiography, or the confession, exposes the original interpretation of personal experience, and modern man has found it increasingly mandatory to write his life in art. There are important reasons for the frequent use of the genre in black South African writing. Among other things, incidents in such works give historical authenticity to the South African situation as it affects individual writers whose desire for credibility in their protest mission hardly needs elaboration. Albert S. Gerard sums this up beautifully when he identifies a two-fold purpose for the imaginative usage of the English language for the South African black:

> One was to convey to the outside world in the words it could understand the violence and the horror of the black man's predicament in an apartheid society ruled by a ruthless minority. The other was not communicational but expressive; it was to discharge their resentment, to seek emotional relief in the artistic reporting of their own experience.[10]

Such are the factors that have helped to make the autobiography a primary form for the South African black writer.

In *A Question of Power* (*AQP*), protest against the South African government is embedded in the author's musings and brooding which together constitute what has largely been branded the 'unreal' or mad world in that novel. In it, communication never really breaks down; all that happens is that the novelist succumbs to the urgency of releasing her mental and psychological anguish and so overtly superimposes these on the main storyline which in itself is a story of inhumanity, oppression, alienation and individual success. In exposing her mental stresses and strains in this way, the novelist also indicts the socio-political conditions responsible for causing them.

Recollection starts only at the age of thirteen for Elizabeth (Bessie for short). The true circumstances of her life and its sordid details spell the beginning of the long and tortuous journey into painful alienation. Before her biological details were revealed she was regarded as a coloured woman but not one with a taint of possible madness – that is, madness as defined by a recklessly ruthless society. The mission school was her initiation into the details of life and oppression in South Africa which before then had hardly taken form in her mind. Even at play she was haunted for traits of the same madness from which her mother was believed to have died. The kind of madness which Head writes about is madness used as a label to denote overt non-conformism in a social set-up as brutal as South Africa's where the merely alienated are untruthfully diagnosed as mad. The experience at the mission school was a traumatic one, as the author effortlessly recaptures in *Maru*.

> It was only when she [Margaret Cadmore] started going to the mission school that she slowly became aware that something was wrong with her relationships to the world. She was the kind of child who was slyly pinched under the seat, and next to whom no one wanted to sit. (*Maru* 17)

Latent hatred for the South African atmosphere coupled with her marriage difficulties causes her on the spur of the moment to leave South Africa for Botswana where there had been an advertisement for teachers. The sequence of events in this text comes out very clearly despite the initial difficulties of grasping the narrative style. The autobiographer's statement is that, although the child is the 'learner dependent on his society for his soul evolution' (*AQP*, 11) and acculturization, South Africa was one which the child Elizabeth was to reject as a teacher:

> She hated the country. In spite of her inability to like or to understand political ideologies in South Africa it was like living with permanent nervous tension, because you did not know why white people there had to go out of their way to hate you or loathe you. They were just born that way, hating people. There wasn't any kind of social evolution beyond that, there wasn't any lift to the heart, just this vehement vicious struggle between two sets of people with different looks ... (*AQP* 19)

Consequently, she gives the verdict that South Africa as a teacher is 'at fault' and that 'conclusions [must be] drawn at the end of each life in opposition to the social trends' (*AQP*, 11). Implicit in this rejection is protest, deep protest.

By the time she exiles herself to Botswana, she had been exiled from all there could be. First exiled at birth and pronounced unacceptable by blood relations who were only races and not people, then exiled from childhood, and later, exiled even from marriage and love life. She turned her back on South African society rejecting all the hatred and cheapness which was all it was capable of teaching.

Lewis Nkosi has written to imply that Head chose Botswana for a place of self-exile because of her pathological need to be close to South Africa.[11] 'This is pure conjecture since nothing in the life she lived up till the point of her departure from South Africa, or later in her artistic creations, gives the impression that she, at any time, believed anything in South Africa worth nostalgic grief. The explanation which seems more readily acceptable is that put forward by Kolawole Ogungbesan, who affirms that it is a proof of her meekness and simplicity of heart that she should choose a 'quiet back-water' like Motabeng in Botswana to live, as against the vogue of black South African writers choosing the big cities of the Western European world as places of exile.[12] Perhaps Head like Makhaya, the hero of her first autobiographical work, 'simply wanted a country to love and chose the first thing at hand' (*When Rain Clouds Gather* (*WRCG*) 17). The autobiographer makes this point strongly in her observation that:

> Well-educated men often come to the crossroads of life. One road might lead to fame and importance and another might lead to peace of mind. It's the road of peace of mind that I'm seeking. (*WRCG*, p. 20)

In *When Rain Clouds Gather*, the will of a free people is shown to be capable of assertion even to the point of toppling bad leadership. This is because a free people have the will and the power to decide their own fate. In the face of economic disaster, the Golema Mmidi farmers form farmers' cooperatives to foster and ensure economic advantages, and with complete disregard for the selfish ambitions of Metenge, their leader. In short, to borrow the author's own phrase, they 'resolved their distress'.[13] This is an outright condemnation of the criminal white minority rule in South Africa 'where a cooperative of any kind ... would cause a riot of hysteria among the white population [whose] wealth and privilege are dependent on the poverty and distress of the black people'.[14]

Ironically, it is Gilbert Balfour, the European, and not Metenge, who works hard, freely imparting his skills and knowledge to the Golema Mmidi peasants in order that the quality of their life might be improved.

The thin thread of protest against black domination begun here is given a wider dimension in her two subsequent novels. In *Maru*, the Masarwa (bushmen) people have been so named not by the white colonizer but by the native blacks. And in showing the various patterns of evil in *A Question of Power*, we see also the exploitation of blacks by blacks as no less evil than that discerned in the white racist's relationship with blacks. As we shall see later in this chapter, it is in fact the wanton preying of one black nation on another that is the single most devastating factor in black South African history.

IV If the autobiography generally attempts to depict historical realities, the utopia on the other hand seeks to transcend the present. This notwithstanding, scholarly interest in utopia as a literary genre reveals that it is ultimately rooted in social and political issues. Plato's *Republic* of around 394 BC was evidently written to condemn Athenian democracy, even as Thomas More's *Utopia* was primarily written in reaction against the medieval upheavals which eventually culminated in the reformation and the birth of modern man. The motivating force behind the realization of Head's utopia is the scientific and technological supremacy vested in her major characters, including the female ones. These are characters who have either had formal education in the sciences or people gifted with remarkable intelligence to grasp imparted knowledge and skills quickly and efficiently. What all her major protagonists – Eugene, the Boer exile from South Africa, Gilbert Balfour, Makhaya and Maru – have in common is that each refuses to recognize colour bars, preferring instead to be useful and productive members of communities of men. Eugene rejects South Africa, lives with Africans in Botswana, works with them and is loved and respected by them. Gilbert, a white man, rejects his bourgeois family background, comes to live and work with African people, and marries a black wife. He gives and is given respect and honour. Maru rejects his traditional rights of leadership and marries a masarwa, convinced that no man should be the object of pity or slave of another. For the apartheid system as well as for the perpetrators of oppressive tribal prejudices, these are recriminatory pictures. Indeed by highlighting what could be and contrasting it with what is, the writer indicts the ugly South African machinery which desecrates human life on both the rural and urban fronts.

Bessie Head pleads mutually rewarding inter-human relationships among people in general and restates this stand variously in her works. In *A Question of Power* she writes.

> I don't like exclusive brotherhoods for black people only ... I have got my concentration elsewhere. It's on mankind in general. (*AQP* 132–3)

Her essay 'For Serowe a village in Africa' is even more insightful. Here is an excerpt:

> We are all really startled by the liberation of Africa, but we have been living in exclusive compartments for so long that we are all afraid of each other. Southern Africa isn't like the rest of Africa and is never going to be. Here we are going to have to make an extreme effort to find a deep faith to help us to live together. In spite of what the politicians say, people are not going to be destroyed. Not now.[15]

Head died of infective hepatitis on 17 April 1986. And now the last vestiges of white minority leadership and domination are fast and steadily ebbing away. Thus it is no longer possible to question her prophetic vision of a South Africa where blacks and whites would necessarily have to forge a symbiotic relationship.

V   In contrast to the utopian genre, historical works instruct as they highlight past mistakes and achievements. And for this purpose Head uses contrasting historical figures. Her last major works, *Serowe,*

Village of the Rainwind (1981) and *A Bewitched Crossroad: An African Saga* (1984), which are non-fictional and historical respectively, reveal the novelist's resolution to challenge the image of the black man as an impotent sufferer who is forever prone to aggression and forever engaged in unmatched battles against his militarily superior adversary. To do this, she has had to unearth prestigious historical African leaders whose astuteness and psychological preparedness stood them in good stead in the face of menacing foreign interests in their land. Khama the Great (1875–1923) and Tshekedi Khama (1926–59) stand out among others. In revisiting history in this way, she achieves two major objectives. First, she presents us possible ways forward out of the nightmarish reality of apartheid. Then again, she uses the contrast technique to reveal to the South African where indeed 'the rain began to beat him'.

Khama's considerate and wise alternative of a resistance of image and prestige with its attendant successes points a possible way forward. On the home front, his contemporaries and subjects confirm that his was the 'calm thoughtful rule of the mind'[16] which 'thought about the man who was nothing'.[17] And on the political scene, Khama ruled with such grandeur and self-respect as to enable him to proclaim to the British that he was 'not baffled in the government of his town, or in deciding among cases among his people according to custom'.[18] Interestingly, Khama's country, Botswana, was never really colonized in the ordinary sense, evidently because as a ruler he made it impossible for the black man's image to be trampled upon.

His son, Tshekedi, followed in his father's footsteps and not even the trumped up charges against him by colonial Britain, which opposed anything he did and exiled him twice from Bamangwato country without a proper trial,[19] could dent his image as the father of self-help projects. In presenting these alternatives as possible ways forward, the novelist enjoins us to reconsider the fire and brimstone war alternative which had largely proved ineffective and even downright senseless at other times. Khama's thoughtful reasoning and inventiveness in dealing with the colonialists produced good and lasting results and his approach is seen in vivid contrast to the indiscriminate and often unprovoked attacks of the Matebele. The Matebele assaults were often devastating and the culminating influence of these wars resulted in the inability of the tribal nation states to present a common front of resistance against white Boer incursion into modern South Africa.

Even the exposition of such sordid historical details as the Matebele's is essential to the restoration of Africa's dignity and self-respect. We find the rationale for Head's attitude in Bernth Lindfors' critique of Armah's histories where he writes that

> the depredations of the past are responsible for the chaos one sees in Africa at present and [that] only by properly understanding that past and present will Africans collectively ... be able to tackle the problems of the future.[20]

A way to tackle the problems of the future is for the black South African to understand that he did not lose all his fights with the white man in the past, neither did he always agree to battles where only physical prowess counted. She points out that mental and psychological warfare was often ill-suited to his opponents and so must be exploited.

VI

The short story in South Africa has since ceased to 'belong to an oral literary tradition centuries old and still very much alive in Africa today'.[21] The genre is now employed in the exposition of the needs and problems of the present day; and thus the impetus which has encouraged its production is drastically different from that responsible for the oral form. Like other South African short story writers, the novelist too has not turned to tradition for the inspiration for her stories. Mbulelo V. Mzamane articulates the reason for this when he writes in his introduction to *Hungry Flames* that

> Under the harsh conditions of the settler colonialism experienced in South Africa, for black writers to dwell on the beauty of traditional culture would be a hollow exercise performed at the expense of more vital issues.[22]

Interestingly, Head's own contribution to this volume, 'The Prisoner Who Wore Glasses', is radically political even if utopian in its vision. Hannetjie, the Boer warder employed to work with Span one, a span made up of ten political prisoners, soon learns a few hard lessons: Brille calmly announces that he is twenty years older and therefore could not bring himself to call Hannetjie Baas; although Brille suffers an immediate physical assault as a result, none of the often predictable reactions takes place; instead a psychological warfare develops between the warring factions.

Predictably, Hannetjie employs all the tools available to white authority whose responsibility, it is believed, is to keep the black man in his proper 'place'. However, he soon oversteps his bounds and awakens to the reality that he is pitched in a battle against opponents he could never hope to triumph over. The writer tells us that 'the battle was entirely psychological. Span one was assertive and it was beyond the scope of white warders to handle assertive black men.'[23] Hannetjie succumbs under this war of nerves and falls harder than all the other warders before him.

First, Brille catches him stealing fertilizer for his private farm and although he accepts a bribe as a condition for keeping quiet about it, he nonetheless betrays him and Hannetjie incurs a huge financial loss as a result. Brille succeeds in the betrayal because he does a thorough psychological study of his opponent and knows how best to get the better of him. In addition, Brille consistently refuses to acknowledge that Hannetjie's skin colour is of any obvious advantage and treats him as he would any other impetuous younger man of whatever race:

> One day, at close of work Warder Hannetjie said, 'Brille, pick up my jacket and carry it back to the camp.' 'But nothing in the regulations says I'm your servant, Hannetjie,' Brille replied coolly.
>
> 'I've told you not to call me Hannetjie. You must say Baas,' but Warder

Hannetjie's voice lacked conviction. In turn, Brille squinted up at him. 'I'll tell you something about this Baas business, Hannetjie,' he said. 'One of these days we are going to run the country. You are going to clean my car. Now, I have a fifteen year old son and I'd die of shame if you had to tell him that I ever called you Baas.'[24]

In Head's vision, there was the possibility of a black man owning a car in the future and employing a Boer to clean it. At the point of writing though, hard core pragmatists could only have dismissed such a vision as utopian. But we now know that today's utopia is tomorrow's truth. To live then with this utopian possibility in mind is for the black South African to live conscious of his black pride and integrity. This is an integral aspect of Head's commitment to the black liberation efforts.

A major authorial statement is embedded in the fact that in reaching some understanding, life becomes mutually enriched for members of Span One and Warder Hannetjie. In return for treating the political prisoners decently, Hannetjie receives his much needed fertilizer without having to do the pinching himself. This goes to confirm the author's stated opinion that exploitation and evil thrive only because there is a lack of communication between the oppressor and the people he oppresses. Once the warder is forced to compare his desire for fertilizer and its theft with the prisoners' desires for food and smoke, he concedes that all are identical offences which must either attract comparable punishment or be dismissed with equal resignation.

This story illustrates another of what Head considers the viable fighting stances open to blacks in South Africa, namely, assertiveness. Only a tactical war of the nature fought by the prisoners of Span One could bring about such a happy result. An overtly aggressive reaction from Brille and his men would have resulted in one of those mass and senseless murders which is abhorrent to Head and to all who ascribe dignity and reverence to human life. Clearly, the two options left to the oppressed in South Africa are aggression and assertiveness. And she chooses assertiveness which is far more subversive and more effective in that the protest it entails is at the same time silent and recriminatory.

Furthermore, she here revisits another of her peculiar stands on the racial problem – a stand which advocates inter-racial integration for the maximization of happiness and comfort for all. This stand is antithetical to the favoured exclusive organizations on either side of the racial line. The set of people she presents to us at the end of the story is a well integrated multi-racial group. Through mutual understanding, they all triumph over aspects of some of the unpalatable South African rules.

The author's stand on inter-racial cooperation calls to mind John Povey's critique of John Pepper Clark's poetic art contained in the article 'Two Hands A Man Has'.[25] Here the critic makes it clear that Clark rightly acknowledges the need to effectively marry his Western education and heritage to his native African circumstances as vital aspects of a unique self-expression in art. In much the same way Head recognizes that the presence of the white man in the African's life and vice-versa is far too much of a reality to be successfully suppressed under prejudices and senseless dichotomies. She sees that there is a need for blacks to do all within their power to fight a war of image and prestige against the South African white man. Her scenario in this story is simply a microcosm of the South African social set-up in which she 'travels along a long road' and, through her artistic devices, especially that of the change and revelation of character, she goes 'deeper, to unravel the mysteries that lie behind appearances'.[26] In this story, she is not just 'a reporter of events and situations'. Here, she teaches a salient lesson.

Her stories collected under the title *A Collector of Treasures* espouse various aspects of the social conditions of her times. They highlight different dimensions of adult delinquencies such as prostitution and other forms of sexual and marital irresponsibility. One of the author's most memorable heroines is certainly Dikeledi, the collector of treasures, whose story compares with Johannah's in another of the author's stories, 'Jacob: the Story of a Faith-Healing Priest'. In both stories the unfortunate fact that women can be as oppressive to women as some men are is shown rather than suppressed as some feminists would wish. The writer exposes it because it is an important fact which women cannot afford to ignore in their fight for emancipation. The French feminist, Antoinette Fouque, has noted rightly that:

> the difference between the sexes is not whether one does or doesn't have a penis, it is whether or not one is an integral part of a phallic masculine economy.[27]

Head's contention is that we must recognize all oppressive stances in our lives and excise them before we women can hope to fight a winning battle on a common front. She is consistent in her commitment to protest against oppression, be it political, racial or sexual. Her stand here compares with her political and racial protest which is directed against both whites and blacks.

In her short stories, especially the two now under study, 'A Collector of Treasures' and 'Jacob: The Story of a Faith Healing Priest', Head shows how a man has the power to determine what kind of meaning an African woman's life can have.

The investigation of the concept of power offers the author fertile ground for protest against forceful governance. Conventionally, power is might and its retention and exercise are the main preoccupations of many rulers. Indeed, many see power as the most vital factor in enlisting acquiesence and loyalty from subjects. However, Head's attitude to power remains radically opposed to the conventional. She finds the fierce passion for power abhorrent largely because it is sadly opposed to those enduring qualities of humane love and understanding which are better suited to the improvement of the quality of a man's life on earth. She contends that fierce authority does not and cannot earn loyalty and respect, at least not the kind that easily comes to humane leadership. Two of her strikingly similar short stories: 'A Power Struggle' and 'The Deep River: A Story of Ancient Tribal Migration', like *A Question of Power* unequivocally repudiate the thirst for power and contrast it with the noble love and friendship which they advocate.

Protest & Commitment in the Works of Bessie Head 75

Conclusion

In all that Bessie Head published, she remained consistent in her vision and commitment. Her quiet human temperament helped her fashion a corresponding introspective and highly philosophical world outlook. The seeming difference between her and her many other major contemporaries can perhaps be explained in the light of this. Yet this difference is basically that of style and the attempt has been to show that this difference does not and can not denote the degree of commitment or otherwise. Bernard Blackstone's criticism helps to unknot and clarify the fundamental differences between the 'fact-finding and recording journalist'[28] and the artist:

> the journalist cannot see the wood for the trees, the artist grasps the meaning behind phenomena. He is something of a *philosopher*, a *seer*, as well as a technician. But the technique comes in too. New wine will not go into old bottles. New thoughts, new ways of experience will not fit the old forms. *Inevitably, originality of thought and spontaneity of emotion create fresh designs, fresh music, new rhythms.*[29] [my emphasis].

NOTES

1. Lewis Nkosi, *Task and Masks: Themes and Styles of African Literature*, Harlow: Longman, 1981: 99.
2. Plato, 'Apology or Socrates's Defence' in *Dialogues of Plato*, ed. J. D. Kaplan, New York, 1950: 25.
3. R. N. Egudu, *Modern African Poetry and the African Predicament*, London and Basingstoke: Macmillan, 1979: 2.
4. 'Social and Political Pressures that Shape Literature in Southern Africa', *World Literature Written in English* 18, 1979: 22.
5. B. Head, 'Some Notes on Novel Writing'. *New Classic* 5, 1978: 4.
6. 'Modern Fiction', *Collected Essays* 2, New York: Harcourt, Brace and World, 1960: 106.
7. 'Social and Political Pressures that Shape Literature in Southern Africa', *New Classic* 5, 1978: 21.
8. James Olney, 'Autobiography and the Cultural Moment: A Thematic Historical and Bibliographical Introduction', in J. Olney (ed.), *Autobiography: Essays Theoretical and Critical*, Princeton NJ: Princeton University Press, 1980: 10.
9. *Metaphors of Self: The Meaning of Autobiography*, Princeton NJ: Princeton University Press, 1972: vii.
10. '1500 Years of Creative Writing in Black Africa', *Research in African Literature* 12, 2, Summer 1981: 154.
11. '1500 Years of Creative Writing in Black Africa', 99.
12. Kolawole Ogungbesan, 'The Cape Gooseberry Also Grows in Botswana: Alienation and Commitment in the Writings of Bessie Head', *Présence Africaine* 109, First Quarter, 1979: 93.
13. 'Some Notes on Novel Writing', 4.

14. 'Some Notes on Novel Writing', 4.
15. 'For Serowe a Village in Africa' *The New African IV*, 10 December 1965: 230.
16. Bessie Head, *A Bewitched Crossroad: An African Saga*, Craighall: Ad Donker, 1984: 121.
17. Khama the Great, 'Preliminary Document for British Protection', 1885, quoted in *Serowe: Village of the Rain Wind*, London: Heinemann (1981) 1986: 13.
18. *Serowe*, 9.
19. *Serowe*, 76.
20. 'Armah's Histories', in E. D. Jones (ed.), *African Literature Today, 11, Myth and History*, London: Heinemann, 1981: 87.
21. Charles Larson (ed.), *Modern African Stories*, Glasgow: Fontana Collins, 1977: 7.
22. Mbulelo Mzamane (ed.), *Hungry Flames and Other Black South African Short Stories*, Hong Kong: Longman, 1986: ix.
23. Mzamane, 69.
24. Mzamane, 72.
25. 'Two Hands a Man Has: The Poetry of J. P. Clark', *African Literature Today* 1, 2, 3, 4, 1972: 216–22.
26. In his preface to *Black Orpheus*, Ulli Beier distinguishes between two types of short story texts drawing largely on the short story writer's point of view. First, there are those stories in which the writer's role is confined to that of 'a reporter of events and situations', who seeks basically 'to mirror the world around objectively'. Then there are those stories in which the writer 'travels along a lone road', and through other devices tries 'to go deeper to unravel the mysteries that lie behind appearances'. *Black Orpheus*, Ibadan: Longman, n.d.: 7.
27. bell hooks, *Feminist Theory: From Margin to Centre*, Boston MA: South End Press, 1984: 2.
28. Lewis Nkosi, 'Fiction by Black South Africans', in G.D. Killam (ed.), *African Writers on African Writing*, London: Heinemann, 1975: 8.
29. B. Blackstone, *Virginia Woolf*, London: Longmans, Green and Co., 1952: 8.

Changing States: Exile & Syncretism in Buchi Emecheta's *Kehinde*

Ana María Sánchez Arce

The study of literature in the former British colonies, including that produced by African authors and/or authors of African descent, has usually been related to notions of migration and exile. Recently I was asked whether I thought that the question of cultural collision had not been dealt with to exhaustion. The specific person – an interviewer for a prestigious scholarship – was touching a delicate point: is 'postcolonial' literature (as he termed it) a trendy field of study in the late twentieth century which spins and spins around the same topics and theories; or is it a way of tackling questions which, though presented in an acute way by certain writers, also belong to a wider range of human experiences?

One of the best examples of the flexibility and adaptability of human mentality and societies can be found in the multiplicity of cultural forms rising in Africa and in places as remote from it as the Caribbean or the United States. There is no question as to the extrinsic differences which compose the outcome of diverse writers such as Tony Morrison, Grace Nichols, Ben Okri or Tsitsi Dangarembga. However, they all share a common characteristic: their writings are informed by a sense of flexible mobility between worlds and a recognition that 'the road' is always hungry for human flesh. Those who are eaten up by the road alienate themselves from fixed, agreed forms of experiencing reality and enter into a dialogue with alternative social structures. This dialogue changes both ends of the road insofar as there are individuals who are unable to end their journey and inhabit the fluid space of exile.

Exile is not only the cause, but also the effect of the changing relationships amongst individuals within social groups – including those assembled in terms of race, religion, nationality, gender, and so on. Curiously enough, in *The Famished Road* (1991), Okri uses the neverending road as a powerful symbol of both a limitless journey for humanity and the desire for a concrete, definite end. The mind is always travelling beyond and, at the same time, trying to get to a safe end of its trip where a utopian world would be waiting. As Derrida pointed out in 'Structure, Sign and Play in the Discourse of the Human Sciences', the metaphysical categories which are used to make sense of the world by limiting the play of signification create an illusionary certitude of presence and meaning. This search for a transcendental signified, which would become the beginning (arche) and the end (telos) of the play of signification within language, is triggered by what I call the 'anxiety of uncertainty'. Humans have been haunted by the need to define themselves and the world (and by defining the world redefining themselves every day). The absence of a reassuring basis on which to lay the foundations of our lives and thoughts makes us panic. Therefore, we install a centre or several centres in our mental structures which help us overcome the anxiety that the 'unknown' creates. The road of progress, the journey, *Bildungs-* and *Kunstler-roman*, and evolution, are but a few of the metaphors for the illusion of a promised land after the desert. However, most writers who have experienced exile – either physical or mental – are increasingly describing a reality which is not clear-cut and defined by a pretty sharp set of rules. Their work reveals that the bottle of cultural beliefs which contained coherent discourses within its boundaries is cracking at some places and definitely broken at others. One of the reasons why this break-up may be so is exile and its consequences for individual subjectivity, the receiving society, and the source society. I intend to develop the first two in relation to the work of Buchi Emecheta, particularly *Kehinde*.

The latest development in Emecheta's expression of her subjectivity is *Kehinde*. In this novel the author gives voice to the contradictions which arise in the migrant's mind after a long period of exposure to the receiving culture. Despite the apparent simplicity of its plot, the narrative does something more than simply showing the experiences of a migrant woman going back to her 'home' country after a long stay in England. Emecheta's narrative explores concepts such as community, kinship, sisterhood, and multiculturalism in relation to an individual's identity. I analyse Kehinde as exemplifying Emecheta's commitment testimony to her own syncretic cultural identity and to a multicultural society.

The celebration of a transgressive identity – which is articulated in the area where cultural identities collide – is constant in Emecheta's writings. This identity, like Kehinde's, is built in a zigzag manner as the author explores different communities and their symbols. This notion of identity as continually shifting results in contradictions and confusion which critics try to overcome or openly criticize.

Emecheta has been accused of being 'too aloof from her people', of 'loving and hating them at the same time', of 'being too feminist to be "one of us"' (Ogunyemi 1983: 70), even of being unpatriotic. Emecheta resents these accusations by defending her right to criticize her culture and her country.

> Some people have said that a talk which I gave at the Africa Centre a few weeks ago is unpatriotic, but I, as a writer, cannot afford to tell my people what they want to hear. If I start doing that, I would be betraying my conscience, my profession and my country.
>
> Expatriates and many so called 'friends of Nigeria' do tell us exactly what we want to hear in order to keep their jobs and to get as much money out of Nigeria as possible before the oil runs out ... but the stories some of them tell behind our backs are different.
>
> As I said, I cannot afford to play this double role. (Emecheta 1981b: 2582)

Emecheta does not tell anyone 'what they want to hear', hence her difficult position in society and literature. While critics from different positionings regret her 'inconsistencies', she writes herself into her books without censoring any of the sides of her self. On the contrary, her multiple narrations and contradictory statements allow her to play with fixed ideas, raising a hall of mirrors that reflect and deflect her selves in an endless play of signification. In Derridean terms, one could say that her different discourses – whether autobiography, fiction, or speeches – open up the play of signification and do not allow for a stable, permanent centre of belief. Emecheta resists stable categorizations, revealing a fiercely independent personality which favours fluidity and introspection as deconstruction favours a continuous revision of beliefs. Emecheta is a living paradigm that destroys the binary oppositions of First World–Third World, Black–White, Feminism–Africanism, and so on. An example of that could be her reaction to being called a feminist.

> The problem of the black woman is beyond feminism. If the black woman is going to be a feminist, she would have to be a feminist-plus. Her cultural burden is the type the average, over-educated, middle class, well-fed white woman can never begin to understand. (Emecheta 1984: 175)

> I will not be called a feminist here, because it is European. It is as simple as that, I just resent that. Otherwise, if you look at everything I do, it is what feminists do, too; but it is just that it comes from Europe, or European women, and I don't like being defined by them. (Emecheta 1989: 19)

These two quotations illustrate two of Emecheta's attitudes towards feminism. They seem at first sight crude, and – in a way – they probably are. But, if taken together, they reveal a confused Emecheta who remains within both discourses at the same time that she undermines them. The two fragments, then, are central to the understanding of her discourses along temporal lines. In the first fragment, she refers to mainstream feminism and explains its limitations for black women. In the second one, she accepts feminism but rejects being classified as such. Emecheta hints at slightly different positionings which are neither feminist nor Africanist. These opinions, which in many cases have aroused polemics, are brought about by her situation as a migrant writer.

Significantly, Emecheta's most explicit celebration of multiple articulated subjectivity comes after her visit to Nigeria and later return to England. Like Kehinde, she does not feel comfortable in her home country after a long absence. 'Two weeks after my arrival in Calabar, I decided that I had had enough. I was going to leave Nigeria and go back to England, which had been my home for the past 18 years' (Emecheta 1981a: 110), she says in a revealing essay in which she exposes her ambivalent feelings. Nigeria no longer is – or perhaps it never was – her 'home'. England, despite the difficult relationship Emecheta has maintained with it from her arrival in 1962, has replaced it in the writer's mind.

In *Kehinde*, the protagonist's thoughts while in Lagos appear as a voicing of Emecheta's essay.

> She [Kehinde] took hold of herself. Surely it was foolish to pine for a country where she would always be made to feel unwelcome. But then her homecoming had been nothing like the way she had dreamed of it ... The Africa of her dreams had been one of parties and endless celebrations, in which she, too, would enjoy the status and respect of a been-to. Instead, she found herself once more relegated to the margins. (*K*: 96–7)

Kehinde's arrival in Nigeria is harder since she dreams of a community which does not relegate her 'to the margins'. She expects that her condition of been-to will mean inclusion in the elite. However, she does not bargain for the secondary place she is given, first in relation to her husband, and second after his sisters and the educated Rike. She – who should be the first wife – keeps the title but retains little power, or none, since she does not know the rules of the competition for power in an extended family. She is rejected and she is not able to learn the boundaries of her native community nor its symbols.

> It [community] is the arena in which people acquire their most fundamental and most substantial experience of social life outside the confines of the home. In it they learn the meaning of kinship through their being able to perceive its boundaries – that is, by juxtaposing it to non-kinship; they learn 'friendship'; they acquire the sentiments of close social association and the capacity to express or otherwise manage these in their social relationships. (Cohen 1985: 15)

During her childhood, Kehinde cannot acquire the symbols of what is going to be her community in Lagos. She is not comfortable in a polygamous household and she does not know how to behave in that society. Her faux pas are not a result of her long stay in England but of her lack of experience within an Igbo community. She is in a weak position since she does not have more relatives than her sister Ifeyinwa and is not integrated in any of the institutions of the community. On the other hand, Rike is supported by her religious community and her family.

The atmosphere of a polygamous household parallels that of Kehinde's father's house in Ibuza. Kehinde feels isolated and ridiculed during her stay at her father's. She has been brought up in a different family and community. Therefore, she has not been able to learn the customs and manners of the Igbo community. She is a stranger and feels estranged from her own family.

> I [Kehinde] had to watch what I said because I did not want them to laugh at me, but I wanted to protest, to say that when I grow up I am going to be like white people. I will look after my own only, since for eleven years I did not know of my family's existence. (*K*: 80)

Kehinde does not seem to miss Nigeria. She only leaves England when she thinks she has nothing left there, her husband and children having returned long ago. As in her delirium after the abortion, she is ready to follow her family to 'the other world', even though it would mean death – physical or psychological – for her. Again, as in her delirium, she is saved from final destruction by a community of women relatives. In the first case it is her dead mother and sister Taiwo who oppose her in order to keep her away from the father; in the second case her only living sister –

Ifeyinwa – and her adopted sister – Moriammo – who stand by her in her fight for survival.

Kehinde's attitude shifts from an almost total acceptance of traditional and patriarchal values to outright rebellion. Until Kehinde's return to England, she seems to be basically passive. She is 'the twin who follows behind' (*K*: 18) whereas Taiwo, even in death, is still presented in a more active way.

> I wanted to come out first. To be the Taiwo, the one who tasted the world first. I tried to hold back what was left of my sister, but even her wrinkled lifeless flesh had a strong stubborn will. Her tiny wizened head came out first. (*K*: 18)

It is Taiwo who urges her to leave England and do something to keep her husband and children. At the same time, Taiwo and Moriammo encourage her to come back to England. Kehinde, then, is indeed 'the one who follows behind'. She does not choose, as Hawley states, 'to step into this brave new world with *no* guide' (Hawley 1996: 340). She follows her husband to England and back to Nigeria. She also tries to follow her aborted child and father into death. Even when Taiwo dies, she 'held her to herself' in their mother's womb (K: 18). Hawley seems to acknowledge as much just after the above quoted statement. He refers to Kehinde's neighbours' story that she had ' "eaten" Taiwo in the womb – and she now carries the twin's spirit, her *"chi"*, within her' (Hawley 1996: 340). However, he concludes by stating that 'there is more to her [Kehinde's] "individualism" ... than may meet the eurocentric eye' (Hawley 1996: 340). That conclusion seems a little strained if we take into account Hawley's argumentation. If Kehinde has Taiwo's *chi* within herself, then she has both a spiritual guide and the help of the eldest twin. At the same time, Kehinde is also the heir of her mother's spirit. Therefore, she does not 'step into the world with no guide', but with both maternal and sisterly help.

> The doctors told our [Ifeyinwa's and Kehinde's] mother to take something to purge you out, because if not she would die, but she said she wanted you to taste life. Since you carried your *chi* and that of Taiwo, letting you die would mean killing two people. When she died giving birth to you, she gave you her *chi* also. (*K*: 80–81)

Ifeyinwa implies here that Kehinde's spiritual world is even more complex. She adds her mother's *chi* to Kehinde's guide and spirit. One could say, then, that Kehinde's subjectivity is torn between different forces that compose the currents of her personality as it is by the different cultures and expectations that collide in the mind of the migrant.

Taiwo assumes the role of guide and advisor, but also of the rebelliousness that must be suppressed for Kehinde to be accepted in society. She is the link with her ancestors and, at the same time, the reason for her alienation from her immediate family and community. Therefore, one could say that in Kehinde coexist two tendencies from her childhood. She is extremely near the spiritual world of the Igbo community, but she does not identify with her living community and family. Kehinde's feelings could be a reflection of Emecheta's ambivalence towards

Nigerian and English – or Western – societies. She takes what she thinks is the best for her from both worlds and stays in the transition area. In this way, her identity is always open and surprising to those who expect coherence from her.

Taiwo acts as Kehinde's other self as well as her *chi*: Kehinde's identity seems to be split before birth by the acquisition of her sister's and mother's *chis*. But the separation from her family after being born is also a reason for her unrooted personality. She is not allowed to live with the family or community during her early childhood. Therefore, she does not develop a sense of belonging to Igbo culture. Rather, she is a mixture of Christian, Yoruba and Igbo communities.

The story of her name is another example of these mixtures. She is christened 'Jacobina, after Jacob; who fought and won a battle against his brother Esau in the Bible' (*K*: 19). But after the discovery that she is a twin, she is always called Kehinde, 'the one who follows'. In her there is a physical and spiritual doubleness which includes being a twin, having the twin's *chi* and her mother's as well as hers, believing both in Christian and African myths, being born in an Igbo community and brought up in a Yoruba village, and, finally, migrating to England.

Taiwo, who is the reason for Kehinde's estrangement from her native community, is a part of Kehinde's identity that Aunt Nnebogo and the rest of her family want to suppress. Kehinde is given in the first place the name of a famous younger twin, Jacob, who fights his brother even in the womb. She is told 'that story [Jacob's] so many times that, for a while, I [Kehinde] thought it was the story of my real birth' (*K*: 19). Aunt Nnebogo and the rest of Kehinde's family – except for Ifeyinwa – seem to want the child to forget Taiwo and the circumstances of her birth. By giving the child the name of Jacob, Aunt Nnebogo is upsetting her relationship with her ancestors, especially with her Taiwo. She seems to be using the West African concept of *nnomo* in reverse. *Nnomo* considers voicing as a procreative act which assures civilizations a connection to past and future generations (Holloway and Demetrakapoulos 1987: 20). Instead of reinforcing Kehinde's tie to her female ancestors, Aunt Nnebogo is naming her after a male of an external community. The Jacob story could then be an imposed discourse – parallel to that of a community or state – which would act as cover for Kehinde's own identity. This part of her identity, since it has been rejected by the community as alien and – in Foucauldian terms – deviant, would be what Kristeva calls 'the foreigner within'.

> The foreigner lives within us: he is the hidden face of our identity, the space that wrecks our abode, the time in which understanding and affinity founder. By recognising him within ourselves, we are spared detesting him in himself. (Kristeva 1991: 1)

Individual subjectivities are usually formed within the symbolic space of a community. Belonging to a given community and sharing its symbols with the other members is reassuring and favours group consciousness as well as a relatively coherent interpretation of life within the symbolic order of the community. As Cohen points out, 'the symbols of community are mental constructs: they provide people with the means to make meaning. In so doing, they also provide them with the means to express the particular meanings which the community has for them' (1985: 19). But the fluctuation band of the symbols is limited. Whatever is beyond it becomes a threat and, thus, must be buried under another discourse.

Jacob's story is one of sibling enmity in which the younger wins over the elder.

> And the children struggled within her [Rebekah]; and she said, If *it be* so, why *am* I thus? And she went to enquire of the LORD.
> And the LORD said unto her, Two nations *are* in thy womb, and two manner of people shall be separated from thy bowels; and *the one* people shall be stronger than *the other* people; and the elder shall serve the younger.
> And when her days to be delivered were fulfilled, behold, *there were* twins in her womb.
> And the first came out red, and all over like a hairy garment; and they called his name Esau [from Hebrew for hairy].
> And after that came his brother out, and his hand took hold on Esau's heel; and his name was called Jacob [from Hebrew for heel]. (Genesis, Chapter 25, Verses 22–6)

The biblical story gives *Kehinde* another dimension. Since Jacob and Esau become the ancestors of two different nations, the building of a nation-community is at stake when Kehinde's family decide to silence her other self. However, the relationship between Kehinde and Taiwo is not one of opposition and conflict. They are not defined by opposition like Jacob and Esau, who are respectively '*the one* people' and '*the other* people'. On the contrary, instead of 'struggling' they share in a sisterly community in the mother's womb.

> There were two of us in our mother's womb. We had no will of our own. We followed the rhythm of everything around us... Soon, we started running short of the water of life... At length, we started to talk to each other, sharing as best as we could for survival, becoming weaker and weaker by the day together. (*K*: 17)

Unlike Esau and Jacob – who do not want to share the father's legacy – Taiwo and Kehinde share the mother's legacy, even when scarce. It is true that Kehinde tries to come out the first 'to be the Taiwo' (*K*: 18). But she does not succeed as her sister demonstrates 'a strong stubborn will' (ibid.). Kehinde, though, is not as aggressive as Jacob. She does not 'take hold of' her sister, she 'hugged her and held her to myself [herself].' (ibid.) She feels more love than jealousy for her sister.

However, Kehinde is forced into exile – presumably since the community thinks it is her fault that her sister and mother die – like Jacob. Her journey parallels that of Jacob in a strange way. Whereas he had to exile himself for twenty years to make amends with his brother, she is pushed into exile to break her relationship with her sister. In Kehinde's first exile from her community, she is extremely close to her *chi*, Taiwo. Berrian examines the relationship between the death of Taiwo and Kehinde's exile.

Since Taiwo, as Kehinde's *chi*, dies in Ibusa in their mother's womb, Kehinde is forbidden to stay there. Hence the spirit Taiwo returns to the physical/worldly realm as a result of Kehinde's two difficult moral decisions: an abortion and a tubal ligation. (Berrian 1996: 171)

Berrian's standpoint in relation to why Kehinde is exiled is not clear. She does not explain why it is important that Kehinde does not live in the place where her *chi* died. I believe that it may be connected to the myth of the *ogbanje* child. The myth of the *ogbanje*, which Emecheta had already explored in *The Slave Girl* (1977), reflects the Igbo and Yoruba belief in the reincarnation of dead children on successive occasions to be borne by their mothers. The *ogbanje* child is simultaneously in the world of the dead and that of the living. Its inclination for one world or the other wavers and this results in a cycle of births and deaths which only stop when the child finally decides to stay in the world of the living and abandon its other self.

Kehinde's family could have been enraged with her for 'killing' her mother and sister, at least, that is what Kehinde herself seems to think but the family's decision might also have been propitiated by fear of losing Kehinde and, with her, her mother and sister's *chis*. If Taiwo is an *ogbanje*, then Kehinde, who carries her *chi*, might be called or attracted to the world of the dead. It is worth remarking that Kehinde is brought back to her hometown when she is eleven. The Igbo believe that when *ogbanje* children are old enough to reject their friends on the other side they do not need protection any more.

Emecheta combines the figures of the *chi* and the *ogbanje* to create a more complex subjectivity for Kehinde. Ogunyemi analyses the *ogbanje* myth in relation to migrant subjectivity.

> *Ogbanje* refers to the iconoclast, the one who runs back and forth from one realm of existence to another, always longing for a place other than where s/he is. It also refers to the mystical, unsettled condition of simultaneously existing in several spheres. (Ogunyemi 1996:62)

Just as the *ogbanje* exists in two worlds, the mind of the migrant also fluctuates between communities. These communities might be represented by their symbols – including geographical boundaries, ethnicity, and so on – in the migrant's mind. Migrant subjectivity could be defined by the adjectives which define an *ogbanje*: 'iconoclast' and 'unsettled'.

Kehinde, then, could be referred to as an *ogbanje*-migrant character. She articulates her identity in a syncretic way, not only between the English and the Nigerian communities but also within her native community. In other words, although people expect her to forget her Taiwo and everything she means, 'I [Kehinde] would grow into a child who would not let her identity die. I kept asking, "Where is my sister? Where is my Taiwo?"' (*K*: 21). She would have to exile herself again to accept and recover her dead twin sister, the foreigner within herself. Like Emecheta, she finds a community – multicultural London – in which being a foreigner is usual. Ifeyinwa, on the other hand, understands that there is something different in her sister – which she attributes to her *chi*, Taiwo – but has not experienced other realities as Kehinde has.

Exile & Syncretism in Buchi Emecheta's Kehinde

> She [Kehinde] had stopped protesting that all her thoughts were hers alone, and started accepting Taiwo's voice as a permanent part of her consciousness. Ifeyinwa had said that she was the most unconventional woman she had ever met, walking out of her marriage simply because her husband had taken another wife. She argued that if every woman left for such a trivial reason, there would be few marriages left, but Ifeyinwa had not travelled out of the country of her birth. She didn't know what it was like to be taken by her husband to a doctor to abort an 'unwanted' baby. Nor would Ifeyinwa understand how she could go out to eat Indian or Chinese with a man who was not her husband or even Nigerian. (*K*: 135)

Kehinde finally accepts Taiwo's legacy and voice. It has taken her a long time to start the process of full, open individuation from the communal discourse. She describes a community which is as dissimilar from the Nigerian as Kehinde is from Ifeyinwa. London is a *locus* of iconoclasm and blending of cultural symbols. This society in which a Nigerian woman and a man from the West Indies can 'go out to eat Indian or Chinese' is the perfect non-frame for the development of the syncretic mind.

Emecheta, like Kehinde, is a paradigm not of hybridity, but of syncretism. Both author and character articulate their identities in what Davies calls 'critical relationality'.

> *Critical relationality* thus means negotiating, articulating and interrogating simultaneously a variety of resistant discourses relationally and depending on context, historical and political circumstances. It is not opportunistic, in the sense of conveniently articulated, but progressively multiply articulated in the face of a variety of dominant discourses ... I [Davies] am asserting an interrogation of a variety of positions and a fluidity of movement which, more like a spider web, asserts itself in multiple ways. I therefore reject the Bhabha notion of 'hybridity' for the same reason and share the position of Becquer and Gatti in 'Elements of Vogue,' [in *Third Text*, 16–17, Autumn-Winter 1991: 65–81] which suggests 'syncretism' and syncretic articulations as '*antagonistic*' ... while hybridity ... offers two essentialized poles from which something new grows. (Davies 1994: 47–8)

'Critical relationality' and syncretism give a more flexible account of identity discourses than the hybridity model, especially in relation to individuals who are experiencing cultural collision, since it implies a non-hierarchic approach to discourses. Davies' rejection of 'hybridity' eliminates the ecstatic quality of that notion, favouring a more dynamic and thus unpredictable process. Syncretism unsettles and questions discourses while hybridity emerges as something new and more defined. The outcome of syncretic practices may be more or less complex. That is to say, representation of identity might include a varying number of 'deviations' from the symbolic order of one of the communities, therefore being more or less recognized by the members of any of the communities as kinship. However, the process itself – whether resulting in a total suppression of one or various of the discourses, or in a chaotic amalgamation of contradictory, transitory fragments of the different discourses – is not simple. Syncretism implies a mainly unconscious process of picking and rejecting, reaching compromises and creating new symbols which belong

86 *Changing States*

to none or to all of the communities with which the migrant has come into contact.

Kristeva's *Strangers to Ourselves* tries to give some insight as to the results of suppressing one side of our identity. She strips the 'foreigner' of a self and turns it into an empty Mr Hyde who is named and defined by others.

> Settled within himself, the foreigner has no self. Barely an empty confidence, valueless, which focuses his possibilities of being constantly other, according to others' wishes and to circumstances. I do what *they* want *me* to, but it is not 'me' – 'me' is elsewhere, 'me' belongs to no one, 'me' does not belong to 'me', ... does 'me' exist? (Kristeva 1991: 8)

However, Kristeva seems to forget the essential quality of foreignness. A foreigner is conceived as different. It is a category charged with antagonistic features which have, rightly or not, been perceived by a community. The last thing one could say about foreignness is that it is neutral precisely because of society's reactions to it. That which is foreign is not 'valueless' and selfless. If this was so, it would not represent such an enormous threat to dominant discourses and it would be comfortably included within them.

> The '*common*ality' which is found in community need not be a uniformity. It does not clone behaviour or ideas. It is a commonality of forms (ways of behaving) whose content (meanings) may vary considerably among its members. The triumph of community is to so contain this variety that its inherent discordance does not subvert the apparent coherence which is expressed by its boundaries. If the members of a community come to feel that they have less in common with each other than they have with the members of some other community, then, clearly, the boundaries have become anomalous and the integrity of the 'community' they enclose has been severely impugned. (Cohen 1985: 20)

Symbols as a 'commonality of *forms*' rather than meanings leads us to Adah's struggle in *Second Class Citizen* (1972) to adapt to colliding ways of behaving. Her final breakdown is represented by her crisis before the caesarian operation. Whereas Adah looks for a unique meaning, Kehinde transcends the closed communalist circle and acknowledges other voices into her mind. One could then argue that Kehinde is to Adah what – in Bakhtinian terms – polyphony is to monology.

Unlike Adah in *Second Class Citizen*, at the beginning of the novel Kehinde accommodates to the community of Nigerians living in London. She is ready to believe that the Nigerian community in London could be transposed to Nigeria without it being altered. However, she does not realize that, although many migrants such as Albert have adapted to the receiving society, they still want to go back to their former ways of behaving. Sometimes in a more strtct way than they used to.

Despite apparent similarities, Kehinde's and Albert's positionings during their stay in England are extremely different. Kehinde 'aborts her father's *chi*' and refuses to have any more children either in Nigeria or in England. In her delirium, her dead mother tells her that she has 'refused to receive him [Kehinde's father]' and therefore she has 'to learn to live without him' (*K*: 31) The abortion, like the substitution of the name of 'Jacobina' for that of 'Kehinde', might symbolize Kehinde's rejection of paternal protection and its tradition. She not only aborts his *chi*, but also refuses to bear any more children into that tradition. Her mother and sister stand in her way when she almost gives in to death and support her in a strong matriarchal community to which she also does not fully belong.

Kehinde believes that, even in her delicate position as a black migrant, she has found a group that backs her up. It is from this presumably safe position that she judges other members of the community such as Mary Elikwu. However, Kehinde's status in the community depends on her husband. Even though she earns more than he does, she is psychologically dependent on him and sees herself mainly as mother and wife.

Kehinde starts by condemning Mary Elikwu, remarking that she is 'a fallen woman who had no sense of decorum' (*K*: 38). She recognizes the fact that Mary Elikwu has gone beyond the limits of their community. Likewise, after living on her own for a while, she also believes herself to be 'a fallen woman'. Finally, however, she accepts her difference and claims it in front of her son, who is reminding her of her 'duties'.

> 'Claiming my [Kehinde's] right doesn't make me less of a mother, not less of a woman. If anything it makes me more human,' she murmured to her Taiwo.
>
> 'Now we are one,' the living Kehinde said to the spirit of her long dead Taiwo. (*K*: 141)

Kehinde's reconciliation with her Taiwo comes after her full individuation. She is no longer only an Igbo 'wife' and 'mother,' but a full individual who has created her own community with other migrants in a multicultural setting. Kehinde, like Emecheta, finally changes states. They both transcend the limits of their community to encompass a volatile community, that of migrants living in London. Emecheta has had a firsthand experience of the problems experienced by young black people during her stay at the youth clubs, The Seventies and Dashiki. She has expanded her narrative to include other black migrants such as in *Gwendolen* (1989).

The mere existence of a character like Kehinde – or Mary Elikwu – is a threat to those migrants who still hold on to all the symbolic structures of their original communities. These characters are affirming their difference and identifying more with the whole black community in London than with the restricted circle of Nigerian migrants. Therefore, they are 'impugning' the limits of the community and creating a space where 'liminality' – Bhabha's notion of the minority position in the borderline of the mental structures of a given community[1] – does not exist.

Kehinde is the story of the permanent migrant. It is the story of those who do not identify wholly with or have not been accepted as they are by any society. Kehinde, as a subject speaking from the changing perspectives of the people who migrate, projects a more active yet flexible identity.

> *Kehinde* is a quasi-mystical novel of human identity, a search for self, and a transcendence of the Igbo limitations of traits which constitute a good mother

and wife.... Neither defeated by indigenous Igbo definitions nor constrained by Western gender definitions, Kehinde conjures up her own self-definition with the aid of her spirit twin Taiwo and embraces only those values which are the most beneficial for her lifestyle. (Berrian 1996: 171)

Emecheta presents a character who starts a process of individuation through a series of adjustments in her life. Kehinde is, like Emecheta, a survivor above all and refuses to comply with any single model of what she should be. She is fluid and variable as the environment she is living in.

With their heads just above water, Emecheta's female characters are a display of her struggle to create herself through a syncretic narrative. Emecheta's writing – her hall of mirrors – is, then, a dynamic space in which the reflections are partial in relation to any image that diverse discourses – such as feminism, Africanism, and so on – would like to impose on her. Adah is the confused migrant facing cultural collision. Kehinde is, at the end of the novel, the fully multicultural self whose essence is syncretic. Emecheta, up to now, is the mind who orchestrates the *ogbanje* narrative. Who she would become is up to her. She has migrated from one geographical community to another, but her mind is still changing states.

I would like to conclude by going back to the question of whether cultural collision, exile and 'postcolonial' literature are exhausted fields of study. As I have illustrated in the above argument, 'postcolonial' literature is not simply another fashionable, useless theory. Academics do not consume their energies in recycling old topics with new authors, or old authors with new topics. Instead, and as always, they are trying to make sense of a world which is crisscrossed by 'famished roads', and the study of the literature of the exiled, the *mestiza*, the alienated, is the best way of understanding the processes of human association and construction of symbolic communities. Progress is not achieved by the confirmation of hypotheses, but by adapting them to existing and future 'exceptions'.

NOTE

1. For more information on liminal spaces and subjectivities see Homi Bhabha's 'Dissemination: time, narrative, and the margins of the modern nation', in *Nation and Narration*.

WORKS CITED

Berrian, Brenda F., 'Her Ancestor's Voice: the Ibéji Transcendence of Duality in Buchi Emecheta's *Kehinde*', in Marie Umeh (ed.), *Emerging Perspectives on Buchi Emecheta*, Trenton, NJ: Africa World Press, 1996: 169–84.

Bhabha, Homi, 'Of Mimicry and Man. The Ambivalence of Colonial Discourse', in Homi Bhabha, *The Location of Culture*, London: Routledge: 1993: 85–92.

Cohen, Anthony P., *The Symbolic Construction of Community*, London and New York: Routledge, 1985.

Davies, Carole Boyce, *Black Women, Writing and Identity. Migrations on the Subject*, London: Routledge, 1994.

Derrida, Jacques, 'Structure, Sign and Play in the Discourse of the Human Sciences', in *Writing and Difference*, London: Routledge and Kegan Paul, 1981 [1978]: 278–93.

Emecheta, Buchi, 'Lagos Provides a Warm Welcome', *West Africa*, London: West Africa Publishing Company, 19 January 1981a: 110–11, 113.

Emecheta, Buchi, 'Nigeria: Experiencing a Cultural Lag', *West Africa*, London: West Africa Publishing Company, 2 November 1981b: 2582–3.

Emecheta, Buchi. 'Culture Conflict', *New Society*, London: Harrison Raison, 6 September 1984: 249.

Emecheta, Buchi, 'The Dilemma of Being in between Two Cultures', in Raoul Granqvist and John Stotesbury (eds), *African Voices. Interviews with Thirteen African Writers*, Sydney: Dangaroo Press, 1989: 17–22.

Emecheta, Buchi, *Second-Class Citizen*, Oxford: Heinemann Educational Publishers 1994 [1974].

Emecheta, Buchi, *Kehinde*, Oxford: Heinemann Educational Publishers, 1994.

Emecheta, Buchi, *The Slave Girl*, Oxford: Heinemann Educational Publishers, 1995 [1977].

Hawley, John C., 'Coming to Terms: Buchi Emecheta's *Kehinde* and the Birth of A "Nation"', in Marie Umeh (ed.), *Emerging Perspectives on Buchi Emecheta,*, Trenton, NJ: Africa World Press, 1996: 333–48.

Holloway, K.F.C. and Demetrakopoulos, S.A. *New Dimensions of Spirituality and Bicultural Reading of the Novels of Toni Morrison*, New York, Westport, CT, London: Greenwood Press, 1987.

Kristeva, Julia, *Strangers to Ourselves*, New York: University of Columbia Press, 1991.

Ogunyemi, Chikwenye Okonjo, 'Buchi Emecheta: The Shaping of a Self', *Komparatistische-Hefte* 8, Bayreuth: Germany [KompH], 1983: 65–77.

Ogunyemi, Chikwenye Okonjo, 'An Excursion into Woman's [S][p]ace', in Chikwenye Okonjo Ogunyemi, *African Wo/man Palava. The Nigerian Novel by Women*, Chicago and London: The University of Chicago Press, 1996: 17–92.

Okri, Ben, *The Famished Road*, London: Jonathan Cape, 1991.

The Holy Bible, London: British and Foreign Bible Society, [1611].

> Exile & the Female Imagination:
> The Nigerian Civil War, Western Ideology
> (Feminism) & the Poetry of Catherine Acholonu

Ode S. Ogede

Exile is not always a condition of existence we associate with the experience of human beings while they are still living in their own homelands. As a matter of fact, as Salman Rushdie points out in an enigmatic passage in *The Satanic Verses*, we usually link the pain of being exiled to territorial displacement, to the sense of being physically separated from the homeland. Conventionally exile is commonly considered to be one of the most harrowing feelings a human being can ever endure because it evidences total ousting from the native land, a sense of physical ostracism:

> émigré, expatriate, refugee, immigrant, silence, cunning. Exile is a dream of glorious return. Exile is a vision of revolution: Elba, not St. Helena. It is an endless paradox: looking forward by always looking back. The exile is a ball hurled high into the air. He hangs there, frozen in time, translated into a photograph; denied motion, suspended impossibly above his native earth, he awaits the inevitable moment at which the photograph must begin to move, and to reclaim its own.[1]

Yet, as I hope to show in this essay, Catherine Acholonu's poetry proves that we also can relate the idea of exile with the condition of being made to feel a stranger in one's own homeland. Although Acholonu's ability to confront extreme pain and cast it in poetic form is evident in all her poems, I begin with her second volume of verse, *Nigeria in the Year 1999*,[2] in which her reaction to suffering occasioned by war emerges with a solidity which renders it unmistakably an expression of the state of mental agitation caused by the sense of being without a country. There, Acholonu objectifies the physical and psychological devastations unleashed by the Nigeria-Biafra war which called into question not just the identity but the very humanity of the speaker in her poems. In attributing the collapse of traditional values to the war, she highlights the far-reaching consequences it had on Nigerians. For Acholonu, one of the most debilitating consequences of the war is that it dislocated the sense of mental equilibrum of Nigerians, to the extent that, though they were still physically attached to their place of birth, they could no longer maintain a firm psychological and mental connection to it. In so far as the moral and cultural confusion as well as the socio-economic anguish

Poetry of Catherine Acholonu 91

suffered by people in contemporary Nigeria pushes them to a sense of utter homelessness, it is tantamount to the affliction of exile. In a brief reference to this text in his article which offers a general survey of the 'New' Nigerian poetry, Funso Aiyejina, who is himself a member of the younger generation of Nigerian poets, describes the volume as follows:

> Acholonu's *Nigeria in the Year 1999* is devoted in its entirety to themes of the Civil War and its consequences. Acholonu employs the details of that dark period in Nigerian history in fashioning a comprehensive philosophy about oppression, dehumanization and the need to struggle in order to survive.... Throughout *Nigeria in the Year 1999* Acholonu sensitively deploys metaphors of loss, rape, personal and collective angst and agonies to erect her threnodic parables which articulate the plight of the twentieth-century African.[3]

One will have to agree with Aiyejina that one reason Acholonu's text makes enormously stimulating reading is because she diagnoses with incisiveness some of Nigeria's current socio-economic and political problems which can apply to the experience of other Africans as well. On the specific level, Acholonu opens the selection with the section entitled 'Poems on war' because she recognizes that the Nigeria–Biafra war was a turning point in modern Nigerian history. Through the Civil War Nigeria experienced what Obi Maduakor appropriately terms 'the death of the national soul' caused by lack of passion.[4] As she re-lives the sense of the human destruction unleashed by the war, the speaker's memory of the war 'saddles' her 'nights and days/with nightmares of the holocaust/and the Years pin me/down with wheels of lead/and my thoughts/are muffled with the/martyred shrieks/of lives unsung' ('Not Yet' 17). Among the ravages of the war graphically depicted in this dramatically intense and imagistically vibrant poem, is the picture of 'dangling bodies/ into mass fermentation grottoes' (18). Though a good number of the people were killed on the battlefield, many also had their lives taken by hunger when 'suddenly evening/crashed into the night/and starvation into strangulation/unicef was blockaded' (19). For Acholonu, the affliction of hunger caused by the use of food as a weapon in the Nigeria–Biafra War is one of the most senseless aspects of inhuman treatments which Nigerians subjected one another to during the war.

It is no wonder that in 'Biafra Days', one of the poems devoted exclusively to providing a graphic picture of the hunger and poverty engendered by the war, Acholonu considers the politics of food used by the Federal Republic of Nigeria in prosecuting the war as perhaps one of the most tragic features of war. By employing the personal perspective of a victim who no longer 'remembers/how bread used to taste' (20) and has 'noticed/the disappearance/of rags from our home' because 'today everybody is in rags' (21), the poet presents a horrifying image of the situation. Moreover, from this poem, we get the sense that Acholonu is equally concerned about the capability of her country to learn any useful lessons from the war:

> What a price to pay
> for unity

fraternity
and oneness
and shall we
twenty years from now
have learnt from this
or simply forget the pain
when the wound is closed ('Biafra days' 21-2)

This poem bears the ring of Acholonu's patriotic anguish; because Acholonu's accounts of the problems thrown up by the war have been presented in relation to the distortion of the people's moral values, she captures a vivid sense of the excruciating pain unleashed by the war. Though the material destructions of the war were undoubtedly unkind, and she gives them adequate coverage in such other poems as 'The refugee' (which employs a matter-of-fact style in exposing the pain of homelessness and pitiless exposure to the elements, the harsh weather), and 'In this concentration camp' (a collage of images of the insecurity due to the ever persistent mortar fire and other physical tolls exerted on people), she makes it pointedly clear that even more brutalizing has been the warping of the psyche of those who survived.

Susan Schweik, who noted in *A Gulf So Deeply Cut*, her monumental study of poetry written by American women about the Second World War, that wars have 'a way of revealing with special clarity how men as well as women are both intensely and uneasily gendered,' adding 'the meanings attached to femininity in war are always opposed to those attached to masculinity (though both unsettle in historical crisis),'[5] might very well be speaking for the Nigerian situation, since in her Biafran War poems Catherine Acholonu lends powerful confirmation to similar issues of gender, war, violence, and representation. For instance, what makes 'Other forms of slaughter' so engaging is the alarming catalogue of the moral and physiological depravities caused by the war. Because the war let loose such an unprecedented wave of violence, a tragic spectacle that defies comprehension, the poet can only gaze at society and helplessly watch the general catastrophe. Rape is one clear manifestation of this violence, 'when hands of sandpaper/jarr at tender tendons/of daughter drums' and 'rods of aggression/rip through sealed valves/of flutes of reed' (32). Appearing as a defender of female dignity, Acholonu's emotional involvement with the female victims of sexual violence is registered effectively by her horrifying reaction to the fearful situation in which 'innocent virgins/basking in the sun/suddenly wake up to/greedy eyes/ lecherous tongues/and devouring breath' (132). Since virginity is a girl's most precious possession in traditional society, it is reasonable that Acholonu should view the taking of it by force as the worst form of a girl's dehumanization.

Apart from rape, the society has other social maladies to battle with, foremost among which is the rejection of the notion that a country is built through love of labour and productive work. This is the theme of the title poem of the collection, where Acholonu produces a horrific image of Nigeria by bearing witness to the morbid birth of her country through a representative monster, an 'adult infant', who is very much conceived in the tradition of the freak, the manchild image, in Ayi Kwei Armah's *The Beautyful Ones Are Not Yet Born*.⁶

But in Acholonu's poetry, the whole question about the ogre takes on added significance, because where Ayi Kwei Armah's harmless manchild merely completes the cycle from birth to old age and death within only seven years, Acholonu's adult infant is a real curse to his country. It is an act of ill-will; not only has the baby already been a smoker, alcoholic, and drug addict right from the tomb (not womb) from which it is born, the new baby is holding in its hand a 'pamphlet of life made simple', on which is inscribed a detailed programme of perverse sensuality, criminality and pernicious behaviour. It is evident that this agenda, which the baby wishes to popularize across the country, can only hasten the doom of the nation. The chapter headings of the book are self-explanatory:

Chapter one – how to run without walking

Chapter two – education made simple
expo 2000

Chapter three – how to make billions without sweat
the secret of the ten per cent

Chapter four – rig yourself into life-presidency

Repudiating the ascendancy of these negative influences on her country, in her next poem 'Tell them Okigbo', Acholonu summons the spirit of the famous poet who died in defence of Biafra, in defence of the ideals of freedom and human dignity, to arrest the 'era of anarchic bestiality' that had been unchained. All Okigbo's dreams are gone, Acholonu warns, because 'the elephants are back in our streets/they are ravaging our farms/our homes are all in flames/oh mister dead town crier/you must wake up from/that grave' (56). The image of the elephant powerfully conveys a sense of the might, insensitivity, and recklessness with which the military dictators and the political thugs are trampling on the freedom of the common people. The poet's exhortation for the re-incarnation among the Nigerian population of the gallant and patriotic spirit for which Okigbo was known, is conveyed through the decreeing formula of traditional incantation poetry because she wishes to invoke the full power of the word in ritual practices, and so echoes of Igbo incantation poetry and Okigbo's modern verses merge harmoniously in her lines:

> thunder must strike those
> that grow fat
> at their brothers' expense
> thunder will strike those
> that rape their brothers' daughters
> thunder must strike those
> that suck the nation dry (56)

These aspersions cast on the nation's wreckers serve Acholonu well in her intention to underline the necessity of positive action; as the poet looks for the men and women who will fight for the liberation of her country, her resort to the use of an avalanche of images of poetic justice reflects the restored world the poet dreams of for her country, a land where justice is inevitably served and where all are made to realize that crime does not pay:

> the boa constrictor that swallowed a man
> now lies limp
> stretched out with its victim
> the child that ate a toad
> can no longer taste of meat
> the eagle now perches exposed
> the hunter is taking his aim (57)

Acholonu's abiding patriotic commitment to her nation is remarkable. Despite the depth of the corruption of those in power and the wide disparity in the standards of living, in spite of the alienating pressure all around her, she bears her country everlasting love and continually wills its liberation.

This love is epitomized in 'Embryonic bride,' where Acholonu, like Dennis Brutus in *A Simple Lust* (1971),[7] paints her country in the image of a woman whose beauty has been violated. Dennis Brutus, though physically exiled from his homeland by the then obnoxious apartheid authorities, responds with love and nostalgia to the land of his birth from which he has forcefully been separated; Acholonu, too, shows similar generosity of mind in the devotion she bears her country. Thus her poem begins by recounting the protagonist's disappointed dream of meeting his wife. They had planned to meet on 'eke' day/at the spot where four roads meet and he defied the morning dew and other dangers to get there; having paid her dowry and bathed her in 'the waters of innocence', ordinarily, his claims on her should have been indisputable:

> With you I swam
> hand in hand
> while you nested in your mother's womb
> Wife that I wooed
> from the very beginning
> from the remote mouths of darkness
> I watched you grow (44)

Though she had always been in his dreams, and he in hers, 'bathing in happiness/we thought would never cease' (45), alas, while he 'waited for her day of maturity/hoping to taste your first up-wine, a rapist stole into your fattening chamber/and planting himself between your laps/drank the wine and broke the pot' (45). The image of the broken pot in reference to the lady's defiled state articulates the feeling of the protagonist that his future spouse has suffered a degradation that cannot be repaired.

And yet the protagonist still demonstrates faith in the intrinsic value of his Intended, testifying to the endurance, forgiving spirit and tolerance with which the poet herself approaches her beloved homeland from which she has been emotionally alienated. The endearing rather than confrontational tone, which the protagonist uses to address his loved one, becomes more than an ordinary rhetorical device; in this case, it reflects the nature of a thoughtful person yearning for a much desired re-union with a significant portion of her identity which had all but been lost completely:

> Where is the wedding garland
> I wove you from the sea weeds
> sprinkled with lotus and water lilies
> on you I placed a white wreath
> to commemorate our eternal
> union for while the water dripped
> from your thick black locks
> I made my declarations
> with my fingers I traced
> the smooth line of your forehead
> through your straight nose
> onto your tender lips
> my hands tremble at
> the touch of your skin
> so babylike and yet so desirable (45)

The swirl of melancholy and tenderness as the protagonist does battle with the sense of despondency which threatens to overtake him in these lines reflects the realism in the attitude that Acholonu brings to the outrageous decay of her nation. Her love is so strong that she cannot bear the sight of the injury done to her country (the violated spouse); and so, she ends the poem with the protagonist's resolute stand to bring the invader of his Intended to book so that he can reclaim her:

> they shall clothe you
> in blood of white cock
> your breasts painted with white chalk
> you shall be offered to me
> on the alter (sic) of the sea
> and with the weeds clinging to your naked skin
> I will consummate our defiled marriage
> and when my lust is alleviated
> I shall throw you to the crabs (46)

The woman's ravished state symbolizes the exploitation which the nation suffers as a result of the action of the greedy privileged class in alliance with their external collaborators; her rehabilitation, for Acholonu, on the other hand, is the restitution of the impoverished masses among whom she counts herself, her total re-unification with her estranged homeland.

Because her second verse volume indicates that, unlike many a liberal writer, she does not view her commitment to the liberation of her country as deriving essentially from altruistic motives but as a practical step that would ensure her own full participation in the socio-economic, political, and cultural life of her nation, in retrospect we see that Acholonu's preoccupation with acts of self-definition and female empowerment in her very first volume of verse, *The Spring's Last Drop*,[8] is her means of searching for emotional anchors as a result of all the brutal life experiences caused not only by war and male domination, but also colonial education, whose object has always been to use ideology to brain-wash the African in order to make him/her feel a stranger in his/her own homeland.

The importance which Acholonu attaches to the female identity is certainly linked to her belief that, being the 'weaker vessels', women have had to bear a double yoke in circumstances such as those created by war and colonization. This picture emerges with clarity in her second volume of poems in which Acholonu's speaker expresses her over-riding ambition as being the desire to be fulfilled in the traditional roles of a mother:

> I Obianuju
> I shall provide my children
> with plenty
> I shall multiply this drop
> they will never taste
> of the wasting fluid
> of the sea (17)

If the speaker now yearns to perform the function of housewife, for a position that could enable her to keep alive the fulfilment of the traditional motherhood roles, it is because she exists in a context (war in a modern postcolonial location) that has denied those possibilities, situations that make the role of a traditional housewife an ideal much to be desired, but unattainable in actuality. This context could refer to materialistic modern society in which individuals are so caught up in the rat race for survival that women (especially) are habitually forced to neglect their primary responsibility for the upbringing of children. This situation is decried by the speaker as an act of irresponsibility forced especially on the Western-educated African woman.

In particular, by deploring the misconception that women's liberation (or women gaining equality) entails the total abandonment of their family roles, the speaker exposes the attitude of the 'new' women who lack moral scruples as criminal. The image of the spring's last drop evokes her sturdy resolve to overcome all odds, every hurdle, as she climbs up the steep crevice to fetch the water for her children; it is a particularly ingenious image, for it is one that embodies all the life-sustaining products – food, clothing, shelter, moral lessons and manners – which the poet is determined to make available to her children as part of her role as a good mother. By this image, Acholonu pointedly asserts her immersion in core traditional African values.

Moreover, the style, like that of many of Acholonu's other poems, beginning with the dedicatory piece to *The Spring's Last Drop*, shows that she employs incantatory and invocational techniques of the traditional Igbo prayer. According to E. I. Metuh, the 'things the Igbo ask for in prayer are many and varied':

> These revolve around worldly goals, which is one of the characteristics of African religion.... In the prayers there are evidences that material goods continue to hold very strong attraction for the people. To obtain these, they sometimes attempt to barter with the spirit forces: 'we brought a hen with us!/To trade with you, by barter!'[9]

It is easy to see why the material dispossesion which resulted from the war has had such alienating effects on the protagonist of this poem in which the protagonist accompanies her words with very important manipulated ritual objects – the rattle of bronze bells – because she is so desperate to make good her relationship with her husband, to restore her balance. If Acholonu's resolve in many of the poems of *The Spring's Last Drop* to be rooted in a family illuminates some of the specific features of what one could call 'African feminism,' it is because, in contrast to some of the irreverent attitudes toward men exhibited by some Western feminists, she believes that the female is made by a man, to whom she must be accountable. In fact, as has also been demonstrated in her second poetry volume, *Nigeria in the Year 1999*, Acholonu not only acknowledges the male energies without which no woman can be a figure of any significance, but also reverses the old Western idea of the muse as a woman, showing the necessity for the female to pay dutiful and obedient devotion to her husband as he is her support and inspiration:

> This space is dedicated
> To your quick silver spirit
> May it bear greater harvests.
> You planted me
> On fertile soil
> Here is your harvest (9)

The socio-cultural underpinnings of Acholonu's seeming veneration of the male are monumental, and must mean different things to the various communities of her readers. For example, because women in traditional African society accept patriarchy as a norm and in no way aspire for equality with their menfolk (they ask only for the right to occupy their own spaces, within which spaces they derive their greatest satisfaction as productive members of their communities), what Acholonu's position says about the character of the ideological project known as feminism is that it varies from space to space as well as from time to time. By the same token, it shows that the war for gender equality, which is currently promoted by Western feminism, is an alien importation into Africa. It is in this context that Western feminism equates nicely with the concept of an exiled consciousness from which Acholonu herself, as a Westernized African woman, might be seeking escape. Indeed, because she began by venerating the male before she moved on to underscore the extraordinary nature of the female personality, the twist in her argument may be all the more persuasive to those who identify with core 'African feminism' – even though it will undoubtedly alienate her more 'progressive' group of readers, those who have been won over by Western feminist aspirations.

Overall, what we must never lose sight of is the fact that Acholonu's newest contribution to the emerging discourse on 'African feminism' lies in the poem entitled 'Surviving', where she ventures that the female was made by man but she has become larger than her creator. This is a shrewd rhetorical style, which shows that Acholonu is prepared to plead the cause of women's liberation in the dominant male group's terms. The viewpoint this poem puts forward is that it is this ambiguous relationship which makes the female an intriguing subject for study and understanding, and Acholonu draws upon her own family history, in positioning the identity of her own female person between a mythical and a physical existence, between legend and history, to show that she is this representative female figure.

In *Nigeria in the Year 1999*, Acholonu establishes a strong relation between nation-state, war (sexual), violence, and gender. This connection is suggested by her mapping of the the strife-ridden and war torn nation as a raped woman in the Biafra poems. In order for her to make her case, she has to move entirely away from the exclusively private concerns of *The Spring's Last Drop* toward the collective destiny of her society. Indeed, the failure of the quest in 'Water Woman' is proof enough of the futility of any essentially personal/inward quests. Like its companion piece in *The Spring's Last Drop*, 'Water Woman' contains a trip to 'the abode of the goddess, where the lotus flower is smiling/ smiling onto my face/beckoning and reassuring/drawing my heavy feet/ along the soft white sand amidst the rumbling of thunder' (42–3); but, the pleasure of the trip, the romantic quest, ending in an illusion, the poet then becomes discouraged from continuing to pursue her self-indulgent goal that has turned out to be a journey into a dead end:

> she beckons with a steady nod
> and I plunge
> making for the river bed
> discarded lifeless figures
> skeletons
> hooked onto mangrove roots
> make little impact
> and I try in vain to reason (43)

The image of 'discarded lifeless figures/skeletons/hooked onto mangrove roots' strikingly captures the claustrophobic horror of the quest, a situation that forces Acholonu to an awareness that her struggle for inner liberation is a luxurious exercise that she must abandon immediately and turn instead to more practical patriotic obligations.

While *The Spring's Last Drop* and *Nigeria in the Year 1999* provide very suitable channels for the outpouring of Acholonu's patriotism, a major achievement of her poetry is the ability to utilize the medium of art as forum for examining the burdens which cause the exilic affliction, problems that are normally left unexamined. By exploring the everyday experience of Nigerians, especially the plight of women in very distressing circumstances such as those created by war and acculturation, Acholonu's poetry clarifies the nature of the disharmony hurting contemporary society. Through recollecting the sense of the pain occasioned by the disappearing ideal society, however, memory empowers her protagonists with an undiminished optimism in the constant search for restoration of the estranged homeland. In adventurously exploring the predicament of being ousted from the homeland, Acholonu's poetry is constantly gripping and absorbing because of the rare elegance, sensuousness, and the long stresses of lyrical intensity which distinguish it. Reading her poetry is pure linguistic delight, for it is a literary *tour de force*, a magnificent accomplishment which raises the profile of African dramatic and lyrical poetry.

NOTES

1. Salman Rushdie, *The Satanic Verses*, New York: Henry Holt and Company, 1988: 212.
2. Catherine Acholonu, *Nigeria in the Year 1999*, Owerri: Totan Press, 1985. Page references to this text are incorporated into the body of the essay.
3. Funso Aiyejina, 'Recent Nigerian Poetry in English: An Alter-Native Tradition', in Yemi Ogunbiyi (ed.), *Perspectives on Nigerian Literature 1700 to the present Volume One*, Lagos: Guardian Books Ltd., 1988: 112–28, 117.
4. Obi Maduakor, 'Female Voices in Poetry: Catherine Acholonu and Omolara Ogundipe-Leslie as Poets', in Henrietta Otokunefor and Obiageli Nwodo (eds), *Nigerian Female Writers*, Lagos: Malthouse Press Ltd., 1989: 75–91.
5. Susan Schweik, *A Gulf So Deeply Cut: American Women Poets and the Second World War*, Madison, WI: The University of Wisconsin Press, 1991.
6. Armah, Ayi Kwei, *The Beautyful Ones Are Not Yet Born*. London: Heinemann, 1969.
7. Dennis Brutus, *A Simple Lust: Collected Poems of South African Jail and Exile, including Letters to Martha*, London: Heinemann, 1971.
8. Catherine Acholonu, *The Spring's Last Drop*, Owerri: Totan Press, 1985. Page references to this text are incorporated into the body of the essay.
9. Ikenga Metuh, Emefia, 'Context, Content, and Spirituality of Igbo Prayers,' *Research in African Literatures* 16, 1985: 319–48, 344–6.

Reviews

Abdourahman Ali Waberi, *L'Oeil nomade*
Photographs by John Liebenberg, Pierrot Men, Yves Pitchen, Ricardo Rangel, Abdourahman Issa, Houssein Assamo, Ramadan Ali, and Amin Mahamoud.
Djibouti: Centre Culturel Français Arthur Rimbaud, and Paris: L'Harmattan, 1997.
ISBN 2-7384-5222-1

The work of Abdourahman Waberi, born in Djibouti in 1965, living and studying in France since 1985, is a poetic and ironic approach to one small region of Francophone Africa. Djibouti has been described as a country without a culture, without a language, without a history of its own, without an economic base,[1] always looking outward: a country filled with transient foreigners, whose presence may beckon the local youth to exile. It was once French Somaliland, an 'invention' of the French empire, carved out of the surrounding territory as a fuelling station, maintained initially to gain access to shipping lanes, to counter the presence of the English, later to ensure a French presence in a largely Communist-dominated area. It was the last French colony in Africa to be granted independence (1977). Although for most Djiboutians, Somali is the first language, the country has two 'official' languages, Arabic and French, neither a native language of the inhabitants. French was imposed by the colonial regime; Arabic was adopted, along with the designation of the country as Islamic, primarily to get support from the rich oil-producing states in the Gulf. It is this country that Waberi seeks to bring to life. His Djibouti can never be seen as a paradise. Geographically it is an almost barren desert; politically its independence from colonial domination has brought no economic stability, no real national identity. One of the narrators in his first book, *Pays sans ombre* (1994), describes the country as the third world of the third world (*Pays*, 87). Another narrator compares Djibouti to a 'blind camel' (*Pays*, 131).

Waberi is one of the few modern writers in French from Djibouti. His stories and *Balbala*, his first novel, a trilogy on his native land,[2] give a rich if unconventional picture of Djibouti. His tales are not so much short stories as prose poems, in which the imagery, the narrative voice and the historical and geographical setting are more important than character or plot. He writes in a sophisticated style; he invents folktales which both describe and gently mock the native culture; he juxtaposes bits from newspapers with local voices to portray the physical horror of the wars in the Horn of Africa. Throughout he is both a sympathetic and a detached observer. The stories are often harshly critical of both the French colonial presence and the corrupt independent government, but also evocative of a land of poor but proud people, with long traditions growing from a nomadic culture in which the camel is the measure of value.

Waberi has said that he is inspired to write to describe his country in a European language. *L'Oeil nomade*, a book of photographs of Djibouti (both the city and the country) with a short text and captions by Waberi, is another attempt to bring his little-known country to the attention of the wider community. The photographs, some by young Djiboutian photographers, some by better-established photographers from other African countries, vary considerably in quality, some needing cropping or clearer focus. Many are, however, fascinating images of a country living in both a modern and a traditional world. Like the stories, they are rather fragmentary juxtapositions, which do not tell a single narrative: 'We will begin by adopting as our own the art of the fragment, for life is too complicated to be comprehended in its entirety' (*Pays* 178).

Waberi's Djibouti was once a tribal society; in his stories he evokes old customs, usually treating them with considerable cynicism. His contemporary Djibouti has a largely imported mass culture. He mocks the 'happy few' who imagine an authentic tribal culture, 'who would like to believe that the nomads of Djibouti – or elsewhere – are coming out from "one hundred years of solitude" and that they live very simply far from urban decay'. Both his written work and his choice of photos show Djibouti not as a land of happy peasants but as an impoverished country which has lost much cultural authenticity.

One recurring theme is Djibouti as the product of a colonial imagination. In *Pays sans ombre* a section of the historical account of De Gaulle's visit to Djibouti in 1966 is entitled 'local colour' and reduces Djibouti to a pretty postage stamp (*Pays* 25). Waberi mocks the foreign writers who come to Djibouti 'to draw upon a stock of received ideas and morbid images' (*Pays* 22). The photographs he chooses give a more varied picture than the Djibouti created by foreigners. There are indeed camels crossing the desert, Muslim women in traditional dress, but also boys playing football by dribbling stones, graffiti in English on a market wall.

Waberi defines his project in *L'Oeil nomade* as the creation of an equilibrium 'between the objectivity of the camera and the subjectivity of writing, between distance and closeness, between irony and compassion' (6). His text evokes the country in terms that give it a richer history than the foreign reader might expect: 'Well before Pliny the Elder, before the domestication of the camel ... this country was there' (6). Often, however, what is now Djibouti can only be considered as part of a larger entity, beyond the artificiality imposed by colonialism. There is a note of pride in his descriptions of the many illustrious visitors, or of the history and geography of his region, as in his mention of the Rift Valley region in Ethiopia where skeletons of the family of Lucy were discovered in 1974.

Like so many third-world writers, however, he can also present a critical image of his country. As *L'Oeil nomade* was sponsored by the Rimbaud Cultural Centre, with financial support from Air France, the text is less critical of both the former colonial power and the present government than Waberi's fiction. One photograph, however, of a French soldier giving medical attention to a Djibouti woman, is ironically titled 'The French army in its best guise'. How to describe faithfully is, he realizes, not easy. In a 1995 newspaper produced for the Festival of the Book in Bron, he wrote: 'How can I evoke, write, draw or recount for instance, Djibouti, this cross-roads country, this city of military installations, this city of transitory visitors, this brothel city ... and with no anchor for nomads who come from the cultural backwaters? How to give a legitimate share to the foreigner who crossed oceans to build this old city only a little over a century ago? One must in any case respect the fragile balance of the various contributions.' The collection of photographs is a valuable part of this project.

Adele King
Ball State University

NOTES

1. Writing in 1977, Robert Tholomier said, Djibouti 'has no historical past, no marked indigenous culture, no linguistic unity, no true discipline, and no economic resources.' *Djibouti: Pawn of the Horn of Africa*, trans. Virginia Thompson and Richard Adloff, Metuchen, NJ and London: The Scarecrow Press, Inc. 1981, 126.
2. *Le pays sans ombre* (Serpent à Plume, Paris, 1994, winner of the Prix de l'Academie des sciences d'outre-mer de Paris and the Prix de l'Academie royale de langue et de litterature françaises de Belgique) and *Pays nomade* (Serpent à Plume, 1996, winner of the Grand Prix de l'Afrique noire); *Balbala* (Serpent à Plume, 1997). All translations from Waberi's works are mine.
3. 'Variations sur le pays réel', in *De Temps à Autre*, newspaper produced for the Ninth Festival of the Book in Bron, 31 March to 2 April 1995, 2.

Reviews 103

Maishe Maponya, *Doing Plays for A Change*
Introduced by Ian Steadman.
Johannesburg: Witwatersrand University Press, 1995. 172 pp., photographs, R64.95.
ISBN 1 86814 242 6

At the Junction: Four Plays by the Junction Avenue Theatre Company
Edited and introduced by Martin Orkin.
Johannesburg: Witwatersrand University Press, 1995. 198 pp., illustrated, R74.95.
ISBN 1 86814 264 7

Barney Simon, *Born in the RSA: Four Workshopped Plays*
Johannesburg: Witwatersrand University Press, 1997. 224 pp., photographs, R42.95.
ISBN 1 86814 300 7

Zakes Mda, *And the Girls in their Sunday Dresses: Four Works*
Johannesburg: Witwatersrand University Press, 1993. 176 pp., illustrated, R39.95.
ISBN 1 868 14 222 1

All titles: Witwatersrand University Press are distributed to libraries and individuals in the UK and Europe by Africa Book Centre, +44(0)171 240 6649; World, excluding UK and Europe by Book Promotions: PO Box 5, Plumstead 7800 RSA +27(0)21 706-0949.

We owe the appearance of the volumes under review to the enterprise of Witwatersrand University Press, which seems to have embarked on a somewhat unexpected but wholly admirable project of publishing play texts, not normally considered one of the more profitable branches of the industry. As the present batch of South African plays amply demonstrates, there is no shortage of interesting material to draw upon. The seventeen plays contained in the four volumes (by the Junction Avenue Theatre Company, Maishe Maponya, Zakes Mda and Barney Simon) were written and in most cases performed between 1979 and 1991, a period which roughly corresponds both to the final phase of the apartheid era and, as these plays so abundantly testify, to the gathering movement of opposition to it.

The value of these volumes, which seems enhanced when they are assessed collectively, is that they so fully document the contribution of the companies and the venues, the playwrights and the directors, the actors and the theatre scholars active in the period. Here is the evidence, if ever we needed it, to bear witness to the excellence of a theatre company as experimental in its techniques and as multiracial in its commitment as Junction Avenue, to the pioneering significance of a venue such as the Market Theatre in Johannesburg, which from the start made its stages available to all those represented here, to the inspiration emanating from a director as innovative as Barney Simon, to the considerable body of work for the stage created by the likes of Zakes Mda and Maishe Maponya.

These volumes, one must emphasize, set down for our scrutiny the theatrical activities of a period now over. What we have in them are some of the building blocks with which to build the new South Africa has moved on, into the post-apartheid age; theatre has entered upon an era of transition. Of those whose work is collected here, Maishe Maponya no longer works in theatre; Junction Avenue has not produced a new play since *Tooth and Nail* in 1989; Zakes Mda's career is burgeoning into other realms such as the writing of much-praised novels; and Barney Simon died, lamented throughout the theatre world, in 1995.

The performance history of these seventeen plays is instructive. With the exception of Mda's *Banned*, broadcast by the BBC's African Service, as well as of Simon's *Born in the RSA* and Maponya's *Gangsters*, both of which were included in the *Woza Afrika* Festival at New York's Lincoln Center, they have all been performed almost exclusively at 'alternative' venues. Ten were staged at the Market Theatre, two at the Nunnery in Johannesburg, one at the University of the Witwatersrand and one at the University of Zimbabwe. Of those performed overseas two (Mda's *And the Girls in their Sunday Dresses* and Simon's *Born in the RSA*) went to the Edinburgh Festival. Taken together, the plays clearly demonstrate the over-riding importance of the Market as the prime testing ground for new South African theatre during the period in question. The Market, which in defiance of apartheid practice, had set out from its foundation to accommodate both multiracial casts and multiracial audiences, had its share of harassment from the authorities, but came to be regarded – especially in an age of incipient reform, as the case of *Gangsters* makes clear – even officially as a venue where politically contentious theatre might be tolerated (presumably on the cynical grounds that its audiences constituted a small and no doubt insignificant elite). It was thus ideally placed to host performances as diverse as Junction Avenue's multiracial *Sophiatown* and Maishe Maponya's Black Consciousness-inspired – and thus black-directed and acted – *Hungry Earth* or *Umongikazi*.

Edited and introduced by Ian Steadman, *Doing Plays for a Change* makes available five works by Maishe Maponya (*The Hungry Earth, Umongikazi/The Nurse, Dirty Work, Gangsters* and *Jika*). The playwright himself contributes a preface which he uses not only to focus attention on the relationship between artistic creativity and political activism evident in all his work but also to stress the importance of developing critical consciousness, his own as well as his audience's, in seeking to end oppression. His brief résumé of his work is interesting for what it reveals about some of the difficulties he had to contend with in the course of his career. His lawyer advised him to suspend performances of *The Hungry Earth* in view of the harassment it might engender; the security branch extended an invitation for a 'friendly chat' after he successfully put on *Umongikazi /The Nurse* at a hospital; his and his lead actress's passports were subsequently withdrawn in an effort to prevent an overseas tour of that play; the Directorate of Publications had *Gangsters* restricted to 'small intimate four-wall theatres of the experimental or avantgarde type'. Like other black dramatists, Maponya encountered obstacles in securing recognition for his work; as long as he performed at township venues (which were then inaccessible to whites), none of the media, not even the black press, reviewed his work, and no sponsor could be found to support it. Only when he performed at the Market did he acquire sufficient profile to warrant attention.

Steadman describes Maponya's work as 'central to a survey of black South African theatre' (xxii), and justly accords him significance both as a practitioner in the Black Consciousness tradition and, generously, as a 'precursor of the new voice of South African theatre' (xxii). He is particularly impressed by the theatricality of Maponya's work, drawing our attention to the resourceful way he uses gesture, tracing his indebtedness both in style and ideology to Brecht, and reminding us of the ongoing process of improvisation and revision to which Maponya subjects his work.

Steadman makes the point that in the case of Maponya 'the final published text is merely an edited scenario of quite spectacular action' (xvi). It remains the reader's task to reconstruct a possible performance – mentally and visually – from the evidence of the printed page. This is no easy challenge since, like those of his fellow playwright Matsemela Manaka, Maponya's plays do not live primarily through their texts, but through their interpretation and elaboration in performance. In *The Hungry Earth*, for example, Maponya supplies a narrator to comment on the action, he supplements dialogue with choral singing, he incorporates gumboot dancing, and frequently has recourse to mimed sequences to represent elements of the performance as diverse as a nineteenth-century military encounter ('the battle of spears against guns'), working conditions on the mines or the Sharpeville massacre. In *Umongikazi/The Nurse* he calls on his actors – as frequently in such performances – to play up to eight different roles and he deploys multiple flashbacks to depict episodes in the history of the nurses' struggle. In *Gangsters* he tellingly juxtaposes the interrogations of the poet with her (spotlighted) recitations of her work throughout the play. And so on.

Steadman makes much of the way the political realities of a turbulent country have affected Maponya's life and work (the forced removal of his own family, for instance), noting how his personal experience of oppression has made of him a playwright of outspoken radical commitment. And indeed, his plays are remarkable for their fearless onslaughts on the abuses of the apartheid system. In *The Hungry Earth* he depicts the exploitation of industrial labour through the migrant labour system and the pass laws, demonstrating both the political consequences (anti-pass demonstrations, strikes) and the human cost (mine fatalities, alcoholism, prostitution). In *Umongikazi/The Nurse* he explores conditions in the health service, exposing racist practices and supporting change through unionization. In *Gangsters* he graphically portrays the interrogation, banning, torture and death in detention of a poet, lambasting police complicity (for it is they who are the 'gangsters' here) and castigating those responsible (his poet Masechaba would have P. W. Botha put on trial as a Nazi war criminal, for example).

Athol Fugard called Barney Simon 'unquestionably the most significant theatre talent to have emerged in South Africa'. Few would disagree with him, for this man of many talents was not only the co-founder of the Market Theatre in Johannesburg, he was also a director, writer and editor. Through his own commitment to theatre as a multiracial and multicultural art, Barney Simon facilitated the performances and careers of so many others who joined with him to make the Market the leading theatre centre in the country. He was also a theatre practitioner, one must record, who could have enjoyed a high-profile international career overseas, but who chose instead to stay on in apartheid South Africa to make his own massive contribution to change. As Lionel Abrahams concludes, Simon's work 'reshaped the culture of the theatre in South Africa'.

The volume under review presents us with Barney the playwright – or, more precisely, as active collaborator with his cast on four workshop productions: *Black Dog/Inj'emnyama*, *Outers*, *Born in the RSA* and *Score me the Ages*. Although it thus does not contain that most famous of all his collaborative ventures – *Woza Albert!*, scripted and produced with the play's two performers, Mbongeni Ngema and Percy Mtwa – it nevertheless provides a welcome opportunity to assess the astonishing range and variety of his work for the stage. Apart from the plays themselves, the volume contains a number of tributes to Simon and a brief, but informative, introduction by Pat Schwartz, in which she focuses on the 'communal creativity' which informed his workshop practice, his interest in personal biography which fed into the storytelling technique he preferred, and his constant search for authenticity, which he took to great lengths, despatching his cast to Soweto to conduct interviews with ordinary people in the street for *Woza Albert!*, to visit people with experience of detention and solitary confinement for *Born in the RSA*, or even to gay pick-up spots for *Score me the Ages*. Undeniably one of the benefits of this procedure has been the unerring sense of language evident in all the works included here. (One wonders, nevertheless, whether in the case of *Outers*, the student – Nicky Rebelo – on whose research with down-and-out white hobos in Joubert Park, one of the seedier parts of inner-city Johannesburg, the play was based, was well-advised, albeit not by Simon, or even morally responsible 'to infiltrate the group with a hidden tape recorder' in an effort to achieve social and linguistic authenticity.)

Simon is quoted here as trying 'to change the molecules of people who come to see our shows' (xxiii). *Born in the RSA* serves as a good example of how he did it. Set against the background of the states of emergency successively imposed in the mid-1980s and using video footage of township violence as a backdrop, the seven performers tell a story of political activism, of betrayal (both sexual and political) and of detention without trial. Addressing the audience directly, they force them to examine their own attitudes to the events narrated. The emerging life-stories undermine, elaborate, corroborate and comment upon one another, intertwining personal histories and political action, laying bare motives for resistance as well as for betrayal, exposing harrowing facets of state repression (the detention and interrogation of children, etc.). Monologues and dialogues alternate, multiple ironies emerge from the juxtapositions within the skilful pattern of the unfolding narrative. The play has the power of courtroom drama, the performers being the witnesses, the audience becoming the jury. No one who saw the show at the time of its first performance in South Africa, when it so courageously bore witness to and took issue with major events then going on in the country, is likely ever to have forgotten the intensity of the experience. *At the Junction* is an edition of four plays by the Junction Avenue Theatre Company – *The Fantastical History of a Useless Man, Randlords and Rotgut, Sophiatown* and *Tooth and Nail* – the last named having been laboriously compiled from the original fragments and now appearing in print for the first time. This collection, then, comprises the best known works of the company, but it is also representative in the sense proposed by the editor, namely that it enables the reader to follow the internal history of the company itself and to trace its ideological and stylistic evolution. The volume has been edited by Martin Orkin who, it must be said, has done a fine job of work. The editorial apparatus is considerably more comprehensive than in any of the other volumes under discussion. Thus, Orkin himself provides a general introduction to the company's history and workshop techniques as well as separate introductions to each of the plays. He also includes much supplementary material comprising an interview with the cast of *Fantastical History* by a very enthusiastic Lionel Abrahams, a background piece on the genesis of *Sophiatown* by the show's artistic director, Malcolm Purkey, and a brief characterization of the place itself together with an account of its destruction by Pat Schwartz. There is also a glossary to assist the reader with the African-language, Afrikaans and tsotsitaal expressions occurring in that text. All of this proves most useful.

Orkin's several introductions virtually constitute a major academic study in themselves. His general introduction is a lucidly presented and cogently argued overview of the work of Junction Avenue. He shows how in each of the plays they draw on other writings for their source material – school history books, for example in *Fantastical History*, an essay by Charles van Onselen from his *Social and Economic History of the Witwatersrand* for *Randlords and Rotgut*, reports from *Drum* magazine for *Sophiatown*, and so on. He then situates the work of Junction Avenue in relation not only to that of Workshop '71 on which it drew, but also to developments in international theatre (Brecht, Beckett, etc.) and theory (Grotowski on poor theatre) by which it was influenced. He follows this with a perceptive account of the nature of workshop theatre practice itself, the group's reasons for adopting it and their espousal, especially in the first two productions, of a 'Marxist/socialist discourse' to articulate an alternative view of history in the particular circumstances of apartheid South Africa where such views had long been suppressed.

These themes recur throughout the analytic close readings which precede each of the texts. In *Fantastical History* Orkin shows how the company set out to explore 'the kinds of knowledge, education and social experience which help to fashion white dissident subjectivity' (16), and to portray the growth of political consciousness (or in the Marxist terms Orkin prefers, the overcoming of 'false consciousness') of a young white male struggling to throw off the bonds of apartheid society. He explicates the episodes (the Great Trek, the Anglo-Boer War) and personalities (such as Rhodes) figuring in their demythologizing of the received version of South African history, delighting in the elements of parody, pastiche and caricature deployed, and identifying the company's debt to Brecht and

Joan Littlewood in their performance style. The 'gesture towards a Marxist narrative' which he discovers here becomes more pronounced – as does the debt to Brecht – in *Randlords and Rotgut*, Junction Avenue's dramatization of an academic study of the conflicting interests of the mining and liquor industries at the turn of the century. Here Orkin shows himself particularly impressed both by the company's emphasis on the workers' growing awareness of their own exploitation and by the way in which they succeed in relating past and contemporary events and communicating to the audience a sense of their own complicity in history ('What you have seen before you/ Is the story of your past/ But history doesn't end there / And how long can you last?' 129).

Sophiatown, too, confronts a South African audience with its past, indeed with one of the most notorious episodes in the whole history of apartheid, the forced removal of an inner city Johannesburg suburb. Their most successful production on stage, *Sophiatown* was a triumphant vindication of Junction Avenue's commitment to evolving alternative views of history on the basis of detailed sociological and literary research. In the play Orkin distinguishes a 'focus upon commonality and a merging of cultures' (136) and, of course, in this sense *Sophiatown* is one of those works (Richard Rive's *Buckingham Palace District Six* is another, for like District Six, Sophiatown was 'an island in a sea of apartheid') which critically confront the lived experience of non-racialism and the segregationist policy of apartheid. In this connection, Orkin interestingly points out how the dialects of the sub-cultures of Sophiatown feature prominently here 'as evidence of the vitality of the communities using them' (138). Again, Richard Rive does the same.

In many ways *Tooth and Nail* represents a quite radical departure from Junction Avenue's previous productions. Developed in collaboration with members of the Handspring Puppet Company, it consists of some 98 fragments, the order in which they are to be performed being arbitrary and the performance style being described as 'obsessive and repetitive'. Without having attended a performance, it is difficult to imagine an audience's response to the extraordinary demands placed on them by a show which must have gone far beyond their expectations. Not for nothing did *New Nation* describe the production as a 'mindblast'. The dialogue between the madam and her servant is sung as opera; some roles are played by life-size puppets (that of Noah by a giant puppet); images of the Biblical flood suggest all-consuming chaos; ritualistic invocations call up the spirits of the ancestors; 'history lessons' recall episodes in apartheid history; the lives of pleasure-seeking whites are juxtaposed with the story of a freedom fighter, and so on.

Orkin is remarkably helpful in enabling the reader to make sense of all this. He relates the project to the violence and the climate of uncertainty about change pervading the country at the end of the 1980s, shows how Gramsci's famous dictum (also taken as the motto to Nadine Gordimer's apocalyptic novel *July's People*) that 'the old is dying. The new cannot be born. In this interregnum there arises a great diversity of morbid symptoms' informs the text, not least in its preoccupation with middle-class obsessions and the abuses of apartheid. Analysing *Tooth and Nail*'s presentation of history, Orkin points out that the company is here turning to contemporary history, reflecting on modes of narrating history through non-linear, non-realistic techniques and the fragmentation characteristic of postmodernism, seeking, as Malcolm Purkey appositely puts it, 'to enrich and extend ... [the company's] own theatre language, while remaining firmly committed to critically reflecting South African reality' (231). Orkin brilliantly analyses Junction Avenue's dramatic style, revealing how the social and psychological atmosphere of the period is captured through expressionist techniques of stylization and grotesque caricature. His perceptive pages on *Tooth and Nail* derive their significance in part from the fact that so little has been written about this most experimental of all Junction Avenue's shows, which, as he reminds us, failed to find favour with audiences unaccustomed to such radically innovative, avantgarde productions. Overall, this excellent critical edition does full justice to Junction Avenue's importance.

And the Girls in their Sunday Dresses is the second collection of plays to have been published by the prolific Zakes Mda, who lived for many years in Lesotho where he gained much experience in theatre for development and who has recently embarked on what looks like becoming a successful career as a novelist. His career differs somewhat from that of many of his contemporaries, a fact which is reflected both in the concerns of his plays and in their performance histories. (This collection does not, for instance, list any performances of these works in South Africa itself.)

The present collection, which comprises two plays for the stage (*And the Girls in their Sunday Dresses*, *Joys of War*), one radio play (*Banned*), and what Mda terms a 'cinepoem' (*The Final Dance*) written between 1982 and 1989, comes with a perceptive introduction by Bhekizizwe Peterson and a brief note by Teresa Devant, who directed the two stage plays for performances in Edinburgh and Zimbabwe. Peterson accords Mda 'unique status' in South African theatre, arguing that 'his work goes against the grain of the performance traditions and politics' (vii) of the black theatre movement of the 1970s, a fact which finds expression in his focus on the lives of ordinary people, his concern to situate the political issues of the day within personal experience and his preoccupation with the kind of neocolonial abuses to be found in independent states such as Lesotho. In Mda's work, the view of South African racism and of apartheid society is largely reflected in their impact on the family, most notably here on women. A further factor which distinguishes Mda's work from that of his contemporaries, Peterson notes, is 'his elegant writing and [...] keen sense of dialogue' (ix). Indeed, it will be immediately apparent to any reader that Mda's writing is qualitatively different in a number of ways; while his texts are almost entirely lacking in a sense of the multilingualism of South African speech, for example, they abound in satirical humour and – in *Joys of War* – even in intellectual debate.

Peterson provides penetrating analysis of each of the four works. In *Joys of War*, he examines Mda's careful handling of the issue of armed struggle, revealing his skill in juxtaposing two distinct narratives – the journey towards self-discovery of his two soldiers on active duty reviewing their past histories and debating the moral nature of their commitment, and the parallel quest of mother and daughter which reveals much of the social background out of which such commitment is born. *And the Girls in their Sunday Dresses* is a lively two-hander focusing on the plight of two women queuing for days on end to purchase rice from a government food aid store. Mda's handling of the various roleplays they perform, the comic banter between them – the 'lady' is in fact a prostitute and her profession is used here as a kind of moral yardstick to measure the shortcomings of others – and the amusing satire of bureaucracy and corruption, not to mention of the wiles of men, offers actresses a wonderful opportunity to develop rounded characterization, again something largely missing in other plays of the period. Peterson points to the 'range of complicated themes' embedded in this 'deceptively simple' (xix) work, prime among them the question of Lesotho's dependence on South Africa and the politics of gender informing the women's social roles. He has both praise and criticism for Mda's political analysis in this play, suggesting that although the tale has relevance for post-apartheid South Africa in that it shows how in other parts of Africa the nationalist struggle has issued after independence into a class struggle, it fails to be specific about the problems directly confronting women, preferring to situate them within the wider liberation struggle. In view of Mda's manifest vindication of the two women, defiant, united and witty at the end of the play, this criticism seems a little beside the point.

In conclusion, let me note one or two editorial shortcomings of these volumes. All the plays except one are accompanied by only one production photo together with one photo of the author or director. This is far too little, especially since such outstanding material is available. In the case of such a highly experimental production as *Tooth and Nail*, for example, it would have been particularly desirable to have had more visual documentation of the actual staging. All the volumes, with the exception of *At the Junction,* could have done with some annotation, particularly from the point of view of an overseas reader for whom plain texts prove of limited use. Unexplained references, such as that to 'the days of Isandlwana and the days of Umgungundlovu' in Maponya's *Hungry Earth* (8), for example, might usefully have been annotated, as might that in the lines addressed by the policeman to Thenjiwe in *Born in the RSA*, where he says: '... and no games, hey? Not like Biko, or Timol, or Aggett, hey.' Only a reader well versed in South African political history is going to be able to make anything of the last two of these names. In the matter of translation, too, the Simon volume is particularly deficient, a pity since it is also this volume which confronts the reader with the most complex linguistic problems – the dialect of Johannesburg's down-and-outs in *Outers*, the songs in African languages in *Born in the RSA*, for instance. Here again some help would have been useful.

Such minor carping aside, however, these four collections of plays constitute a major step forward in documenting theatre practice in South Africa during the final decade of the apartheid era, and as such are very welcome indeed.

Geoffrey V. Davis
Institut für Anglistik, RWTH, Aachen

Chirikure Chirikure, *Hakurarwi*
Harare: Baobab Books, 1998, 65pp., £3.50, pbk.
ISBN 1-77909-007-2

Charles Mungoshi, *The Milkman Doesn't Only Deliver Milk*
Harare: Baobab Books, 1998, 69pp., £3.50, pbk.
ISBN 1-77909-006-4

Chenjerai Hove, *Rainbows in the Dust*
Harare: Baobab Books, 1998, 61 pp., £3.50, pbk.
ISBN 1-77909-001-3

Zimbabwe Women Writers, *Poetry and Short Stories Written by Members of Zimbabwe Women Writers from 1990–1998*
Zimbabwe Women Writers, 1998, 108 pp., £6.25, pbk, no ISBN.

Baobab Books and Zimbabwe Women Writers are distributed by African Books Collective Ltd, 27 Park End St, Oxford OX1 1HU.

Zimbabwe has seen considerable growth in locally published literature since the late 1980s. Of the writers I shall be discussing, only Charles Mungoshi had an established reputation before Independence. Chenjerai Hove and Alexander Kanengoni's work dates from the early 1980s but both have become better known over the last ten years. Chirikure Chirikure and most of those published in the Zimbabwe Women Writers anthology are new writers whose concerns are those of 1990s Zimbabwe.

Baobab's publication of the performance poetry of Chirikure Chirikure will be welcomed by the student of contemporary Zimbabwean poetry. However, despite the claim on the back cover, *Hakurarwi* is not a bilingual edition with translations into English by Charles Mungoshi set beside Chirikure Chirikure's original Shona poems. Instead, Mungoshi has set about explaining to the non-Shona reader what each poem means and has added his own critical commentary which allows both Shona and non-Shona readers to understand how the poems work as poetry and dramatic performance.

In his introduction, Chirikure Chirikure writes of the diverse early influences on his poetry, 'traditional song and dance, the rhetorical devices of the Christian preachers, and the more carefully honed, selfconscious techniques of urban performers' (ix). He adds that while at university he read the poetry of South African and black British performance poets and this led him to experiment further with his own style and delivery.

Employing a range of different voices in his work, Chirikure Chirikure often allows the tyrant to condemn himself. In *'Utsi hunokachidz'* ('Teargas'), the poet takes on the persona of an authoritarian father who advises a visitor that children who ask difficult questions or make demands will be brought to their knees if water hoses and tear gas are used on them. The poem achieves its satirical purpose through parallelism. The speaker refers to those who ask questions without answers, seek explanations for what cannot be explained and cry for food when there is none in the granary:

Kubvunza mibvunzo isina mbinduro
Kutonongora zvausina tsananguro
Kuchemera chausina kuisa mudura (33)

However, the poet is not just concerned with condemning tyranny through novel ways of mocking the repressive state apparatuses. In 'Yakarwiwa nesu' ('We fought this war') he warns different groups of Zimbabweans that there is little point in celebrating history and extolling the role they played in the struggle for independence if they cannot attend to the injustices of contemporary society. Each group is allowed to present its claim before the main speaker tells all of them that, yes, we are grateful for your efforts to liberate the country, but who holds the key to the country's wealth so that they can feed the hungry children?:

Ativhurire tinokorere vana zviyo tivabvuwire kasadza,
Hezvo miromo yavo yati papata kunge vapoteri vehondo. (5)

The poet takes on a developmental role, raising social and collective consciousness at different levels. Even in a short poem like 'Munyama' ('Fate') he deals both with specific conditions – if people let lizards shit in their cooking pots, then children will die of diarrhoea – and also with the more general lethargy and resigned belief in fate which prevents people from changing their conditions, *'Ndinoona ndipo pachazofumhwa munyama'* (13).

The social criticism expressed may be directed against targeted groups but it requires a response from the audience at large. In 'Chomozeza chii?' ('What are you afraid of now?') the speaker purports to address white Zimbabweans, asking them why, when they have faced dangers as pioneers, they are now afraid to live with black Zimbabweans. Mungoshi points out that the last line, *'chomozeza kunwa mumukombe mumwe nesu chii?'* (45) which he translates as 'Why are you afraid to drink from the same cup with us now?', carries a strong message. However, that message will be more readily understood by black Zimbabweans.

Mungoshi's own poetry collection *The Milkman Doesn't Only Deliver Milk*, originally published in 1981, has now been published by Baobab in a revised and extended form. Mungoshi, unlike the other writers discussed here, tends to steer clear of politics in his own work and this led to criticism of his pre-Independence novel, *Waiting for the Rain* (1975) which was seen to be showing the disintegration of Shona society and to be cynical about the liberation struuggle. However, in his poetry Mungoshi conveys a sense of the general continuity of Zimbabwean life despite specific disruptions and irritations.

The opening poem in the collection, 'Before the sun', reveals the delight the poet takes in remembering the everyday pleasures he enjoyed as a child. His simple, but humorous and effective language, realistically depicts the game playing of a boy taking a rest from routine work:

I tell the sun to come share
with me the roasted maize:
and the sun just winks
like a grown-up.

> So I go ahead, taking big
> alternate bites:
> one for the sun, one for me.
>
> This one for the sun,
> this one for me:
> till the cobs
> are just two little skeletons
> in the sun. (4-5)

This poem, like other Mungoshi poems, illustrates the American modernist poet William Carlos Williams's famous dictum 'no ideas but in things' and, like Williams, Mungoshi starts with the local and stresses place. In 'Lazy day' he describes a scene in which he and a woman friend visit his family to tell them that they have decided to live together. The relationship between father and son is a familiar, comfortable one which is set within a natural scene. Gender roles are understood and not questioned and the speaker and his partner seem set upon an idyllic, even traditional relationship as his father is able:

> to paint
> our future portraits
> into the family canvas. (16)

The companion piece to this poem 'The same lazy day, later' concentrates on the relationship between the two lovers. The reader who is conscious of gender issues will be disturbed by the way in which the poet sees the female body as territory to be explored and as Freudian mystery but the images are handled confidently and successfully:

> And now, my dreams
> are being carved and shaped
> to house the perfect mould
> of your body.
> And my fingers
> are being ground into the perfect telescope lens
>
> to probe the furthest stars in your
> endless
> darkness. (18)

Mungoshi will never be a politically correct writer. 'What are you going to do now, Virginia?' and 'Neighbours' deal directly with prostitution and extra-marital sex and 'Location miracle' recounts the story of a young woman with only one eye who meets a young man with one leg and one arm. But Mungoshi is witty and inventive. He tells Virginia 'everyone knows you have fought too many/bedroom wars/to have any claws left' (31); he refers to his neighbour's 'sex-on-the-side-sated voice' (35) and we are told that Liza, the one-eyed girl, 'worried herself beyond the point/it is legal to worry any more' (37).

Mungoshi is a humorous poet and he tells his stories well but he is also able to focus, sharply and concisely, on cultural clashes and the resulting absurdity of continuing with traditions when they are inappropriate. Anyone who has stayed in Harare in December will appreciate the contrasts Mungoshi draws out in 'Christmas':

> Here is neon-bright First Street
> A kaylite feast of imitation fir trees
> snow-sledge-pulling reindeer
> silent featherweight bells
> a heavily-laden, heavily-clothed
> cheerfully-bearded Santa Claus
> under sweltering southern stars.
>
> And here am I: born to fear the lion
> abhor the vulture, turn back
> on seeing a squirrel crossing my path
> decipher dark meanings
> from an otter's droppings, or a hyaena's laugh
> ward off the potency of the owl's hoot
> with charms, amulets and roots. (56)

Chenjerai Hove's *Rainbows in the Dust* lacks the coherence of his earlier poetry collections *Up in Arms* (1982) and *Red Hills of Home* (1985). Like his collection of newspaper essays *Shebeen Tales: Messages from Harare* (1994), *Rainbows in the Dust* is concerned with the state of the nation. As I read through the collection, I recalled Stewart Brown's assertion that much Nigerian poetry has been concerned with opposing successive authoritarian regimes. Brown argues that this 'can seem, after a while, like nothing more than a self-aggrandising style, a relatively safe way of asserting one's radicalism'.[1]

To apply this to a writer as original as Hove may seem like a harsh judgement. Yet Hove does appear to be taking on the role of people's bard condemning tyranny and injustice wherever he sees it. In 'power' Hove describes the external trappings of power:

> this is how we dress
> power:
> with whistles and muskets and gunpowder
> from outriders
> flashing lights
> smoked glass windows
> motorcades
> titles (33)

The problem with this is that it does not tell the reader anything that they did not know already; nor does it defamiliarize to present what we already know in a new and interesting way. Another overtly political poem 'I will not speak', which in terms of its content is central to the collection, veers between explicit statement in a declamatory manner and experimentation with words. Hove, ironically, insists that he is unable to speak out because to do so is to be condemned for opposing the state and spreading discord and, besides, words are debased when they come from the mouths of politicians. The poet employs hyperbole to create a shock effect:

> i will be silent
> i will not speak
> even when flames engulf the clouds of conscience
> roasting children for the minister's take-away lunch:
> i will be silent.
> i will.
> i will utter, no words. (13)

Hove's stand is a courageous one which implicitly foregrounds the ways in which different factions, before and after independence, tried to silence those who wanted to speak the truth. But the rhetorical device of speaking out by denying that you are doing so has now been used so often that it has become clichéd. Moreover, if you insist on using dramatic imagery, as Hove does, then you cannot re-work the same or similar images. The reader familiar with Hove's work will compare the line 'roasting children for the minister's take-away lunch' with the line 'and roasts brother for sister's lunch' from 'Uprising' and the recognition will detract from the impact of the metaphor in the more recent poem.

Emmanuel Ngara has suggested that Hove 'tends to focus on images as words, as verbal expressions, confining himself to the significance of an image purely as a linguistic form'.[3] In some of these poems, Hove does appear to use images as words rather than conceptually. In 'restraint' he writes:

> let us peep through the windows of self
> if we go in
> we drown
> and the earth trembles
> to shatter the few dreams left. (4)

We can guess at what he means by the first line but 'the windows of self' seems inept and the imagery which follows is incongruous.

Similarly, in 'tributes', Hove weaves a poem out of the titles of works by Zimbabwean writers but it seems pointless to look for meaning in the poem.

The most impressive poems in the anthology are the last ones which are collected under the title 'on the death of ken saro-wiwa (november 10, 1995)'. In the poems, Hove recalls his friendship with Saro-Wiwa and in direct but evocative language writes a lament for his fellow writer which is also a lament for Africa. Hove questions the essentialism of African literary movements and dares to confront what Africans have done to themselves:

> They were wrong
> the negritudes
> about the beauty of the land,
> the land of our fathers;
> they were wrong
> for not seeing our ugliness
> for we are, indeed, ugly.
> the DARK CONTINENT.

a continent that bleeds
and does not know it. (57)

Hove is a fine writer, as his novel *Bones* (1988) amply demonstrates, but none of his subsequent work has matched the quality of *Bones* and one suspects that he is writing too much too quickly.

Poetry and Short Stories written and published by Zimbabwe Women Writers raises serious questions about the relationship of literature to development and consciousness raising. The collection consists of poems by a number of new non-professional women writers around specific themes such as nature, sports and emancipation, and it concludes with a selection of short stories. What we have in the collection is writing in the raw – an engagement with themes which matter to the women and which may act as therapy – but which have been published more out of a concern for development than literature.

This is not to decry publishing work which has been produced by amateur writers. However, the reader needs a context for this book. Since the poems are organized thematically and some of them have the same titles, like 'Dawn' or 'Street kid', I assume that they originated as exercises undertaken in workshops. If so, then there are a number of questions I would have liked answered in an introduction: why are there more poems than stories? Was there any teaching of creative writing? Why are all the poems and stories in English?

Encouraging new writers is, of course, important and this type of collection has a place in the history of Zimbabwean writing. To cite two examples: *Life with a Long Spoon* (1975) is a well-known anthology of writing by pupils at Highfield High School and *The March and Other Pieces* (1983) is a collection of writing by participants at a Zimbabwe Literature Bureau workshop. Almost twenty years after Independence, though, one does need to ask whether this type of anthology benefits anyone other than the participants. At the very least it needed an editor to cut out some of the more obvious errors.

The one piece of writing by an established author is Barbara Makhalisa's poem 'Woman', part of which has already been published as the dedication to a resource book, *Zimbabwe Women's Voices* (1995).[4] Comparing this latter book with the Zimbabwe Women Writers anthology suggests that it is contextualization that makes the difference. *Zimbabwe Women's Voices* is glossy and was more expensive to produce but what it does is to include some poetry in a text which is concerned with women's contemporary realities. Autobiographies, statistical data, photographs and social commentary give the reader a sense of how women's creative writing emerges from their social and economic environment.

Only two of the poems from *Poetry and Short Stories* will remain in my memory. The first, 'The River God's Hunger' by Sonia Gomez, is an aesthetically pleasing poem with vivid imagery to describe landscape and people. However, it reads like a visitor's poem, written by someone who is fluent in English and who is describing a scene which is new to her:

> We buy some shriveled fruit
> and watch the woman
> with an ebony carved face,
> ugly enough to tempt
> the river god
> to send rain. (6)

Would a Zimbabwean write of an African woman in this way? Although I cannot be sure, I think it unlikely.

The other poem which I shall remember for different reasons is Perpetual Kabunze's 'Charged with Murder'. This poem is not as controlled as Gomez's and Kabunze is less sure of where lines should begin and end but she portrays forthrightly the pain of a woman forced to live with a brutal man because he has paid *lobola* for her:

> Like melting ice in scorching heat,
> So tears from my eyes endlessly ooze
> Choices; if only I had known
> Too deep in to turn back,
> Yet, too painful to stay in. (30)

Pauline Dodgson
Thames Valley University, London

NOTES

1. Stewart Brown, 'Daring the Beast: Contemporary Nigerian Poetry' in Abdulrazak Gurnah (ed.), *Essays on African Writing 2: Contemporary Literature*, Oxford: Heinemann, 1995: 59.
2. Chenjerai Hove, 'Uprising' in *Up in Arms*, Harare: Zimbabwe Publishing House, 1982: 45.
3. Emmanuel Ngara, *Ideology and Form in African Poetry: Implications for Communication*, London: James Currey, 1990: 126.
4. Ciru Getecha and Jesimen Chipika (eds), *Zimbabwe Women's Voices*, Harare: Zimbabwe Women's Resource Centre and Network, 1995: 5.

Bernth Lindfors, ed., *Conversations with Chinua Achebe*
Jackson: University of Mississippi Press, 1997, 197 pp., $17.00.
ISBN 0-87805-999-7

Ezenwa-Ohaeto, *A Biography of Chinua Achebe*
Oxford: James Currey and Bloomington and Indianapolis: Indiana University Press, 1997, 326 pp.
ISBN 0-85255-546-6 £25.00 (cloth), 0-85255-545-8 £12.95 (paper)

Judith E. McDowell, in *An Interview with Chinua Achebe*, the second of the twenty-one pieces collected in Bernth Lindfors' *Conversations with Chinua Achebe*, offers a characterization of Achebe in 1962 which continues to have some validity to the present:

> [Chinua Achebe] ... a slender ... man with a bearing both hesitant and determined [who] reaching manhood at the time of Independence, examines social and political events with an eye at once lucid and objective and which, especially in Nigeria, does not allow itself to be impressed with former greatness. (7)

Not only does the interviewer catch or sense the quality of Achebe the man but also by implication an awareness of the purposes to which Achebe puts his art. (The interview is interesting in many ways, not least for one of the only, if not the only suggestion, that *Arrow of God* – not yet named – is the second novel in the planned triptych of which *Things Fall Apart* is the first and *No Longer at Ease* the third.)

Lindfors has chosen his twenty-one pieces from more than three times that many available to him. (There are seventy-three *Interviews with Achebe* listed in Ezenwa-Ohaeto's bibliography.) Lindfors' purpose has been to reveal answers about Achebe's life and art to the following questions:

> How did he get started? What kind of upbringing and education did he have? Which writers influenced him? Were there any teachers or mentors who encouraged and guided him? What prompted him to write fiction when few other Nigerians were doing so? How did his first manuscript find its way into print? ... How does [Achebe] explain himself. (ix)

Lindfors' selection is judicious in aiming to provide answers to the questions posed. And his questions provide a useful way into comment on the biography of Achebe by his former student Ezenwa-Ohaeto. The *Biography* answers the questions posed by Lindfors fully and usefully for anyone who wants to know about Achebe's life – his writing, his general social and political views, his activities as teacher, editor, political activist and reputation as a writer and an African.

Lindfors does not include the *Paris Review* interview with Achebe by Jerome Brookes of 1994. And while much of the conversation with Brookes finds an equivalence in other interviews, Achebe, perhaps as a passing remark, provides an interesting answer to a question persistently posed (and repeatedly answered) about which writers influenced him. Achebe has said many times that Joyce Cary's novel, set in Nigeria, *Mister Johnson* was a seminal influence – if that was the best that could be done to evoke Nigeria and the Nigerian character then perhaps he, Achebe, ought to have a go. (There are six references to Cary in the Lindfors volume and five in the *Biography* – and doubtless many more in the interviews given over the years.) To Brookes' reminder that he has said Cary's book prompted him to write *Things Fall Apart*, Achebe replies: 'I wish I had never said that' – a comment interesting in itself and in relation to references by Achebe to other Cary opinions. 'We are doomed to be free' says Cary and in expounding and in expiating the quality of this doom we become creative, free individuals. Cary describes Johnson as 'the artist of his own joyful tale' and the telling of Johnson's doomed story as 'creation in the act'. Perhaps the initial links were deeper than at first conveyed.

Much of the biographical material in Lindfors' volume is repeated in various forms and at various lengths over the course of years spanned by these interviews – from 1962 to 1995. What changes over those years, as Lindfors notes in his Introduction, is a shift from an emphasis on the literary background and concerns to current pressing political and social problems. Art is always at the service of the people and concern with making good art is at the forefront of Achebe's agenda. But social and political problems, as these reflect the needs of the generality of Nigerians, are what prompt Achebe to speak. These concerns are revealed in the Interviews and expounded to the fullest measure in Ezenwa-Ohaeto's biography.

It is in many ways astonishing to have recorded and described the number of public speeches, talks, interviews and lectures that Achebe has given in Nigeria, principally, but also abroad, on the subject of Africa and Africans. Clearly, it remains necessary to contest the clichés of colonialism as these still have surprising currency. There is also a need to face fearlessly, and make proscriptions about, the possible salvation of a country with such promise as Nigeria, as it is progressively dismantled by a series of civil and military hegemonies in the post-Independence period.

What is implied in so much of the comment in Lindfors' selection of interviews is enlarged and explicated in Ezenwa-Ohaeto's book. His is a biography and not a literary critical biography. Literary criticism is kept to a minimum and used only to suggest the ways in which Achebe's reputation as a writer developed. There is ample quotation from addresses that are not generally available, especially those given at various convocations, and at university and school meetings in Nigeria. As with the Lindfors book, readers will find that different aspects of Achebe's life engage their attention. One can note that the Biafran War and the circumstances surrounding the 1983 elections and Achebe's central roles in both historical events are given detailed and thorough explication.

Ezenwa-Ohaeto has been at work on his study since the early 1980s when, as result of a diffident approach to Achebe, he was given 'my general approval to his project'. Between then and the final preparation of the book, Ezenwa-Ohaeto consulted in one form or another – through letters, published materials, interviews – more than two hundred people (all duly listed in his Acknowledgements) who had contact with Achebe.

His bibliography provides three and one half pages of writing by Achebe – Books; Short Stories; Poems, Essays, Talks and Miscellaneous Work; two pages of Interviews and four pages of Secondary Sources related to Achebe's writing. The thirteen-page Index is comprehensive and reliable. Lindfors' *Conversations* also has a dependable Index. Some users might wish some biographical information on the interviewers whose work has been chosen for inclusion in the *Conversations* volume. Such was the demand on Achebe's time and such his willingness to respond – before the road accident in 1990 that seriously injured him and made travel difficult and tiring – that the final several chapters of the *Biography* read like an epic catalogue of events described and attended. What redeems a certain sameness of presentation are Achebe's words, in these sections amply cited.

Central to the interviews and the larger *Biography* is the position of art in the life of the subject but more impressively in the life of the community. Achebe's words are familiar to those who know his work and will impress those who come upon them for the first time. Art is crucial to society, for Achebe it provides a new handle on reality. It offers choices, allows a community to reach beyond itself because it mitigates against inward-lookingness. More than this, art is a celebration of the human spirit and for Achebe, in Africa at least, art connects with life and the realities which are connected with social living. There are many ways in which one might display Achebe's convictions about the place and function of art as these are found in the interviews, speeches and other documents. None says what Achebe means better than the following in relation to the trouble with Nigeria: 'It is a lack of imagination which is at the root of cruelty' (119).

These two books go together, adumbrating the opinions expressed by Achebe on a variety of subjects. What they reveal is Achebe's willingness to discuss in detail his purposes and methods as an artist, defining with no false modesty his fiction as one continuous consideration of the history of modern Africa beginning in the imperial-colonial period and seen from many different perspectives. We see in the interview with Kalu Ogbaa a full explication by Achebe of all his novels as a long response to questions concerning the nature of Igbo culture, and the ways in which it has reacted to various pressures since the beginning of European annexation and influence. We see what might be called his 'committed disinterestedness' in, for example, his comments on Chinweizu et al. in the interview with Nwachukwu-Agbada, where extreme artistic proscriptions prompt serious discussion when there emerges a too 'comfortable' artistic or cultural milieu.

Readers of Lindfors' collection, as with all such collections, will find favourites among the interviews selected. There are two interviews, fugitive in nature, not mentioned by either Lindfors or Ezenwa-Ohaeto which Achebe gave to Peter Gzowski for the Canadian Broadcasting Corporation programme, 'Morningside'. These were recorded when he was Senior Commonwealth Fellow at Guelph and shortly after the military coup which followed the publication of *The Trouble with Nigeria*. They are available from the Archives of the CBC and I mention them because, against the possibility of a reissuing of the Lindfors volume, Achebe said of them that they were the most searching interviews he had experienced.

Together, these two volumes outline the achievement and importance of one of the most widely read and influential authors of the century. Ezenwa-Ohaeto's *Biography* is a monumental tribute to an author of international reputation and influence. It is an act of enthusiastic yet diffident celebration of its subject, a work of tireless, devoted and thorough research over an extended period in a style which is, for the most part, as engrossing and compelling as the life it celebrates.

G.D. Killam
formerly Professor of Commonwealth Literature,
University of Guelph, Ontario

R. E. Obeng, *Eighteenpence*.
Legon: Sub-Saharan Publishers, 1998, 163 pp., £4.95 /$8.50.
ISBN 99 88 550 146

Ama Ata Aidoo, *The Girl Who Can and Other Stories*
Legon: Sub-Saharan Publishers 1999, 146 pp., £5.95/ $9.95.
ISBN 99 88 550 111

Sub-Saharan Publishers are distributed by African Books Collective Ltd, 27 Park End St., Oxford OX1 1HU, UK.

Amma Darko, *The Housemaid*
London and Portsmouth, NH: Heinemann, 1998, 107 pp., $11.95.
ISBN 0 435 91008 6

The publishing histories of these three titles suggest the routes taken by African authors in the last seventy years, and hint at directions in which the African book trade is moving. It is certainly encouraging that the texts are available, but, in various ways, each prompts proposals about development into other, more accessible, forms, on the stage, through video production, or by means of television documentaries. Since each text draws, in one way or another, on popular forms, it would be wonderful to take them out of the elitist code of print and return them to strongly oral and visual, more popular forms.

When school-teacher R.E. Obeng completed *Eighteenpence*, he sent the manuscript off to Ilfracombe. His choice of this quiet North Devon town was guided by the presence there of a vanity publishing house that had become known to a generation of West African authors. Under the terms of a memorandum of July 1938, Obeng paid Arthur Stockwell of Ilfracombe £78 for a print run of 1000 copies of his book that, delayed by war, was eventually delivered in 1943. I owe this information to Kari Darko's 'Introduction' to the 1998 Sub-Saharan edition of *Eighteenpence* which benefits from her scholarly and passionate concern for what she describes as 'the first true novel to be published by a Gold Coaster'.

Considering that it is relatively little known, *Eighteenpence* has appeared in a surprising variety of forms. The Stockwell edition was followed by another produced at the author's expense, this time by publisher/printer Willmer Bros. and Co. Ltd (1951). In due course, there was a Ghana Publishing Corporation edition, a gesture of respect to a pioneer author by the state enterprise that was part of Nkrumah's vision for a newly independent West African state. The text now appears, with J. B. Danquah's 1941 'Foreword' and full academic supporting apparatus, from an enterprising independent Ghanaian imprint, Sub-Saharan Publishers. It has been designed and typeset by another private Ghanaian outfit, Woeli Publishing Services, and this 'speaks volumes' about the direction in which publishing/printing is moving in West Africa.

Reading *Eighteenpence*, one is constantly struck by 'editorial opinions'. There is a strong urge to intervene in the text, to contact the writer encouraging him to stick to his task, to cut out distracting material, to maintain a consistent focus and to cultivate a style that draws on locally observed phenomena. But, of course, this is not an option. There seems to have been some minor editorial intervention in 1938, but that was not really part of Stockwell's operation. They were paid to print and bind, and print and bind they did. Now, in 1999, *Eighteenpence* exists to be enjoyed as a product of its time, place, and circumstances, and the absence of extensive Devon-based editorial intervention actually contributes to the novel's interest and significance.

Kari Darko, who lectures at the University of Ghana, is a helpful and conscientious guide. For example, she shows the tension within the author's mind between writing a moral fable and following the strong characters, notably Konaduwa and the sometimes heroic Obeng-Akrofi. In the 'Introduction' and in footnotes to the text can be found the fruits of Darko's historical enquiry and of the comparison she has made between different versions of the text. Her comments indicate where there have been changes. For example, in an early edition, Obeng-Akrofi, the impoverished would-be farmer whose desire to purchase an 18d cutlass takes up the first page, is described as wearing a 'loin cloth'. This is changed, or changed back, to 'cloth' with the observation that a loin-cloth is 'an article of clothing not found in Ghana'. In other cases obviously alien idioms are allowed to stand, evidence of the importance of British points of reference in the English that was taught and written in Ghana sixty years ago. Thus Obeng-Akrofi is described as rising 'with the lark'.

Obeng-Akrofi's story is one of extremes of good and bad fortune, and includes a staple of Ghanaian folk-lore as the discovery of 'a pot of gold'. In addition to encouraging good farming practice by showing Obeng-Akrofi benefiting from visits to Aburi Botanical Garden for advice, the novel also includes a powerfully presented example of the ingratitude of relatives. However, the central character, Obeng-Akrofi, has to compete for his creator's and the reader's attention with a woman he scorns, Konaduwa. Darko describes her evocatively as

> The traditional Akan woman whose cantankerous yet courageous voice is heard in all the fora in the colony: traditional and modern. She is made the voice of the Kwahus. (xvii)

'Cantankerous' is a word that falls easily from the lips of many Ghanaians. Indeed it is so familiar and so good at squeezing into other languages that I have met Ghanaians who have been surprised to discover that it is an English word. Norwegian-born Kari Darko's use of it in this context is absolutely justified. Konaduwa is very cantankerous, very self-assertive, very morose. But, in her defence, it should be said that the tactics that earn her this adjective are often effective in the situations in which she finds herself. By becoming involved in protracted litigation she also provides an excuse for a certain amount of the action in the novel. Her encounters with various, inevitably male-dominated, legal institutions give Obeng opportunities to expose the tensions in Kwahu society, and the dissatisfaction with colonial institutions. The process of her case through the various courts allows the author to indulge his own interests and to incorporate within his text accounts of court proceedings.

There are inconsistencies within the text and there is a considerable amount of confusion in this unpolished work. However, I think readers will come to welcome these qualities, especially when they can, with Darko's help, recognize how different versions of the text relate to one another. Through the shortcomings we can understand more about Obeng's achievement in bringing different kinds of writing within the compass of his distinctive novel.

The Girl Who Can and Other Stories is also published by Sub-Saharan Publishers, behind whom should be discerned the figure of Akoss Ofori-Mensah. This title has passed through three incarnations in the short time since it was launched during the Ghana International Book Fair in 1996, a launching that lingers in the memory for the combination of warm sisterly support and academic interest. At moments during the evening one felt as if one were present at a Wesley Girls High School reunion, and it was delightful to share the pleasure old friends took in the author's achievement, an achievement that was, in part, a celebration in prose of the resolution and determination of Ghanaian womanhood. The input from Vincent Odamtten indicated the serious academic interest that has developed in Aidoo's work and the recognition of her contribution as a forceful presence in African literature. Although the occasion was one of almost unalloyed pleasure there were shortcomings on the printing side. In fact, the invitations had actually spelt Aidoo's name incorrectly, and there was evidence of haste too in the printing and binding of the volume that was launched.

That edition was followed by one that was much better produced and had an attractive cover. On opening it, however, the contents page was revealed to be replete with errors. This has now been put right in a volume that looks and feels good and is packed with Aidoo's energy, observation and resolve. A quick comparison with the 1996 edition shows that typographical errors have been corrected, a more sophisticated approach to transcription of Fanti adopted, and certain stylistic changes made. The full import of these will have to await a full study, but one example, the substitution of *tsotsis* for 'thieves,' may be taken to reveal evidence of Aidoo's willingness to import a Southern African township term into a Ghanaian story (69).

The collection includes examples of work originally presented in the early seventies, some of which has been 'completely restructured.' The concerns remain deeply felt, there are certainly moments that recall the anger and sensitivity of stories in Aidoo's earlier collection, *No Sweetness Here*. However, there is no denying the passage of time and the widening of Aidoo's experience. The collection includes recent writing that reflects Aidoo's personal involvement with Pan African politics, her long struggle to survive as a writer and a mother, and her existence as a woman engaged with the feminist movement. The story that appears in the title of the collection was originally published in *MS!*

In reading the stories, fragments of a novel, and commentaries that make up the volume, the presence of Aidoo as dramatist and oral artist is constantly felt. There is a deliberate evocation of the speaking voice so that the reader repeatedly feels like an eavesdropper, a partner in a conversation, or part of an audience at a performance. Aidoo as playwright seems to belong to the past. Her work for the theatre was, after all, written in the sixties when there was a sense of a burgeoning national theatre movement. Aidoo was drawn into writing plays, and was able to see her student composition *Dilemma of a Ghost* brought to life on the stage, and then, through Longman, in printed form. Since then there has been a period of relative stagnation that has affected both the staging of plays and publishing in Ghana.

Aidoo, together with other African women writers, has suffered painful neglect during the last thirty years. In a powerful account of what it means 'To be an African Woman Writer,' a document that provides background to some of the points she makes in her creative writing, she indicted critics and publishers. She also issued the following call to women writers:

> Fish our books out, for either they exclude them, or even worse, where they also are present, they hide them behind shelves that carry the books of authors who are considered more displayable, racially or genderwise. (In *Criticism and Ideology*. Ed. Kirsten Holst Petersen, Uppsala, 1988: 171)

It is to be hoped that the Sub-Saharan edition marks a new stage in author-publisher relationships, and that the link with the African Books Collective in Oxford will lead to many orders for a book that is a compelling read, full of energy and of insistent voices. After all, there is plenty of room in a catalogue for all titles to be displayed.

Amma Darko's *The Housemaid* is one of the few new titles in Heinemann's African Writers Series. It has been produced with characteristic professionalism, and, one hopes, to the mutual satisfaction of author and publisher. Once upon a time, Heinemann used income generated by the best sellers on its list to subsidize a torrent of adventurous new titles each year. Now, while the best sellers have been repackaged and still make a distinctive contribution to bookshop shelves, few new titles appear. Some of them, as in the case of *The Housemaid*, border on catering to tastes usually satisfied by Macmillan's Pacesetters. However, *The Housemaid* has some qualities that interest.

From the very beginning of the novel, the reader is button-holed by an insistent narrator with a clear message, one that picks up certain of the refrains recited by Aidoo and hinted at by Obeng. Opening the book, we read:

> In Ghana, if you come into the world as a she, acquire the habit of praying. And master it. Because you will need it, desperately, as old age pursues you, and mother nature's hand approaches you with a wry smile, paint and brush at the ready, to daub you with wrinkles.

The concern is not in doubt in this passage which predictably moves on to discuss accusations of witchcraft; the quality of the writing is. Does Mother Nature's *hand* have a 'wry smile'? Is it possible to 'daub' wrinkles? Further into the novel we read:

> Indeed, the gender and generation tensions are such that we are not surprised to read of one mother-in-law who regularly screams 'Useless!' at a son-in-law who routinely screams 'Witch!' in reply. (45)

The issue of gender thus boldly, though clumsily, introduced is partly resolved by marginalizing men. Men are present in the novel: they enjoy positions of influence, they behave irresponsibly, they chorus their disapproval. However, they are rarely more than incidental to the main drama: the truck driver who gives the city-struck Akua a lift to Kumasi in return for her favours is typical. The episode is described in abrupt, staccato sentences: 'Akua unbuttoned her blouse. The driver's eyes blazed with consent. She removed her pants. He grinned, and stopped the truck in a secluded bend.' (30–31). While there are good reasons for not describing what follows the lines just quoted, these do not extend to Akua's experience after the driver drops her at Kumasi railway station. Darko makes little attempt to bring before the reader what happened next, the urban encounter. Quickly, and unsatisfactorily, she skips on to 'a month following Akua's arrival' (31).

Amma Darko employs an extended flashback to provide a structure for her book. She moves from the discovery of the body of a dead baby to investigate the ambitions, frustrations, and scheming by which Akua's friend Efia was brought to bed of a still-born child and how she concealed the body. The focus in all this is very much on the role of women, but not in an unbiased manner. Darko is, as we have seen, fully aware of a tendency to brand unfortunate women witches, but she herself creates some desperately twisted, evil matrons. Foremost among these is Efia's grandmother, who, quite cantankerous by nature, and motivated by resentment, greed and, to use an expressive word encountered in Ghana, 'envyness', encourages Efia to fall pregnant while working as a house-girl for Tika, a wealthy businesswoman. The plan is that Efia should then name one of her madam's business partners, one of those who regularly 'discussed business' in the bedroom, as the father of her unborn child. This wicked manipulation of a young woman misfires in a way that it would be unfair to reveal in a review, and Efia is cast out. Pregnant, alone and desperate, she gives birth and conceals the body of the still-born infant which is subsequently discovered. The circle has been completed.

The novel is not without sophistication. In addition to the use of the flashback, there is the contrast established between two young women, Akua and Efia, and a certain subtlety in the way the plots develop. (We read that people have schemes; in subsequent pages we learn what these are). There is also a brief foray into a kind of stream of consciousness, or what might be called, in view of the point made below, 'voice over.' 'Tika,' we read, 'was standing on her porch, staring into space and thinking of about three things in order of importance: the algae...' (63).

In addition to the interest in gender and generational tensions, and the ambiguous engagement with the issue of witchcraft mentioned above, the novel also communicates an acute awareness of the inequalities of present-day Ghana. Imbalances in distribution mean that Akua and Efia make or take opportunities to leave Kataso, their 'village in the eastern hills, (which) had no flowing water, no electricity, no entertainment centre, nothing' for the cities (29). The attractions of the 'greener pastures,' whether at Kumasi railway station or in service to a wealthy businesswoman, are all too obvious to village children.

The Housemaid feeds off conventions and concerns that are flourishing in Ghana through the popular democratic video industry. Like many local video productions, it is characterized by sensationalism, exaggeration, and the demonization of women. It would not take much to produce a screen adaptation and one suspects the novel was written with an awareness of the video options it offered! Might *The Housemaid* have made it to Kataso if there was an 'entertainment centre' there? All too easily one fears. Yet, in fact, the other books reviewed actually offer much more rewarding material for treatment that would make them accessible to a wide public. It would be wonderful if Aidoo were approached by a company keen to bring her prose to life on the stage. It would be heartening if the wealth of material assembled by Kari Darko about R.E. Obeng could be used in a television documentary so that Ghanaians, and others, could learn about the person responsible for 'the first true novel to be published by a Gold Coaster'. In the meantime, we should be grateful that publishers and printers exist that can bring these stories into our hands, and we should be encouraged that the production values of Sub-Saharan are rising.

James Gibbs
University of the West of England, Bristol

Chukwuemeka Ike, *To My Husband from Iowa*
Lagos: Malthouse, 1996, 268 pp., $12.50/ £6.95.
ISBN 9782601438

Femi Olugbile, *Batolica*
Lagos: Malthouse, 1995, 230 pp., $11.50/£6.50.
ISBN 9782601241

Malthouse are distributed by African Books Collective Ltd, 27 Park End Street, Oxford, OX1 1HU, UK.

To My Husband from Iowa is an account of a Nigerian writer participating in a three-month residency and tour organized by the International Writing Program of the University of Iowa. It seems to have been written to fulfil an obligation incurred by participating in the programme. As narrator, Ike assumes the identity of Ify, a happily married young woman writer with two small children.

The book is a travelogue in which the various encounters and incidents give rise to reflections on American culture and comparisons with the Nigerian way of doing things. Ike as Ify conscientiously interviews other writers on the trip about their respective countries of origin and the position of the writer therein. He records sights seen and places of interest visited, which include model farms and local factories. He comments on the diverse facets of American life that the writers on the tour were fleetingly exposed to: tele-evangelism, the primary elections,

Native American pueblo culture, TV chat shows. The result is an eclectic collection of opinions and impressions. Sometimes these are reactionary, as with Ike's conflation of homosexuality with child abuse, and sometimes unexpectedly refreshing. (On divorce we read 'after struggling with your husband over the years to build him up, why lock yourself out only to let in another woman to reap where she did not sow?')

It is hard to see what purpose has been served by making the narrator a woman, apart from enabling Ike to make the occasional coy comment about having a man in 'her' room or being embarrassed by dirty jokes. Ify expresses contentment with married life and conventional values – this is of course a valid and acceptable point of view but since these are presumably Ike's opinions there is no reason why he could not have expressed them on his own account. The lack of published West African women writers is hardly going to be addressed by having a man speak on their behalf.

Ike's portrayal of Ify is respectful but tends towards complacency. Ify has a supportive, loving husband and expresses acceptance of the sexual status quo in West Africa (polygamy, patriarchy) unlike Ama Ata Aidoo or any other female writer one could think of. She also experiences a problem-free separation from her baby and toddler for three months. The book ends with the not unexpected conclusion that Nigeria could learn a lot from the US but had better hold on to some traditional values in order not to become (sexually) demoralized.

Batolica is the story of an idealistic anti-government uprising taking place on the University of Ife campus. People familiar with Nigeria will find the characters realistic and the progress of events plausible – the situation described is not as far-fetched as it may appear to the European reader. Olugbile portrays the University as an enclosed world, an intellectual enclave, separated economically and socially from the larger society. The physical segregation of campus life that makes the Batolica secession possible is also shown. Tellingly, and accurately for Nigeria, the uprising begins at a literary event based at the Drama Department, involving politically aware lecturers taking the lead from student protesters. The trigger is an announcement of the further devaluation of the naira. However, throughout the novel, workers, 'the People' on whose behalf the revolution is supposedly taking place, seem to be as shadowy a concept for the author as they are for the ideologically-motivated revolutionaries.

Olugbile vividly depicts the characters, their motivations and the politicking they indulge in, as, during the course of the novel, recklessness, stupidity and thuggery combine with impractical idealism and political manoeuvring to produce a hopeless and dangerous situation. He interrupts the main action with flashbacks into the background of the major characters providing sometimes rather touching portraits of people and events from the past. These supply complexity and depth to the characters. The technique is most successful with regard to the most fully realized and sympathetic figure, the psychiatrist Professor Olabintan.

In spite of the gallows humour and occasional scurrilous anecdotes, the novel is pessimistic. It is implicit from the beginning that the revolution is doomed and the characters self-delusory, clutching at straws to rescue themselves from a state of chronic disillusion and dislocation. The flash-backs are one of the better parts of the book, exploring as they do the characters' motivation and the background to their current predicaments. It is no surprise to learn that Olugbile, like his protagonist, is a psychiatrist.

What underpins the story but is not explored by the author is the complexity of social and familial ties that underpin the life of a West African individual. These ties mean that no adopted Western ideology is ever going to be complete enough, or flexible enough, to supply all the answers and give a workable framework for living. It is the characters' tragedy that they are carried away by revolutionary feeling without having the means to be truly effective in society. They assume, in a shallow way, a series of ideologies – Marxism, liberal socialism, born-again Christianity – yet it is clear that these ideologies have not managed to penetrate their real lives. The author is very good on the alienation produced in the characters by their various attempts to live by untenable philosophies, and, in Professor Olabintan's case, his efforts to reconcile these with indigenous traditions. However, because the characters are not seen against a realistic wider (as opposed to familial) social background, there is a sense of incompleteness about the novel.

Olugbile's characterization of women is sympathetic, though it becomes shallow when he attempts to imagine a woman from the inside, so to speak, in the character of Aneta. Sometimes the narrative is not coherent, as when the author presents the internal life of a character or an incident from their past, without making it immediately clear who the person is. The author should make things a little easier for his readers: there are too many characters and plot lines for this sort of puzzle to be anything but hard work.

Having said that, the book is enjoyable, and a plausible fictional reconstruction of a situation that may even have happened in the past. Malthouse is to be congratulated for building up a list of topical, lively books, creating opportunities for Nigerian authors to see their work in print, and supplying the public with thought-provoking reading material.

Folake Shoga
Bristol

Rayda Jacobs, *Eyes of the Sky*
Oxford: Heinemann, African Writers Series, 1997, 231pp., £6.99.
ISBN 043591006X

W.P.B. Botha, *A Duty of Memory*
Oxford: Heinemann, African Writers Series, 1997, 229 pp., £6.99.
ISBN 0435910078

Eyes of the Sky is an adventure story, following the fortunes of a young eighteenth-century Afrikaner who becomes alienated from his family, forms links with the San desert people, and in the end returns to his inheritance. It reads like a summing-up of the Boer experience, an exposition of a critical moment containing the seeds of future development for inter-cultural relations within South Africa, and it links the evolution of events in the story to the earliest moments of the Boer adventure. The book is well written, the language expressive, and the author uses intensely visualized physical descriptions of each scene to move the story along. There is an epic feel to the narrative, although the main action takes place within three years.

By plainly describing the physical presence of smells, objects and sounds, the author very economically suggests the harshness of the environment, the violence surrounding the competition for scant resources, and the dogged, frugal materialism through which culture is transmitted down the Afrikaner generations. Still, Boer life is evoked here with a certain amount of that folksiness which Afrikaner critics tend to complain about in English-language South African texts. Moreover the author does not treat her characters impartially: her favourites do not suffer from a sort of harsh determinism half as much as the secondary figures. The author's treatment of Zokho, the San woman, is particularly unresolved. The woman's behaviour could be productively explained in modern psychological terms, but instead a magical explanation is invoked, reducing the character to inscrutability, removing meaning and relevance from her encounter with the hero. 'Zokho has lost favour with the gods, her spirit is tainted.' And: 'That was the difference between them. ... The old father was right, he didn't understand. He didn't want to.' Once her humanity has been thus excised from the text, the hero is free to pursue his aims with integrity.

The technique of visualization Rayda Jacobs uses is often practised by writers to bypass their own internal set of conventions and prejudices. However, Jacobs has not managed to do this. In spite of creating a very vivid text, her conscientious liberalism keeps succumbing to the potency of the Afrikaner pioneer myth – a myth that has been crucial in sustaining the brutalities of its power structure.

'Eyes of the Sky!' is the name given to the hero by the San people. 'He had come to the right place. Those who had never seen him watched in awe as a tall figure clothed in the same sunbaked colours as the Karroo, white hair flying off broad shoulders, came striding towards them.' Passages such as this identify the novel as romantic escapism, and as such perhaps one should not have too high expectations of it. Readers will be perfectly well able to make up their own minds whether the picture of the perfect Afrikaner is unduly benign, or optimistic, or not.

> Ag, when Jo called me Bin Ears it wasn't really because my ears was big as bins. It's just Bin Ears is the reverse of Eeben, Earbin, as they say in English, and my sister she didn't speak anything only English. Now that, I tell you, made us all spitting mad.

In these first three sentences, with what compression and economy does Botha set out the themes of his novel, *A Duty of Memory*. He touches on the violence and anger integral to the Afrikaner heritage, the sense of siege, the interconnectedness and antagonism between Afrikaner and Englander, and the dislocation that reaches into the most intimate, domestic areas of life to tear up families and individuals from the inside.

By the end of page ten these themes have been comprehensively elaborated, and the phrase 'can of worms' may occur to the reader before the translation of '*hele gemors*' is given. Now we know that Eeben is a perpetrator as well as a victim, and see that the process that turns him into a little baas also undermines his belief in himself. We see the interdependence of white farmers and black workers, and that it is the workers who provide family, security and mentorship to the profoundly dysfunctional Hartzenbergs. We observe a sort of cod militarism active in the domestic detail of Afrikaner life. And always, whenever Botha sets up a proposition, he undermines it: there are no essentials, only a shifting, dazzling network of relationships. The conceptual fabric of the novel seems unstable, it wrongfoots the reader, who has to keep adjusting her/his understanding to the different voices used to tell the story. Swinging between Eeben's demotic and the cool lyricism of the author's 'objective' voice, within these first ten pages we are also introduced to some of the metaphors that work through the book almost like living organisms, growing and diminishing, echoing and amplifying the action.

Eeben's voice, laconic, pithy, using conventional phrases, is as expressive in its pauses and omissions as in what he actually says. As the story progresses, he keeps returning to the gaps to fill them in with skimpy details: '... he knows about dirty tricks operations – or if you prefer the military speak, counter-insurgency. Or diplomatic speak: the battle for hearts and minds. Though in the end it's all the same: people vanishing never to be found. At least not in one piece.' His manner of speech reiterates the process of recapitulation, reworking, that goes on throughout the novel. The same chain of events is described over again by different people, with different voices, methods and circumstances. There is a competition for truth within the text, just as there is in the storyline. The truth is what can be rescued from the 'hele gemors,' and this is the very least that is owed to the future: the duty of memory.

The text of the novel is dense, allusive, finely crafted. Content and structure are as organically interdependent as in a piece of poetry. There are superficial thematic similarities between this and Rayda Jacob's book: the pithy flavour of Afrikaans folk culture, the mystique of the pioneer adventure; the hard struggle with the land; the endemic violence. There is also the occasional startling correspondence of story detail. But the two books are not in the same league. I can detect neither residual racism nor romanticism in Botha (nor sexism for that matter): he writes with a frank, painful and truly poetic humanism. He is also aware to whom the future belongs.

An Afrikaans-speaker, writing in English, Botha uses words in a way that resonates between the two languages, carrying a charge of meaning from one to the other. For instance, talking of the Boers, which of course means 'farmer,' he says: 'Hell, let me tell you how we farmers *farmed*. How we sowed the land with dragons' teeth.' The apocalyptic Afrikaner names: Engelbrecht, Draak, Staal, Tonder – Angel-bright, Dragon, Steel, Thunder – these carry echoes of Anglo Saxon myth into the English, and with them a historical consciousness of the trail that leads from there through nationalism to fascism.

Botha is an author who is firmly embedded in two cultures, with an alive and tortured awareness of his place in each. He has the sort of critical 'double consciousness' more usually discussed in connection with authors from the Black Diaspora. He brings a paradoxical ambivalence to bear in his descriptions of people, emotions and events, which always maintains an emotional distance from the action, even when dealing with the most horrifying things. The distance engages the reader, allowing her/him to enter the world of the book without too many reservations, without feeling manipulated. Writing from a position which must be difficult and insecure, Botha has created a novel which is elegant, beautifully written, amazingly constructed, moving and challenging.

Folake Shoga
Bristol

S.N. Ndunguru, *A Wreath for Father Mayer of Masasi*
Dar es Salaam: Mkuki na Nyota Publishers, 1997, 172 pp., $7.95/£4.25, pbk.
ISBN 997 697 33 49
Mkuki na Nyota titles are distributed by the African Books Collective Ltd, 27 Park End Street, Oxford OX1 1HU.

Ndunguru's *A Wreath for Father Mayer* is a curious mixture of a sort of modern morality and a not very convincing thriller. The village setting rings splendidly true and the character of Father 'Moyo' as he tackles the problem of cholera and the villagers' reaction (they think it witchcraft) is engaging and credible, as are the practical steps he plans, the theft of the tetracycline from the presbytery and the murder which follows. But the further the story moves into mystery, the less believable it becomes. Drug-smuggling and the victimization of a naive priest are possible but that the Airport Customs authority would recruit him as a decoy is not presented believably; that a trial could take place so rapidly seems extremely unlikely; the conversion of Dr Bennett to enable the good father to escape after his kidnapping is obviously contrived, and the happy ending with all the ends tied off shows all too clearly the controlling hand of the author. The terse style which carried the narrative effectively in the initial chapters becomes a little irritating. The dialogue becomes less characterized and the willing suspension of disbelief becomes increasingly difficult. The visionary dreams of the good Father are a little hard to swallow. But the story never palls as it moves from the village to Dar es Salaam, to Britain, then the Continent and back home. There is plenty of adventure, even if some of it is somewhat naively told, and there is an optimistic view of the essential goodness of humankind and a belief that evil will fail which is heartening. A story which secondary students may well enjoy, and which will improve their command of English.

Margaret Macpherson
Windermere

A.M. Hokororo, *Salma's Spirit*
Dar es Salaam: Mkuki na Nyota, 1997, 135 pp., $7.50/£3.95, pbk.
ISBN 997 697 33 30
Mkuki na Nyota titles are distributed by the African Books Collective Ltd, 27 Park End Street, Oxford OX1 1HU.

Father Moyo has true dreams. The whole of Hokororo's well-written *Salma's Spirit* depends on the reader's acceptance of the possibility of there being an occult world, on the possibility of people who have died appearing to the living, even to strangers. The way in which the story is told makes this acceptable. The young narrator, Sam Mbogho, sees a beautiful girl, gets to know her, and discovers by a series of unnerving revelations that she is the daughter of his boss and that she had died in a car crash a year before. Her father who was driving had been attacked by a swarm of bees which caused him to swerve into an anthill on the Tanga road (which is well described). His wife and daughter were killed and he suffered terrible sorrow which has led to him seeing his dead relatives. This terrifies him, he tries to stifle the vision with drink and is desperately afraid that his fear of the dead will destroy his love for them. This is a ghost story with a difference.

The Dar es Salaam setting is brought vividly to our eyes, as is the medicine man's home near Tanga. The verisimilitude of the detail, including some very fine descriptions of the scenery at different times of the day and night, as seen by Sam, forms the background to the growing closeness of Sam, his boss and his second wife, who emerge as basically nice human beings. And the matter of fact account of the happenings and Sam's reaction to them lead us constantly forward into the prolonged climax which begins in Chapter 7 with the first visit to the practitioner ToboaTobo who finally exorcizes the spirits of the dead wife and daughter. This is a splendidly combined series of seances where the detail keeps the reader deeply absorbed from the initial car parking arrangements and the scene in the waiting room. It would make a most dramatic act in a play. Once we have set out on the road to Tanga it is hard to put the book down.

Margaret Macpherson
Windermere

Charles Mungoshi, *Walking Still. Nine Short Stories*
Harare: Baobab Books, 1997, 162 pp, with a glossary, $8.50/£4.95, pbk.
ISBN 0908311990
Baobab Books are distributed by African Books Collective Ltd, 27 Park End St, Oxford OX1 1HU

Charles Mungoshi is an established writer in Zimbabwe and his short stories, *Walking Still*, reveal his mastery of the form. A short story requires different skills from those required for a novel. The events need to be concentrated, the number of characters limited, and the narrative shape controlled.

The variety of interest in this selection is notable. The last tale, 'The Little Wooden Hut in the Forest', reveals his individual skills and economy. It is a kind of fairy tale in approach as the young forest worker tries to take his pregnant wife to deliver her first child at her mother's home. They are lost and find asylum in the little hut where the child is born and named. The last line is the climax: 'He comes home and he is crying.'

Each story has a strong narrative line and addresses an important issue. Mungoshi examines the contrasting aims of an ambitious wife and a conservative husband; the friction that can arise in a village with the advent of a stranger; the terrible cruelty of children to one another (this story is told by a child who has been deeply involved); the problems of homosexuality and the impossibility of genuine friendship between recently independent locals and apparently liberal expatriates.

'The Slave Trade' appears simple but contains economically presented punch as the drunken Marara reaches the important conclusions that these apparent friends 'do not come in peace and good will', that his taking of their whiskey is a new enslavement and that in future he will not be deceived. The story is told from the viewpoint of the wife, Ravi, who is both an observer and, because of her relationship with Marara, also involved. The idea of sacrifice in the story of that name is seen from the viewpoint of the girl who is to be the sacrifice to solve the problems of her extended family. An interest here is that Tayeru has to sacrifice an independent future in a modern world to marry traditionally, and the simple sequence of events develops to the quiet 'I am ready' as her frail greybearded husband is seen in the doorway. In this story as in others

there is a sense not only of the conflict between tradition and modernity but a feeling of the past and of the spirit world.
The stories reveal both urban and educated society. Traditional rural village communities and the changing world of Africa are presented in a series of vividly told and well-constructed tales. Detail is clearly presented and dialogue is used skilfully. Each story leads to an effective conclusion and convinces that Mungoshi is a fine short story writer.

Margaret Macpherson
Windermere

Julius Ocwinyo, *Fate of the Banished*
Kampala: Fountain Publishers, 1997, 164 pp., $7.50/£3.95, pbk.
ISBN 997 002 10
Fountain Publishers are distributed by African Books Collective Ltd, 27 Park End Street, Oxford OX1 1HU.

It is worth noting at the outset the notable improvement in presentation and proof-reading from these Kampala-based publishers. As a result, the reader is able to become absorbed in a horrifying story without being irritated by typographical errors. The banished of the title, a Foreword explains, are the children of Adam and Eve, subject to afflictions and temptations and flaws because of that original sin. They appear in the first novel of a young man who is also a poet and interested in drama. He writes very well about an area which he obviously knows intimately and handles the dual threads of the story very competently. The structure, which includes flashback sequences that could have been confusing, is admirably clear.

We follow the development of Apire as a resistance fighter and at the same time watch his lonely wife, Flo, in the village where she is attracted to a young priest. The progress of the story makes more understandable the bitterness with which many people in the north of Uganda regard any form of authority. But far more gripping is the psychological dimension of the narrative through which we understand the behaviour of a range of characters, learning about them sometimes as they themselves think back over a past, which is shown in flashbacks. Apire and his bush companion, Erabu, who joined the resistance to avenge himself on the raiders who destroyed his farm, are initially portrayed as violent young men in the bush. They subsequently become much better acquainted so that when Erabu dies a lingering death beside Apire it is understandably the last straw and sends Apire back to his lonely wife and child. Tragically he returns too late and the violence of his recent existence accounts for his reaction to finding his wife with the priest. This is the 'second strand' and we have simultaneously followed the village events where the young and energetic priest and the lonely Flo, a member of his choir, have been drawn together. When they finally succumb to temptation, we can understand the motives of both of them.

The meticulous detail in which each incident is described and the understanding with which Ocwinyo handles the relationships contribute to our involvement. The melodrama of the denouement is reduced because we have known from the beginning that the priest and Flo are going to die. We are prepared too for the aftermath when Apire gives himself up to the authorities, and for the press report which forms the epilogue. The reader is brought back to less violent 'normal' life, with a greater understanding of what sets such events in motion.

Fate of the Banished is a violent and gripping tale. The author may be less artistically sophisticated than Mungoshi but this is an original and very powerful story, well handled with high seriousness and with real knowledge of both the area and the complexities of human nature. Ocwinyo has another novel coming out soon and it is hoped that it will fulfil the promise of this book.

Margaret Macpherson
Windermere

Sue Kossew, *Pen and Power: A Post-Colonial Reading of J. M. Coetzee and André Brink*
Amsterdam-Atlanta, GA: Rodopi, 1996, 258 pp., £14.00.
ISBN 9042000945

Sue Kossew's *Pen and Power – A Post-Colonial Reading of J. M. Coetzee and André Brink* is a well-written, carefully argued study, which fulfils the contract announced in the sub-title. The post-colonial framework underpinning the book is of the Ashcroft/Griffiths/Tiffin persuasion, quite an understandable choice since this represents the most comprehensive and cogently expressed approach available – though its very comprehensiveness and cogency may sometimes be found too good to be true. However, this theoretical approach is no doubt more appropriate to the object of study than the structures and deconstructions which seemed inescapable twenty years ago. In a detailed introduction, Kossew sets out the issues clearly and (re)places South African literature in the context of post-colonialism without obfuscating jargon, pinpointing the 'double inscription', or fundamental ambivalence, that defines the position of the two novelists.

The main weakness of the book – let us make it clear from the start – stems from its origin as a doctoral thesis, and one based on a comparative study of two novelists. All scholars have experienced that awkward moment when a subject has to be defined under the pressure of various constraints. The final choice, which may have appeared satisfactory at the time, sometimes reveals unexpected pitfalls. This is a case in point, although some of the results could easily have been predicted. To embark upon a comparison between the two writers amounts to stating the obvious: they are not of the same calibre. Coetzee's narratives are extremely elaborate, thought-provoking, his imagery original and immensely varied. Brink tends to be too explicit when he wants to make a point, unnecessarily complex when he decides to deal in the metafictional, and repetitive when, casting about for solutions, he resorts to the *deus ex machina* of interracial love. Therefore, setting him against Coetzee in a literary study cannot but put him at a disadvantage, and indeed *Pen and Power* does not attempt to play down Brink's weaknesses as a writer. Likewise, a comparison with Nadine Gordimer would have been quite as damaging, since it would have shown how many of Brink's themes and situations are derivative of Gordimer's and how, in particular, *Rumours of Rain* is a pale remake of *The Conservationist*. However, in all fairness, it should be said that Brink is a courageous writer who has greatly contributed to making the South African situation known to a larger audience (especially in France where he has a wide and faithful readership).

As for Kossew's yoking together of novels within each chapter, this method lays the author open to endless quibbling, as a measure of arbitrariness will always prevail. So let us just mention the surprising pairing of *Looking on Darkness* with *In the Heart of the Country*, and the treatment of *On the Contrary*, which might have been better analysed under the heading 'History, Mythography and Colonial Fictions'. In addition, as each novel is dealt with separately within a chapter, the text contains a profusion of cross-referencing formulas such as 'interesting parallel' between the two novelists, or 'like Coetzee' and 'unlike Brink', which still smack of the palimpsest doctoral thesis (see for example p. 98). Similarly, the verbatim repetition of Nkosi's judgement on Gordimer (p. 10, footnote 9 and p. 181), and of Redman's quote about the Nuremberg defence (98 and 112) could have been avoided. As for the 'C. M.' mention referred to in the discussion of *Michael K* (128), it should be added that this disappeared from later editions. Lastly, one notices some wavering as to Coetzee's 'first language', defined as being English on page three, whereas page seven mentions 'his mother tongue, Afrikaans'. Actually his mother's tongue was English, and only English was spoken at home (see Coetzee's *Boyhood*, 1997: 105–6, 126).

Once these qualifications have been made, there is no denying that the pages devoted to each novel offer an excellent assessment of its place in post-colonial writing. Not surprisingly perhaps, the section on *Foe* comes off best, since this metafictional novel lends itself well to theorized argument. On the whole, *Pen and Power* favours the antimonologic stance of Bahktin and Bhabha, but staunch opponents of hybridity (such as Benita Parry) are amply quoted and discussed. In short, the book constitutes a balanced and well documented introduction to the current critical debate as it affects South Africa, and more particularly J. M. Coetzee and André Brink. As such, it will be of great value to researchers looking for more than a superficial survey of the subject.

André Viola
University of Nice

Hans M. Zell (comp.), *The Electronic African Bookworm: A Web Navigator*
(With an introductory essay by Kofi Arthiabah)
Oxford: African Books Collective, 1998, 134 pp., £8.95 / $15.00.
ISBN 0952 126 958

As part of its support to university libraries in Africa, the International Network for the Availability of Scientific Publications (INASP) is managing a programme of university-based workshops on 'Using the Internet.' An account of the continent-wide programme (in *INASP Newsletter*, 12 May 1999) points out that 'For Africa [the Internet] offers an opportunity to save time and money in information acquisition. It is also a means to promote local information to a wider audience.' However, the author of the article is well aware of the problems and adds 'finding good and relevant information on the Internet is not easy. The World-Wide Web contains a vast amount of information, but it is neither categorized, nor scrutinized. Many academics do not have the time or expertise to sift the Internet for those sources that could support their work.' INASP is not alone in assessing the opportunities offered by the Internet and in encouraging researchers to make the best use of it.

Hans Zell, whose life has included managing book shops on West African university campuses, organising book fairs in Ife, helping to found the African Books Collective, publishing a series of prize-winning titles, and leading workshops on producing journals in Africa, has set up a carefully focused 'web navigator'. That is to say, he has compiled a 'quick-access guide and pick-list to some of the best Internet sites on Africa, African and development studies, and on African publishing and the book trade'. The result, *The Electronic African Bookworm*, is a practical, well-presented, and immensely valuable tool for African researchers and librarians.

The Internet has been described as a 'great hunter-gatherer' and Zell helps the timorous surfer or novice browser to move onto the information superhighway. There is an on-line version of the *Electronic African Bookworm* (web site http://www.hanszell.co.uk/navtitle.htm) that some readers will have more or less instant access to, but my concern here is with the 'print version'. This includes 'Getting wired', using 'search engines', a 'cyber glossary', and the Navigator itself. Kofi Arthiabah, who is Technical Assistant and a Systems Operator at the Association of African Universities in Accra, contributes an essay, 'Connecting to the Internet in Africa', that provides practical advice and comparative costs for those using Cybercafes, 'E-mail only' and 'Full dial-up'. In many instances expense will be prohibitive, but for those who want to assess the options and can get some time on-line Arthiabah's essay is essential reading.

For many years there were two kinds of researchers: 'Those with access to free photocopying, and those without'. More recently, a new distinction has emerged: 'Those with access to free time on the Internet and those without'. Undoubtedly researchers 'paying by the minute' will feel very differently about the length of time spent looking at the hour-glass icon. (The WWW has been dubbed the 'world wide wait'.) They may respond with cyber irritation or cyber rage to on-screen 'advice' about 'Application errors' and to the information that 'The requested URL could not be retrieved'. They will know only too well that, though the web can offer much, it is always necessary to bear in mind that at present the system has many imperfections. Even 'successful' searches often produce only out-of-date, sadly inadequate information: the average electronic bite is often only a little bit more substantial than the average sound bite.

Claims for the net are often exaggerated, the death of the book has been prematurely announced, and speculators think 'virtual' fortunes can be quickly made. In this context the level-headed contributions of 'man of the book' Zell and 'systems operator' Arthiabah are particularly welcome. The print version of *The Electronic African Bookworm: A Web Navigator* is, it should be noted, freely available to those in certain categories. A note on the back cover indicates that the book: 'is published by the African Books Collective Ltd (ABC) as part of their range of resource materials and is supplied free of charge to the African book communities, and to writers and scholars in Africa'.

ABC's Oxford address appears elsewhere in this publication, but in the present context its website (http://www.africanbookscollective.com) may be more pertinent. Those academics and librarians who have not made use of the *African Bookworm* should acquaint themselves with it today. If they do not, they will be saying 'had we known' tomorrow.

James Gibbs
University of the West of England, Bristol

Arthur Gakwandi, *Kosiya Kifefe*
Nairobi, Kampala and Dar es Salaam: East African Educational Publishers, 1997, 351 pp., $11.25/£6.25, pbk.
ISBN 9966468382

Alexander Kanengoni, *Echoing Silences*
Oxford: Heinemann Educational Publishers, 1998, 136 pp., $13.95, pbk.
ISBN 0435910094

Yvonne Vera, *Butterfly Burning*
Harare: Baobab Books, 1998, 130 pp., $12.50/£6.95, pbk.
ISBN 1779090161

Marjorie O. Macgoye, *Make It Sing and other poems*
Nairobi, Kampala and Dar es Salaam: East African Educational Publishers, 1998, 112 pp., £4.25/ $7.95, pbk.
ISBN 9966466479

East African Educational Publishers and Baobab Books are distributed by African Books Collective Ltd, 27 Park End Street, Oxford OX1 1HU.

Post-independence Uganda is the setting for Arthur Gakwandi's entertaining *Bildungsroman*, as it narrates the progress of Kosiya Kifefe in a rather conventional rags to riches trajectory, from the days as a naïve, impressionable boy, ecstatic about buying his first pair of shoes, to his commercial success and political prominence.

Just when one feels the storyline is about to drag through excessive build-up to individual events, there is a leap forward in time, into a new setting, so that seemingly important transitions in Kifefe's life are skipped altogether. Examples include his move to the city, his university years and the birth of four of his children. Yet what this in effect supports, and indeed explicitly states time and again, is that the anticipation and display of *status* in society — as a city-dweller visiting the village, as a graduate in the city, or as a father — is seen as of greater importance than the experience itself.

Much of the time, the narrative is ironic, so that the reader appears to be laughing both with and at Kifefe. His obsession with the etiquette of status lends the novel ambivalently both humour and exasperation at the pettiness of mind, which expands into full-blown corruption. His insecurity is depicted as a wider political insecurity which involves proving one's capability in the face of post-Independence pressure. Kifefe's resultant alienation from the vast majority of his compatriots is poignantly and subtly depicted in the novel.

The length of the novel indicates the extent of some of the detail, very little of which is excessive or uninteresting, to my mind. Gakwandi is skilful in depicting evocative settings, the hustle and bustle of activities, the hope and anticipation of Independence and later post-Amin Uganda, and in sympathetically recounting the tensions of changing human relationships. However, at times the language falls into the racy clichés and stereotypes of sensationalist story-telling, particularly when romantic passions run high. For instance, we read: 'Too weak to fight back and too shy to shout, Dora abandoned herself to his passionate embrace' (113). In fact, the relationships between Kifefe and his numerous lovers are disturbing for the amount of force they involve, and the fact that this is not explicitly criticized. The narrator leaves it up to individual readers to interpret, for example, Dora's resistance, 'The outcome was so ambiguous that Kifefe could not decide whether he had made a conquest or had simply made a fool of himself' (114).

Kifefe takes on an increasingly emblematic role; the older, stereotypically beer-guzzling, womanizing, bribe-accepting Kifefe has little in common with the clumsy dupe of the early pages of the novel. The narrative of the novel, which reaches an ironic closure with Kifefe's badly timed death, just as he is about to embark on his ministerial career in the new post-Amin government, invites humorous sympathy for the protagonist, but the conditional oversight of his deep faults may be too uncomfortable for many readers.

Another account of political change, Alexander Kanengoni's *Echoing Silences*, provides the reader with a powerful, horrifying representation of the dislocating effects of war, both physical and mental, by a writer who has first-hand experience of combat in the war for Zimbabwe's independence. As Terence Ranger sets out in an essay that provides useful historical contextualization of the novel, spirit possession and healing played a far greater role in the war than many contemporary accounts acknowledged. It is these complex interactions between material and psychic, or spiritual, experiences which Kanengoni so skilfully depicts in a shifting, non-teleological narrative which enacts the workings of memory and trauma.

The story follows the fate of Munashe, as the ex-fighter is haunted by the figure of the wife and child of a rival faction leader, whom he was forced to kill brutally during the war. Without a physical break on the page, the narrative moves back to the day of the murder, yet leaving the scene incomplete until later in the novel, when after several traumatized returns to that day, the narrative reaches the point of completing the disturbing scene of the killing. The style of shifting locations and temporalities is at first disorientating, but as the reader learns to recognize them, the effect is of a powerful dramatization of trauma and possession. Munashe, we read, 'no longer had a self. He was the war' (41).

The second part of the book, in which Munashe returns to his parental home for communal spiritual healing through a totemic lion-possession ritual, is particularly effective. Kanengoni vividly recounts the event, recreating the excavating, purging action of the healing process, as the narrative memory continues to evoke Munashe's war and post-war experiences in scenes which shift, merge and resonate in dream-like fashion. Munashe finally manifests his guilt by becoming possessed by the spirit of the dead woman, and returning her upon divine instruction to her home, where she is recognized and received. In a final destructive act, indicating the relentlessness with which Munashe is possessed by his war traumas, he is killed in a forest gully as he chases a vision of his female lover who was also killed in the war.

At moments of stress, the language reflects rambling delirium, in contrast to other scenes, as in the homestead, in which it idiomatically echoes formal vernacular interchanges. Shona songs are inserted in the text, and translated in the glossary, though, unfortunately, it is not noted which language is being translated. A novel both shocking and sensitive, *Echoing Silences* skilfully deploys understatement to communicate horror and futility. In centring as a recurring motif the mindless killing of the woman with the baby, Kanengoni denies the idealism of stories of struggle against domination in the mould of the heroic tales recounted at Independence.

Another important recent publication from Zimbabwe is Yvonne Vera's latest novel, *Butterfly Burning*. The title strongly symbolizes the main female character, Phephelaphi, as she delicately floats from the ecstasy of all-consuming love with Fumbatha, to her final burning destruction. The first shadow falls as, due to pregnancy, she is forced to cancel her ambitious desire to train as a nurse. Her response is abortion, shockingly and movingly described in intense and symbolic detail as she carries it out herself with a long thorn, alone in the desert landscape (98–108). Fumbatha's rejection of her and his unfaithfulness with her female mentor, Deliwe, is the final tragedy in this story of destructive desire.

The novel is deeply poetic, shimmering with crystal images in lyric prose, certain symbols reappearing to provide a verbal rhythm to the novel. Yet also featuring strongly are the politics of late nineteenth and mid-twentieth century Zimbabwe. Fumbatha is still deeply affected by his father's hanging by the colonial authorities in 1896 (23), Phephelaphi is among the first intake of black student nurses to be enrolled in 1948 (84), and oppressive economic conditions and township uprisings punctuate the story.

For me, the main discomfort is the over-determined sexuality of all the main female characters, implying a male gaze. Indeed, many of the women earn their existence in the township by selling their bodies, and at moments the gaze is reversed onto the male sexual bodies, for example where Zandile traces her clients' histories by tracking the scars on their bodies (34). Yet I wish that, having creatively re-imagined so much else in the novel, Vera could have moved beyond standard representations of sexualized bodies in, for example, 'The girls wait in tattered skirts which waver over their thin thighs, their breasts are flat like the bottle-tops' (13).

This irritation aside, I find *Butterfly Burning* a novel of immense vividness, both in horror and in beauty, leading the reader through a turmoil of emotions. At times these emotions may conflict, as poverty and deprivation are represented with empathetic beauty, as in the description of a tank of oil. 'In the distance, a large tank. So large that the children along Sidojiwe E2 could all drown in it at once. The tank is full of oil. It must be filled with rainbows too. Oil and rainbows' (16). My admiration is greatest for the skilful crafting of vocabulary, symbol and imagery to form a language that, in Vera's own words, is 'laced, dipped in a fragrance soft like milk, words chiselled like stone, words with wings to touch the sky' (41).

Make it Sing is an eclectic, distinctly Kenyan collection of poems by a woman writer who has previously contributed to the country's fine literary tradition through the novel genre. In this new volume, extensively introduced by Philo Ikonya, Marjorie O. Macgoye brings together unpublished work with poems which have appeared previously in local journals, newspapers and anthologies. She has organized them appropriately into five sections, which read as a form of narrative of the poet's life. The first section reflects on art, poetry and the 'labour' of composition. This noun is deliberately used as a common link in Macgoye's favoured extended metaphor, connecting, through birth and regeneration, the notions of womanhood, nationhood and, importantly, writing. African motherhood here gives birth to vocal poems depicting injustice and intolerance, challenging compromised interpretations of freedom. The opening title poem, 'Make It Sing', whose background is detailed in the introduction, is a moving poem in verse and refrain form, urging the use of verse as a changing force in a disturbing world.

Section Two is made up of the long, deeply layered, personal song cycle 'Song of Nyarloka', in which, as the notes explain, 'nyarloka' is the Luo term for a woman born overseas, as in the poet's case. This is an appropriate lead into a third section, 'Crossing Over', referring as much to the poet's physical crossing from Britain to Kenya, as the continuing crossings which her everyday life demands. 'Leonida' and 'Pillars and Angels' are two such poems reflecting on separation and convergence, whilst 'Letter to a Friend', by far the most personal, first published in 1970, is for me the poem with the most immediate impact. Far from displaying the conventional anxiety about her immigrant, 'in-between' or 'crossing' status, she refreshingly states,

Changing continents in midstream
is likely to create a mild upheaval:
there is no need to lament loudly (58)

She replies, at the height of the era of 'black pride', to the racism she and her children suffer, 'Why should I mind/ being out of fashion, which being white is?' and 'Half-black? They are not half anything' (57). Her method of living is much like her method of writing, constructing something new from both British and Kenyan cultures, 'I act no part, learn no lines, improvise/from two lives that I have' (59).

'Songs of Freedom' is the title of the fourth section, which remakes the stories and myths of Kenya's Independence struggle and continuing repression. The poet here celebrates the heroic figures of Harry Thuku and Mathege, pleads in a dignified lyric for Ngugi's release, yet also challenges the abuse of the emblematic 'poor relative' child-servant Atieno, who slips beyond definitions of freedom in modern Kenya. The poet thus subverts and reinterprets the conventional political associations made with 'songs of freedom'.

The final section, 'Public Events', contains a variety of reflections on places, such as 'Muoroto', and 'A Suite for Uganda'. Macgoye vividly paints impressionistic scenes using a mosaic of evocative detail, as in depicting the razed Muoroto township the night after the bulldozers arrived, 'the river crawls with its curd of refuse,/scamperings, whimpers, flicker of flame,/plop of excrement, slither of slime' (82). Other poems reflect on the present condition, such as 'The Melting Pot: Fusion or Fission' and the final despairing 'Bitter Waters'. In these poems, the struggle in the poet's mind expresses itself in dense, opaque language which, read in different lights or at different times, reveals new layers of meanings. Thus, read repeatedly, this poetry provides an ever more thought-provoking, personal testimony to Kenya, of sadness, anger, but above all, deep affection.

Fiona Johnson Chalamanda
University of Stirling

F. M. Genga Idowu, *My Heart on Trial*
Nairobi and Kampala: East African Educational Publishers, 1997, 186 pp., $8.50/ £4.95, pbk.
ISBN: 9966465995

Barbara Kimenye, *Beauty Queen*
Nairobi and Kampala: East African Educational Publishers, 1997, 133 pp., $6.95/£3.75, pbk.
ISBN: 966460144

Ciarunji Chesaina, *Oral Literature of the Embu and Mbeere*
Nairobi and Kampala: East African Educational Publishers, 1997, 211 pp., £11.00/ $19.50, pbk.
ISBN 9966464077

J. Roger Kurtz, *Urban Obsessions Urban Fears: The Postcolonial Kenyan Novel*
Trenton, NJ: Africa World Press, Inc; Oxford: James Currey, 1998, 238 pp., £12.95, pbk.
ISBN 0-85255-550-4

East African Educational Publishers are distributed by African Books Collective Ltd, 27 Park End Street, Oxford OX1 1HU.

My Heart on Trial, set in contemporary Kenya, intricately and enigmatically plots the story of three generations of one family, pivoting on Laorenti, or 'Lawrence', Yada, a wealthy, self-made man who reaches high office in government. The novel opens in a crowded café in the US, where the first narrator is disturbed at her table by two Kenyan couples who join her in succession, the younger couple, Yada's daughter and son, throwing accusations of murder at the older couple. From here, the narrator takes on the role of judicial magistrate, 'That was the beginning of what I had to pursue for a couple of months. I have discussed, cross-examined, and listened ... and as I searched and questioned, I unearthed what makes my very being curdle.' (unpaged).

Excavations and burials are common motifs in the novel as the non-teleological narrative shifts between consciousnesses, recounting the views and memories of a number of characters. A story of Yada's life emerges out of the fragmented sections, as it negotiates the familiar conflict between 'tradition' and 'modernity', as the boy is educated and moves from his position as a village schoolteacher to the city to pursue an ambitious government career. His relationships with his rather conventionally characterized wives, firstly the 'village girl', then the 'sophisticated gold-digger', and thirdly the 'independent woman', indicate his relationships to the various societies they represent. Yet the outcome is negative, as Yada is destroyed, ashamed, desperate and haunted by his alienation from all societies. There are a number of sub-plots and family sagas which are entwined in the main plot, though enigmatic ellipses and unfinished digressions, such as Yada's son's appearances and disappearances, or the fate of the doctor, Ondiala, are too clumsy to be satisfying.

The strengths of the novel lie in two areas, firstly in the imaginative use of dialogue, where expressions evoke conversational Luo and Kiswahili and their idioms in subtle translation. The second area of strength is in the consistent, well-managed use of imagery and motifs which subtlely echo and reverberate to link disparate fragments of the novel at a level beyond action and character relationship. Dominant examples include images of dismemberment, which occur in descriptions of medical procedure as well as in irrational hallucinations of self-mutilation. Similarly, the general motifs of burial and suppression are consistently countered by excavations of events and traumas. Indeterminate signifiers and pronouns serve, together with the disorientating narrative structure and incomplete sentences, to replicate an experience of an irrational and incomprehensible world which ruptures the coherent existence (or narrative) a reader desires. The novelist is clearly fascinated by psychological processes, thought-provokingly engaging with the uncanny. As Yada's son concludes from his father's experience 'there was a wisdom in the shadows of what the human eye can see, and a danger in the familiar that could not be ignored' (182).

The didactic, illustrated novel, *Beauty Queen*, aimed maybe at a younger teenage audience, follows the life of Adela, a young woman entrapped on the beauty queen circuit by her avaricious entourage, as they tempt her from the 'straight' path of academic education to the lure of earning glamorous millions. Adela is contrasted with her school friend, Keti, in a familiarly structured moral tale, in which the innocent Adela is destroyed by following temptation, whilst the saintly Keti pursues a path of religion and caring as a novice in a hospice for AIDS patients. Predictably, it is Keti who at the end cares for the ill, destitute, abandoned Adela. Like many popular publications, the language is racy, the action fast, the characters stereotypical and the circumstantial facts extreme. Adela, for example, secures a contract for five million dollars to promote cosmetics in the West after winning her first beauty contest in Kenya. She is transported around in a private jet, mingles with the famous, and has sex with a Hollywood icon, who infects her with the HIV virus.

Yet I feel that it is misplaced to assume that this book is aspiring to formal literary criteria, and thus to demolish it accordingly. My discomfort in reviewing it in an academic context is countered by my opinion that academics of African literature should acknowledge these popular moral tales, which are avidly consumed in their regions of origin, as J.R. Kurtz notes below. The author herself sets out the 'message of this book', that is, her didactic intention, in the introduction. She states that the story is intended for pubescent girls, and is validated for accurate detail by a medical doctor. Its harm, of course, is that in presenting its central message as true and factual, it also validates some of the novel's conservative conventions, particularly the underlying assumption about gender roles in the various partnerships described. Whether such didactic material is effective is of course a debate which rages between disciplines, the arguments well-rehearsed. Yet despite some caricatured situations and clumsy inconsistencies, forming rather unconvincing characters, there is a gripping narrative, and the story has much pathos and urgency.

The didactic tone of Ciarunji Chesaina's study of the oral literature of the Embu and Mbeere reveals it as another educational book. It is, in fact, written by a professional teacher. The rather simplified language and generalized statements make it less attractive to the academic specialist, who might refute some of the forms of classification, particularly the division of 'traditional' and 'modern', where 'modern' is the automatic label given, for example, to texts containing references to bicycles, syringes or Kenya.

As a secondary or undergraduate textbook, however, the study cannot be faulted on organization and clarity of structure, with diligent use of headings and sub-headings. In the introduction, Chesaina sets out her aims, layout and methodology of collection and transcription, though the politics of interpretation are not mentioned. She also introduces some basic points of development in the field, such as the re-casting of oral literature as a dynamic, contemporary process, whose performer and performance context are crucial, rather than as an archaic activity of handing down petrified texts from generation to generation. She does, however, occasionally lapse into the past tense, seemingly contradicting her earlier assertions. For example, we read 'There were no hard and fast rules as to where stories were told' (21).

The book is divided into two parts, 'Theoretical Framework' and 'Literary Texts'. The first chapter gives a fairly encyclopaedic introduction to the Embu and Mbeere historical and cultural background, followed by chapters on genre and performance, form and style, and the social functions of oral literature, little of it exclusively relevant to the ethnic grouping of the Embu and Mbeere.

A substantial Part Two, three times the length of Part One, provides texts in both Embu and Mbeere, described as distinguishable 'dialects of the same language' (xii). Each text is followed by an English translation; it is, however, only in the chapter of narratives that the language of origin is specified together with the place of origin and field notes on the name, gender and age of the narrator. The language and sources of the oral poetry, proverbs, riddles and puzzles remain undisclosed. I would be most interested in the sources of the puzzles, six out of fourteen of which I was familiar with in European settings, including the puzzle of how to transport a leopard, goat and sweet potatoes across a river using only a small boat, and where the survivors of the car crash on the international border should be buried (208–9). An index and a bibliography of further reading would also have been particularly useful for this kind of text book.

In contrast, the last sixty pages of Kurtz's *Urban Obsessions Urban*

Fears provide a bibliography and plot summary of over 200 Kenyan novels, published between 1964 and 1997, which is a valuable resource. Curiously there is no bibliography of critical works consulted; when they are mentioned, they occur without publication details in the text, and the index is unreliable. The book opens with the statement that there is a growing body of critical analysis of Kenyan literature, but the writer does not indicate its stages nor position himself within it. The title implies a psychoanalytic approach, but does not deliver it; the essential critical method is categorization of the novels, simple plot summary, and impressionistic evaluation. The informative material about Nairobi is not theorized by any conception of the literary expression of urban spaces.

The focus on Nairobi is potentially interesting, but the ways in which the city is constructed are described rather than analyzed, so that, for instance, the fragmented narrative demands on the reader's imagination of Ngugi's *Petals of Blood* are not distinguished from the politically evasive technique of Imbuga's *Shrine of Tears*. There is re-iterated reference to Kenya by the end of the 1970s 'having established a full-blown literary tradition' (46) in English, and to Kenyan writers setting out to provide 'a new set of myths' (156), both problematic concepts. Having effectively applied Bakhtin's formulation of the carnivalesque, the writer then refers to 'unreal language' (84) rather than exploring heteroglossia in relation to the hybridity of city speech. Similarly the writer needs a methodology, which is well-established in the analysis of African fiction, for analyzing popular novels to reveal their political and social agendas.

Fiona Johnson Chalamanda and Angela Smith
University of Stirling

A Note from the Publishers

With reference to the review of Breitinger (ed.) *Defining New Idioms* printed in *ALT 21*, Eckhard Breitinger would like to point out that this review was factually incorrect and that none of the contributions in the earlier Beyreuth publication *Theatre and Performance in Africa* were reprinted in *Defining New Idioms*. He also states that the reviewer's reference to an 'overwhelming presence' of German scholars is misleading as only 7 of 31 contributors were in fact German. Furthermore he wishes to express his concern at the ideas behind such a statement.

Index

Abrahams, L., 107
Abrahams, P., 64
Achebe, C., 118; *Anthills of the Savannah* vii; *Arrow of God*, 53, 54, 118; art, 19-21; CBC interviews 120; characters vii, and Christianity vii; on his fiction, 14, 120; Igbo culture, 120; influences, 118; *No Longer At Ease*, vii, 53, 62, 118, 119; opinions, 120; *Things Fall Apart*, 53, 62, 118, 119
Acholonu, C., African 96; and colonial education, 95; 'Biafra days', 91; 'Embryonic bride', 94; family history, 98; feminism, 92, 95; imagery, 93, 96; lyrical intensity, 99; motherhood, 96; *Nigeria in the Year 1999*, 90, 91, 98; Nigerian social problems, 91; 'Not Yet', 91; patriotic anguish, 92; patriotism, 98; 'Poems of War', 91; realism, 95; *Spring's Last Drop, The*, 95; style, 97; 'Surviving', 97; 'Tell them Okigbo', 93
Ade, Sunny, 38
African Books Collective, 111, 125, 139
Africa(n), 96; languages, 35; leaders, 71; liberation, 51, 70; oral literature, 34-6; redemption, 51; religion, 96
Aidoo, A. A., 128; feminism, 124; *Girl Who Can and Other Stories, The*, 122; launching 1996, 124; *No Sweetness Here*, 124; oral artist, 124; pan-Africanism, 124
Aiyejima, F., 91
Akwanya, A. N., 'Crisis of filiation: ... in John Munyonye's Trilogy', 53–63
alienation, viii, 7, 9, 18, 64, 68, 94, 129, 140; *see also* exile
ambiguity, 44, 66
anthropologists, 35
apartheid, vii, 13, 14, 24, 33, 65, 66, 70, 71, 93, 103, 105, 106, 108
aporia, 42
Arce, A.M.S., 'Changing States ... in Buchi Emecheta's *Kehinde*', 77–89
Armah, Ayi Kwei, *Beautyful Ones Are Not Yet Born, The*, vii, 44, 45, 49, 93; biography, 51; *Fragments*, 44, 45, 48, 49, 51, individual: in family, 46, in society, 45-6; irony, 51; *Why Are We So Blest?*, 44, 49
Arrow of God, see Achebe
Arthiabah, K., 138
At The Junction, 103

Auden, W. H., 'The Capital', 1, 6
Bakhtin, M.M., 147
Baobab Books, 111, 112
Barthes, R., 40, 60
Beautyful Ones Are Not Yet Born, The, vii, *see* Armah
Berrian, B., 84
Beti, M., 44
Bhabha, H., 87; myth, 13
Biafra(n) war, 90, 91
Bible, 83
biblical influence, 36-7, 42
Biebuyck, D., *Mwinde Epic, The*, 40
Biko, S., 25, 26, 110
bildungsroman, 78, 140
biography (auto), Armah, 51; Head, 14; Marechera, 2-10, 16
Black Insider, The, 2-3
Blackstone, B., 75
black writing, 64, 65-7; exploitation by , 69; South African, 66, 71, 73, 74; theatre movement, 109; women, 79
Botha, W. P. B., *Duty of Memory, A*, 130
Botswana, 71
Bourdillon, M., 14
Brecht, B., 107; *Caucasian Chalk Circle, The*, 54
Bridge to a Wedding, see Munonye
Brink, A., 136
Brown, S., 114
Brooks, J., Achebe interview in *Paris Review*, 118
Brutus, D., 33, 44, 64; apartheid, 24; Chipasula on, 29; exile, 23, 24, 28, 29; exile poetry, 28-9; 'For the Kent State Martyrs', 28; freedom fighters, 24-5; 'A Friendly Question...', 27; imagery, 23, 26, 29; 'In London the News Comes', 24; 'In London it is Dark', 25; 'In the Dark Lanes of Soweto', 25; 'In Memoriam...', 26-7; 'In Memory', 28, metaphor, 27, 28, 30; paradox, 24, 25; prison poetry, 28, 29; rational voice, 23-30; Robben Island, 29; Salton, 24; *Salutes & Censures*, 23-31; 'Salute to our Allies', 24; *Simple Lust, A*, 23, 93; 'Sorrow for the Children of Soweto', 25; South African enigma, 23; Tejanai on, 24; 'Terrible

148

Knowledge', 28; 'There was a Girl', 25, 26; 'Tonight', 29; 'A Tribute for Steve Biko', 25; western indifference, 25; 'You May Not See the Nazis', 29
Bunyan, J., *Pilgrim's Progress*, 42
Buuck, D., 1

Cabral, A., 5
Caribbean, and African culture, 77
Cary, J., *Mister Johnson*, 118
Caucasian Chalk Circle, The, see Brecht
Césaire, A., 5, 27
Chalamanda, F., 144
Chesaina, C., *Oral Literature of the Embu and Mbeere*, 144
chi, 81, 82, 83, 86, 87
Chinweizu, et al., 120
Chipasulu, F., on Brutus, 29
Chirikure, C., *Hakurarwi*, 111; influence, 111; 'Munyama', 112; social criticism, 112; 'Teargas', 111
Christianity, vii, 61, 82
civil war, Sierra Leone, vii
Clarke, J. P., 73
Coetzee, J. M., 136
Cohen, Anthony, 82
colonialism, 5, 8, 36, 71, 72, 95, 96, 101; post-, 7, 21, 77, 88, 96, 136; and sexuality, 18, 50
community, see society
cultural identity, 78
culture, refugee, vii, European, 4, 9, 19, 35, 61; African: multiplicity of forms, 77; American vs Nigerian, 127; Djibouti, 100
cultural identity, 78

Dairo, I. K., 38
Damas, 27
Dance of Fortune, see Munonye
Dangarembga, T., 77
Darko, A., feminism, 125-6; flashback, 126; *Housemaid, The*, 122; male characters, 126; witchcraft, 125, 126
Daiko, K., on Obeng, 122, 123
Davies, C. Boyce, 85, 110
Dead Roots, 1
de Beaugrande, R., 40
Demetrakapoulos, S. A., 82
Derrida, Jacques, 77; aporia, 42
Devant, T., on Mda, 109
diagesis, 19, 20
diaspora, 35
discourse, 77, 82, 83, 85, 88, 97
Djibouti, culture, 100; geography, 100, 101; history, 101; languages, 100
Drum magazine, 64

Egudu, R., 25, 65
Eilersen, G. Stead, 15
Emecheta, B., 78; concept of role, 78; contradictions, 77, 81; criticism of, 78; cultural identity, 78; discourse, 79, 82, 83, 85, 88; and England, 79; and feminism, 78, 79, 88;

Gwendolyn, 87; Kehinde, 77-89; migrant writer, 79; myth, 82, 84, and Nigeria, 79; *Second Class Citizen*, 86; *Slave Girl, The*, 84; subjectivity, 78, 79-81, 82, 84; syncretism, 85; syncretism vs hybridity, 85
Empson, W., ambiguity, 41
ewi poet, 38-9
exemplum 57
exile, vii, viii, 1-99 (passim), 23, 24, 28, 29, 33, 45, 53-63, 64-5, 77, 90; Babylonian, viii; *Exile and the Narrative Imagination*, 1, 13; writers in, 44, 78
Ezenwa-Ohaeto, *Biography of Chinua Achebe, A*, 118; 'Rational Voice of Dennis Brutus in the Poetry of Exile in *Salutes and Censures*', 23-31

family, in Igbo society, 54-62
Fanon, F., 5, 8-9, *Wretched of the Earth, The*, 7
Farah, N., 44; *Sardines*, 1
feminism, 74, 78, 79, 92, 95-6, 124, 125-6; African, 97
Finnigan, R., 34, 35
flashback, 20, 126, 128, 135
folklore, Shona, 8
foreigners, 86
formalism, Russian, 32
Foucault, Michel, 40, 82
Four Plays, Junction Avenue Theatre, 103; *Sophiatown*, 106
Fragments, see Armah
Fraser, R., *Novels of Ayi Kwei Armah, The*, 48
freedom fighters, 24-5
Fugard, A., 105; on Simon, 105

Gagiano, A. H., 'Concepts of Exile in Dambudzo Marechera's Early Works', 1-10
Gakwandi, A., *Kosiya Kifefe*, 140
Gambia, bards, 40
Gaylard, G., 2
gender, 113; see also feminism
Gerard, A., 67
Ghana, society, 47
Gibbs, J., 127, 139
Gomez, S., imagery, 116; 'The River God's Hunger', 116
Gordimer, N., 137
griot, 40
Gurnah, A., 2, 19
Gurr, A., *Writers in Exile*, 1
Gwendolyn, 87

Hawley, J. C., 81
Head, B., 64-76; alienation, 64; ambiguity, 14, 66; and apartheid, 13, 14; apartheid and sexual exploitation, 14-15; assertiveness vs aggressiveness, 73; autobiography, 66; *Bewitched Crossroad, A*, 71; biography, 14, 64-5, 67, 68, 69; and black Africans, 66; black exploitation, 69; and black struggle, 15; criticism of, 16; 'The Deep River', 76; female characters, 70, 74; on God, 16, 19;

150 Index

compared with *The House of Hunger*, 16, 21; iconography, 13-16; Ku Klux Klan, 16; literary technique, 65; madness, 68; male characters, 70; *Maru*, 67, 68; mental affliction, 13, 14-15; narrative style, 68; Nkosi on, 64; power, 74; 'A power struggle', 74; 'The Prisoner Who Wore Glasses', 72; protest, 64-6, 68, 74; protest writing, 64-6; *Question of Power, A*, 13, 69, 70, 74; racial integration, 73; relevance, 65; *Serowe Village of the Rainwind*, 71; spirit possession, 14-16; utopiansm, 16, 21, 73; *When Rain Clouds Gather*, 67, 69; witchcraft, 13-15; world outlook, 75
Healers, The, 51
Heinemann, publishing policy, 125
Heron, G., A., 33, 36
hibridity, 85, 137, 147; vs syncretism, 85
Hokororo, A. M., *Salma's Spirit*, 133
Holloway, K. F. C., 82
Horn of My Love, 35
House of Hunger, The, 2, 8, 13-22; see Marechera
Hove, C., 111, 116; imagery, 115; 'I will not speak', 114; literary movements, 115; metaphor, 115; 'power', 114; *Rainbow in the Dust*, 114; *Red Hills*, 114; *Shebeen Tales*, 114; stand, 114; style, 114; *Up in Arms*, 114
Hutcheon, L., 32

iconography, 13
identity, 85, 86; culture, 78, 121
Idowu, F. M., *My Heart on Trial*, 144
Igbo, family, 50-62; incantation: poetry, prayer, reincarnation, 58, 59; society, 53-8, 80-2
Ike, C., opinions, 128; *To My Husband from Iowa*, 127
Ikonya, P., 142
imagery, 18-19, 23, 26, 29, 33, 37, 40, 41, 93, 96, 115, 116; 118-9
Imbuga, F., *Shrine of Tears*, 147
incantation, poetry, 93; prayer, 96
independence, *see* liberation
Innes, G., *Sunjata; Three Mandinka Versions*, 40
Interpreters, The, vii
intertextuality, 36-8, 40, 41-2
Inyama, N., 'Shades of Home and Exile in Ayi Kwei Armah's Novels', 44-52
Iowa, University of, 127
Irele, A., 42
irony, 5, 102
iwi poet, 38-9

Jacobs, R., escapism, 130, 131; *Eyes of the Sky*, 130
Jones, E. D., vii-viii
Junction Avenue Theatre Company, 106; *At the Junction*, 110; dramatic style, 109; *Fantastical History...*, *The*, 106; *Randlords and Rotgut*, 107, 108; *Sophiatown*, 107, 108; staging, 108-9; *Tooth and Nail*, 107, 110

Kabunze, P., 'Charged with Murder', 117
Kanengoni, A., *Echoing Silences*, 140-1
Kanute, B., 40
Kanute, D., 40
Kenya, Embu, 146; Mbeere, 146; novels, 147
Kerr, D., 'Mindblasts: Narrative Technique and Iconography of Social Stereotyping in Bessie Head's *A Question of Power*, and Dambudzo Marechera's *The House of Hunger*, 13-22
Khama the Great, 71
Khama, T., 71
Kimenye, S., *Beauty Queen*, 144
Kossew, S., *Pen and Power*, 136
Kristeva, 54, 82; *Strangers to Ourselves*, 86
Ku Klux Klan, 16
Kunene, M., 64
Kunstleroman, 78
Kurtz, J. R., *Urban Obsessions*, 144

La Guma, A., 64
Lamming, G., *Pleasures of Exile, The*, 1
Langa, M., *Naked Song, The*, viii
language, 65; Djibouti, 100; English, 67; European vs African, 35, 36; Shona, 8, 14, 111
Larson, C., 59
liberation, 51, 70, 95, 97, 98, 117
Lindfors, B., 28; ed. *Conversation with Chinua Achebe*, 118
literacy, 38; vs orality, 34-9, 40
literary technique, 65
literature, feminist, 14, Medusa and, 14; oral, 34-8, 146; post-colonial, 77
Littlewood, J., 107
Lukacs, G., 55
Lyrical Ballads, 34

Macgoye, M. O., 'Bitterwaters', 143; 'Crossing Over', 143; 'Leonida', 143; 'Fusion or Fission', 143; 'Pillars of Angels', 143
Macpherson, M., 133, 134, 135, 136
Maduakor, O., 91
magic realism, 38
Makhalisa, B., 'Woman', 116
Malthouse Press, 127, 129
Manaka, M., 105
Maponya, M., Black Consciousness, 104; commitment, 105; *Doing Plays for a Change*, 103; *Hungry Earth, The*, 105; obstacles, 104; staging, 105; style, 109
Maru, see Head
Marechera, D., 1; alienation, 7, 9; on art, 19; anti-nationalism, 2; auto-denigration, 19; biography, 2-10,16; *Black Insider, The*, 2, 3, 4; *Cemetery of Mind*, 2, 7; colonialism, 5, 7, 8, 21; and sexuality, 18; cont. with Africa, 5; criticism of, 5; and European culture, 4,

9; and exile, 2-10; and Fanon, 5, 6, 8-9; flashback, 20; Fr Pearce on, 5; on God, 19; *House of Hunger, The*, 2; comp. with *Question of Power, A*, 16, 21; mental affliction, 13, 17; *Marechera: A Source Book ...*, 24; *Mindblast*, 7; narrative voice, 4-10; nihilism, 21; 'Night on my Harmonica', 2; 'Oxford Black Oxford', 2, 5; Oxford, New College, 2-3; plot, 20; Protista, 8; satire, 9; *Scrapiron*, 7; Shona folklore, 8; 'The Sound of Snapping Wires', 2; style, 3-10, 19-20; utopianism, 16; 'The Writer's Grain', 9
Market Theatre, 105
marxism, 71
Mbiti, J., 15
McDowell, J. E., *An Interview with Chinua Achebe*, 118
Mda, Z., *And the Girls...*, 103, 109, 110; *Joys of War*, 109
Medusa, and feminist literature, 14
mental affliction (madness), 13, 14-15, 17, 68
metaphor, 23, 27, 57, 77, 91, 115, 131, 143
Metuh, E. I., 96
migrant, 79, 84, 86; black, 87
modernism, 32, 112
Modisane, B., 64
More, T., *Utopia*, 70
motherhood, 96
Mphaphlele, E., 44, 64
Mungoshi, C., 135; 'Before the Sun', 112, 'Lazy Day', 112; *Milkman ..., The*, 111, 112; *Waiting for the Rain*, 112
Munonye, J., *Bridge to a Wedding*, 53, 56, 57, 58, 59, 60; characters, 56-7, 59; *Dance of a Fortune, A*, 53, 60; family, 54-62; historical novel, 55; narrative style, 55-7, 59; comp. with Nigerian writers, 62; *Obi*, 53-6; historical novels: *Oil Man of Obange*, 53, 57, 60; *Only Son, The*, 53, 56-9; *Walking Still*, 134
myth, 13, 82, 134
Mzemane, M. V., *Hungry Flames*, 72

Naked Song, The, viii
narrative, 4-10, 13-22, 54, 55-7, 59, 68, 101, 109, 141; Marxist, 107
Ndunguru, S. N., *Wreath for Fr. Mayer of Masasi, A*, 132
negrophilists, 64
Nichols, G., 77
Ngara, E., on Hove, 115
Nigeria(n), 79, 92-3, 127; poetry, 91, 114; social problems, 91
Ngugi, characters, viii, 35, 44; *Petals of Blood*, 147
nihilism, 21
Nkondo, G. M., 28
Nkosi, L., 7, 44; on Head, 16, 64, 69
nnomo, 82
No Longer At Ease, vii
Nortje, A., *Dead Roots*, 1
novel, genres, 67; historical, 55, 69, 70, 71; Kenya, 147; traditional, 53; utopian, 16, 21, 69-70
Nwachukwu-Agbada, 120
Nzakwu, O., *Wand of Noble Wood*, 58

Obeyi, E., 38
Obeng, R. E., *Eighteen Pence*, 122; pioneer author, 122
Obi, see Munonye
Ocwinyo, J., *Fate of the Banished*, 135
Odanatten, V., 124
Ofori-Mensah, A., 124
Ofuani, O. A., 41
ogbanje, 84, 88
Ogede, O. S., 'Exile and the Female Imagination: The Nigerian Civil War ... Catherine Acholonu', 90-9
Ogunbesan, K., 69
Ogundele, W., 27
Ogunyemi, C. O., 84; on Emecheta, 78
Ogwude, S. O., 'An Exile Writing on Home ... Bessie Head' 64-76
Oil Man of Obange, see Munonye
Ojaide, T., 25
Okai, A., 39
Okigbo, C., 33, 93; imagery, 37; oral literature, 34-8, 72, 124: vs. literacy, 34-9, 40; western influences, 37
Okpewho, I., 35, 38; *African Oral Literature*, 34
Okri, B., 77; *Famished Road, The*, 77; symbol, 77; magic realism, 38
Olney, J., 67
Olugbile, F., *Batolica*, 127, 128
Ong, W. J., 34, 38, 39
Only Son, The, see Munonye
oppression, 24, 25, 66, 67, 68, 73, 74
Orkin, M., ed. *Four Plays*, 107-9
Ovid, 1
Oxford, New College, 2-3, cont. with Africa 71
Oyegoke, L., 'Cultural-Textural Exile ...' 32-43

pan-Africanism, 124
paradox, 24, 25
patriarchy, 97
patriotism, 98
Pattison, D., 2
p'Bitek, O., 32-4; biblical influences, 36-7; and Christianity, 37-8; *Horn of My Love*, 35, 41; imagery, 33, 40; intertextuality, 36-42; *Song of Lawino*, 35; *Song of Malaya*, 35; *Song of Ocol*, 35, 42; *Song of Prisoner*, 35; style, 33; *Two Songs*, 34, 36; and western culture, 36, 42
Pearce, Fr., on Marechera, 5
Peterson, B., on Mda, 109
Pilgrim's Progress, 42
Plato, 39; *Republic, The*, 70
Pleasures of Exile, The, 70
poet, African, 39; ewi/iwi 38-9, griot, 40; national, 39; praise, 38-9
poetry, Acoli, 35, 40, 41; African, 33, 35; definition, 34; ewi/iwi, 38-9; incantation, 43, 96; Kenyan, 143; Nigerian, 91, 114; oral,

152 Index

34-8; praise poetry, 38-9; Yoruba, 38-9
polygamy, 80
Pope, A., 34
post-modernism, 32, 34, 39-40, 41, 42, 109
Povey, J., on J. P. Clarke, 73
protest writing, 64-6, 68, 74
Purkey, M., 107, 109

Question of Power, A, 13-22; *see also* Head

racial integration, 73
Ranger, T., 141
realism, 95
refugee, 7; culture, vii
re-incarnation, 58, 59
religion 96
Rive, R., ... *District Six*, 108
road, as symbol, 77
Roscoe, A., 29
Rureke, C., 40
Rushdie, S., *Satanic Verses, The*, 90

Said, E., 'Reflections on Exile', 1
Salt, M. J., on Brutus, 24
Salutes and Censures, 23-3
Sardines, 1
Sarup, M., 'Home of Identity', 1
Saro-Wiwa, K., 115
Satanic Verses, The, 90
satire, 9
Schwartz, P., on Simon, 106
Schweik, S., *Gulf So Deeply Cut, A*, 92
Second Class Citizen, 86
Seidel, M., *Exile and the Narrative Imagination*, 1
Senghor, L., 27
Senegambia, griot, 40
sexuality, 18, 98
Shakespeare, 1, 37, 42
Shoga, F., 129. 132
Shona, 8, 14, 111
short story, South African, 72, 134
Simon, B., *Black Dog*,106; *Born in the RSA*, 103,106; and Market Theatre, 105; *Outers*, 106; *Score me the Ages*, 106; *Woza Albert*,106
Slave Girl, The, 84
Smith, I., 2
society, 86; Igbo,53-8; 80-3; twins in, 80-4; and the individual, 44-5; Nigerian, 90; in London, 86; Western 49, 82 (London), 85
Socrates, 65
Song of Lawino, 35
Song of Malaya, 35
Song of Ocol, 35
Song of Prisoner, 35
South Africa, culture, 130; enigma of, 23; Market Theatre: Junction Avenue, 103; society, 27, 74; writing, 64, 65-7
Soweto, 35
Soyinka, W., *Interpreters, The*, 33, 38
spirit possession, 14-16

Steadman, I., on Maponya, 104, 105, 106
Stockwell, A., printers, 122,123
Strangers to Ourselves, 86
stream of consciousness, 20, 126
style, 33, 66, 97, 111; dramatic, 109; narrative, 55-7; 68, 109
subjectivity, 78, 79-81, 82, 84; migrant, 84
Suso, B., 40
symbol, 80, 82, 85, 86
syncreticism, 77-89

Tejani, B., on Brutus, 24
Theatre, Market, 105; staging, 105, 108; workshop, 107
Things Fall Apart, vii, 53; and Christianity, vii
twins, in Igbo society, 80-4
Two Songs, 34,36
Two Thousand Seasons, vii, 51

United States, and African culture, 77
Utopia, 77
utopianism, 16, 21, 69-70, 73, 77

Vera, Y., *Butterfly Burning*, 140; poetic style, 142
Veit-Wild, F., ed. *Black Insider, The*, 2; *Marechera: A Source Book ...*, 2
video productions, 127
Vigne, K., 16
Viola, A., 137

Waberi, A., 100; colonialism, 101; irony, 102; narrative technique, 101; *L'Oeil nomade*, 101; *Pays sans ombre*, 100
Wand of Noble Wood, 58
war, Biafran, 91; sexual 98
western, anthropologists, 35; education, 96; idea of muse, 97; indifference to oppression, 25; society, 49-50
When Rain Clouds Gather, see Head
Why Are We So Blest? see Armah
Williams, C. W., 113
Williams, R., *Long Revolution, The*, 44-6, 47, 51
witchcraft, 13-15
Woolf, V., 65
Wordsworth, W., *Lyrical Ballads*, 34
Wreath for the Maidens, see Munonye
writers, Black South African, 64; Djibouti, 100; in exile, 44, 45, 78; liberal, 95; migrant, 79; Nigerian, 62; and society, 44-6; women, *see* feminism
Writers in Exile ..., 1
Wylie, D., 29

Yoruba, 82, 84; Ifa, 41; praise singer, 38-9

Zell, H. (comp.), *Electronic African Bookworm, The*, 138
Zimbabwe Women's Voices, 116
Zimbabwe women writers, 116; *Poetry and Short Stories*, 111, 116

Printed by Libri Plureos GmbH in Hamburg, Germany